OTHER BOOKS BY GIAN N. G. ORSINI

La poesia di Alfred Tennyson, 1928
Milton e il suo poema, 1928
Bacone e Machiavelli, 1936
Studi sul Rinascimento italiano in Inghilterra, 1937
Fulke Greville tra il mondo e Dio, 1941
Benedetto Croce, Philosopher of Art and Literary Critic, 1961

Coleridge

AND GERMAN IDEALISM

A Study in the History of Philosophy

with Unpublished Materials

from Coleridge's Manuscripts

By G . N . G . ORSINI

SOUTHERN ILLINOIS UNIVERSITY PRESS
Carbondale and Edwardsville
FEFFER & SIMONS, INC.
London and Amsterdam

ACKNOWLEDGMENTS

THIS BOOK IS DEDICATED to the memory of Bernardino Varisco (1850–1933) and of Giovanni Gentile (1875–1944), under whom I studied Kant at the University of Rome, Italy, in 1921–1925. The light they gave me in understanding Kant and his successors has remained with me ever since.

The writing of the book was rendered possible by grants from the Graduate School of the University of Wisconsin, by a period of residence in the Institute for Research in the Humanities also at my University in 1962–1963, and by a grant from the Guggenheim Foundation in 1964–1965.

I have also a debt of gratitude to the librarians of my University and to those of the British Museum and Victoria College, University of Toronto, for all the help they have unstintingly given me.

I am also grateful to Mr. A. H. Coleridge for granting me permission to quote from copyright MSS, to Dean A. A. Suppan, of the University of Wisconsin at Milwaukee, for granting me permission to quote from the MS "On the Divine Ideas," and to Professors K. Coburn, E. Garin, G. Whalley and J. R. Jackson for answering my questions and supplying information.

Finally, the students who have taken the seminar I held on this subject have been a source of stimulus and enlightenment. I particularly mention Miss Patricia Ward, who has already published the result of her research.

Copyright © 1969, by Southern Illinois University Press
All rights reserved
Printed in the United States of America
Designed by Andor Braun
Standard Book Number 8093-3562-x
Library of Congress Catalog Card Number 69-11512

Preface

THIS BOOK AIMS at providing the answer to one question: what did Coleridge derive from Kant and the post-Kantians in his most productive intellectual period, i.e., from approximately 1800 to approximately the eighteen-twenties? The question has already been investigated by a number of scholars —Shawcross, Muirhead, Wellek, Winkelmann, Schrickx, and Chinol, in chronological order. Upon their work my book is founded, especially Wellek's. An attempt has been made at a synthesis; but there are still a number of questions to be solved. For one thing, the chronology still presents uncertainties; for another, there is still much Coleridge material that awaits publication. A complete edition of his works, both published and unpublished, is now in progress under the general editorship of Kathleen Coburn. She herself made a superb beginning with the edition of Coleridge's long-lost *Philosophical Lectures* (1949), followed by a selection from Coleridge's unpublished works in her *Inquiring Spirit* (1951), and the annotated edition of the integral *Notebooks* now in progress (1957 *et seq.*). In progress is also Griggs' splendid edition of the *Letters*. This book includes some unpublished material (spelling and accents, especially Greek spirits, in my quotations generally follow the original). Until the whole of the unpublished writings are available, a final estimate of Coleridge as a philosopher is not possible. Therefore this book must be considered in the nature of an interim report.

However, even now it is high time that his connection with the German thinkers be fully recognized. The definite results of the studies of the philosophical scholars above listed have never gained general acceptance among the purely literary scholars, some of whom still poohpooh Coleridge's indebtedness to Schelling and shrug away his derivations from Kant. Ideas which

v

Coleridge obtained indubitably from the Germans are still extolled as his original creations, and in general the German influence is minimized in favor of native sources. I shall bring forward a number of examples of this.

While there are several sides to particular questions of derivation, a full estimate of Coleridge's intellectual achievement cannot be made until his sources are fully explored and the genetic development of his ideas made clear. This does not mean raising again the contentious charge of plagiarism. For one thing, it is my firm conviction, ever since the year 1923 when I first read the *Biographia Literaria*, that Coleridge *is* a genius, and I believe that a genius can be creative even when he is borrowing. But it is a fact that, during a time to be determined (the chronology is still uncertain), Coleridge was a zealous defender and expounder of transcendental idealism in England, thus bringing to his country the most important development in Continental philosophy. His services to this cause cannot be estimated until they are examined in connection with the advance of idealism from Kant to Fichte, and then to Schelling and to Hegel. This whole movement, as students of philosophy well know, is one of the most closely connected and at the same time richly diversified progresses in the history of philosophy, and Coleridge's actions and reactions to it (some of these thinkers attracting him more than others) constitute an interesting episode in this history. For instance, it is from Schelling's earlier works, as Wellek pointed out, that Coleridge derived much of his criticism of Kant. I have tried to show in detail what there is in Kant and in the others that Coleridge saw in them, and at the same time note some significant differences and divergences.

Sometimes one hears of the notion of a "total Coleridge" in which all his various activities, poetic, philosophical, political, critical, and personal, are brought together and derived from the single concept of the "personality" of Coleridge. This results in the notion of a philosophy that is not philosophy, a poetry that is not poetry, a religion that is not religion, but a mixture of all these, each participating in the others and losing its own character. Here these activities have been kept carefully distinct, and the less pertinent ones have been excluded altogether.

Furthermore I have tried to treat philosophy as Coleridge considered it, i.e. as a science—not as mere aimless conjecture, fantasy, or wishful thinking. Philosophical doctrines must be defined precisely, while many of the purely literary scholars content themselves with dubbing Coleridge's philosophy by some such general term as "Platonism" (or "Neoplatonism," as if the two were the same). Too often by "Platonism" is meant a vague, general belief in God and immortality with some mystical overtones. In this area clarification is most required; it is precisely on Plato that Coleridge is least satisfactory. Also, when a later philosopher like Kant is brought into this kind of thinking, he may be presented as nothing more than another "Platonist": for did he not believe in God and in immortality? so what's the difference between him and any other metaphysician—i.e., between Kant and Cudworth, Kant and Berkeley, and even Plato and Plotinus—didn't they all believe in God and immortality? Thus the most disparate systems, with the most divergent conclusions, are boiled down to an indistinct mass and lost to view.

To define these systems, and to answer the question as to Coleridge's specific derivations in a manner accessible to the purely literary student of Coleridge, it becomes necessary to do something which to some may appear supererogatory, while to others it may be frightening: viz., to explain Kant. Boldly venturing into a field full of dangers, I have attempted just that. The bulk of this book consists of an exposition of Kant's critical philosophy in simple language, to make intelligible the doctrines so often referred to by Coleridge. For instance: for the philosophical scholars it is sufficient to say (as most of them have said) that Coleridge adopted Kant's doctrine of the categories, without giving any explanation of them. But what are Kant's categories? What is their significance? To the non-philosopher the term "categories" may appear just another tiresome detail of an unintelligible system. Actually, they constitute one of Kant's most elaborate and most influential doctrines, one with which Coleridge was thoroughly familiar. To it he makes a number of references, some of which have escaped previous scholars partly because of Coleridge's habit of not making exact quotations.

To another doctrine of Kant, that of the transcendental ego, I have dedicated the whole of Chapter 4 because, even though Coleridge's discussion of it is limited, it accounts for the developments after Kant. All of this will, I believe, be found useful also for the study of the hitherto unpublished works.

This being mainly a study of sources, I have not discussed Coleridge's most famous critical ideas, such as the Creative Imagination, considered in itself. No general discussion of aesthetics is attempted, but derivations from Kant's and from Schelling's aesthetics are indicated in Chapters 6 and 9. I have said elsewhere something about his doctrine of Organic Form and hope to say more about it in the future.

To evaluate fully Coleridge's derivations I have found it necessary to determine what philosophical ideas Coleridge had absorbed before going to Germany. This is the subject of Chapter 1 and relates only to his earlier years, which were not only rudimental as all first efforts are, but are also insufficiently documented. The necessarily negative conclusions on the early influence of some philosophers on Coleridge does not exclude their influence in his later life: for instance, the whole influence of Berkeley on Coleridge's mature thinking remains to be investigated. But this, important as it is, must be left to others.

Upon the ultimate question about Coleridge's own philosophy—whether there is in him a coherent body of doctrines, original or derived—I am not prepared to be definite. I admit that when I began this inquiry I was more confident of a positive answer than I am now. My final word is at the end of my Conclusion. In view of the unpublished material, some of which I have not seen, I remain with an open mind: my repeated experience of the sudden and surprising shifts of this great and tormented genius leaves me uncertain.

Finally, I would stress my belief that Coleridge is primarily a poet, and a great poet. But he wrote splendid prose. I cannot help feeling compunction as to my own shortcomings in the matter of style, pardonable perhaps in a writer whose native tongue is not English.

G. N. G. ORSINI

Madison, Wisconsin
October 1968

CONTENTS

A	Kant, I. *Critique of Pure Reason.* 1st ed., 1780, in the Kemp Smith translation, London, 1929.
Abbott	Kant's *Critique of Practical Reason* &c. Trans. by T. K. Abbott. London, 1873.
Aids	Coleridge, S. T. *Aids to Reflection and Confessions of an Enquiring Spirit.* London, 1904.
AP	Coleridge, S. T. *Anima Poetae,* ed. E. H. Coleridge. London, 1895.
Appleyard	Appleyard, J. A. *Coleridge's Philosophy of Literature.* Harvard, 1965.
B	Kant, I. *Critique of Pure Reason.* 2nd ed., 1787, in the same translation as A.
Beer	Beer, J. B. *Coleridge the Visionary.* New York, 1962 (1959).
BL	Coleridge, S. T. *Biographia Literaria,* ed. J. Shawcross. 2 vols. Oxford, 1907.
BL2	Coleridge, S. T. *Biographia Literaria,* ed. H. N. Coleridge and Sara Coleridge. 2nd ed.; New York, 1882.
Boulger	Boulger, J. D. *Coleridge as a Religious Thinker.* New Haven, 1961.
Brinkley	Brinkley, R. F. (ed.). *Coleridge on the 17th Century.* Durham, 1955.
C&S	*On the constitution of Church and State,* &c. London, 1839.
Cassirer	Cassirer, H. W. *A Commentary to Kant's Critique of Judgment.* London, 1938.

Chinol   Chinol, E. *Il pensiero di S. T. Coleridge*. Venezia, 1953.

CL   Griggs, E. L. (ed.). *Collected Letters* of S. T. Coleridge. Oxford, 1965 *et seq.* (in progress).

Co   Smith, N. K. *Commentary to Kant's Critique of Pure Reason*. 2nd ed.; London, 1923.

Deschamps   Deschamps, P. *La formation de la pensée de Coleridge (1772–1804)*. Paris, 1964.

F   Coleridge, S. T. *The Friend*. London, 1865.

Gillman   Gillman, J. *Life of S. T. Coleridge*. London, 1838 (no other volumes published).

GW   Fichte, J. G. *Sämmtliche Werke*, ed. J. H. Fichte. Berlin, 1845.

Hanson   Hanson, L. *The Life of Coleridge, The Early Years*. London, 1938, reprinted 1962.

Haven   Haven, R. "Coleridge, Hartley and the Mystics," *JHI*, XX (1959), 476–94.

IS   Coburn, K. *Inquiring Spirit*. London, 1951.

JHI   *Journal of the History of Ideas*.

LR   Coleridge, S. T. *Literary Remains*, ed. H. N. Coleridge. 3 vols. London, 1836–39.

Misc. Crit.   Raysor, T. M. (ed.). *Coleridge's Miscellaneous Criticism*. Cambridge, 1936.

Muirhead   Muirhead, J. H. *Coleridge as a Philosopher*. London, 1930.

NB   Coburn, K. (ed.). *The Notebooks* of S. T. Coleridge. London, 1957 *et seq.* (in progress).

Paton   Paton, H. J. *Kant's Metaphysics of Experience*. 2 vols.; 3rd impression. London, 1956.

PhL   *The Philosophical Lectures* of S. T. Coleridge (hitherto unpublished), ed. K. Coburn, New York, 1949.

Piper   Piper, H. W. *The Active Universe*. London, 1962.

PW   *The Poetical Works* of S. T. Coleridge, ed. E. H. Coleridge. Oxford, 1912.

RLC   *Revue de Littérature Comparée*.

RX	Lowes, J. L. *The Road to Xanadu.* 2nd ed. Boston, 1930.
S&C	Coleridge. *On the Constitution of Church and State,* and *Lay Sermons.* London, 1839.
Shedd	*The Complete Works of S. T. Coleridge,* ed. Professor Shedd, 7 vols. New York, 1874.
Snyder	Snyder, A. D. *Coleridge on Logic and Learning.* New Haven, 1929.
SW	von Schelling, F. W. J. *Sämmtliche Werke.* 14 vols. Stuttgart, 1856 *et seq.*
TT	Coleridge. *Table Talk and Omniana,* ed. T. Ashe. London, 1884.
UL	*Unpublished Letters of S. T. Coleridge,* ed. E. L. Griggs, 2 vols. New Haven, 1933.
W	Wellek, René. *I. Kant in England.* Princeton, 1931.
Winkelmann	Winkelmann, E. *Coleridge und die Kantische Philosophie.* Leipzig, 1933 (*Palaestra,* No. 184).
Wolff	Wolff, R. *Kant's Theory of Mental Activity.* Harvard, 1963.
Z	MS. "On the Divine Ideas" (so called from the title of its first chapter) in the Huntington Library, San Marino, California.

Coleridge

AND GERMAN IDEALISM

May this mixture of philology, throughout the whole, sweeten and allay the severity of philosophy to the readers. But for our parts, we neither call philology, nor yet philosophy, our mistress; but serve ourselves of either, as occasion requireth.

R. CUDWORTH, Preface to *The True Intellectual System of the Universe*, 1678 *

Questa medesima degnità dimostra aver mancato per metà così i filosofi, che non accertarono le loro ragioni con l'autorità dei filologi, come i filologi, che non curarono d'avverare le loro autorità con la ragion de' filosofi.

G. B. VICO, *Scienza Nuova Terza*, 1744*

* CUDWORTH, *True System*, ed. 1845, I, xliv, slightly adapted; VICO, *Scienza Nuova*, giusta l'edizione del 1744, a cura di F. Nicolini, Bari, 1911, I, 120.

CHAPTER 1

Early Beliefs and Speculations:
c. *1787 to 1799*

FOLLOWING R. H. Shepherd,[1] one can distinguish three main periods in the life of Coleridge: 1) early youth up to the age of twenty-six (1798), which includes his great creative period in poetry; 2) the period of his prime, approximately from 1800 to 1816, mainly dedicated to aesthetic criticism, lectures, and journalism; and 3) the Highgate years, or from 1816 to his death in 1834, dedicated to philosophy and theology.

This book will deal mainly with the second period; but we will begin with a chapter on the poet's earliest speculations.

The sequence of this chapter is biographical, and the philosophers read by Coleridge are shown not in their chronological order but in the order in which they came to Coleridge's attention. In the chapters that follow, this method will be reversed, and Coleridge's ideas will be shown not in their chronological development but in function of the history of philosophy. Coleridge there takes second place in the order of exposition, and the main subject will be the philosophy of Kant, then of his followers, and what Coleridge found in it. There the philosophers will be placed in their historical background, not given in the first chapter.

i

DIRECT ACQUAINTANCE with German intellectual life dates for Coleridge from the academic year 1798–99, which he spent

3

at the University of Göttingen when he was twenty-six. The full impact of Kant and of the post-Kantians on his mind begins after that period, but since he had begun to read philosophers and to think about philosophical problems before it, something must be said about his philosophical and religious interests before that journey. This is especially necessary since it has been sometimes claimed that he had reached philosophical conclusions before he came to Germany, and even conclusions which anticipated the doctrines of Kant and of the post-Kantians. These conclusions were based, it is argued, on his study of the ancient Neoplatonists and/or of English thinkers of the seventeenth and eighteenth centuries. In this chapter we will therefore discuss Coleridge's early readings in these thinkers and the ideas he obtained from them. As we shall see, such an anticipation, very unlikely in itself, is not confirmed by the examination of the evidence.

Coleridge's earliest beliefs were of course Christian and traditional. Born in 1772, he was the son of a clergyman of the Church of England and, on the death of his father when he was eight, was sent to a famous school for clergymen's orphans, Christ's Hospital in London, from which the best pupils were directed to a clerical career. In his childhood years Coleridge was unhappy at this school, but as he grew to adolescence his mind developed and he was recognised as a brilliant scholar. He soon manifested two of his permanent characteristics, an insatiable love of miscellaneous reading and a capacity for talking endlessly and fascinatingly. In later years he reminisced about "a circulating library in King Street, Cheapside," to which he was given a subscription when he was still at Christ's Hospital (we barely hear of a school library): "I read through the catalogue, folios and all, whether I understood them or did not understand them, running all risks in skulking out to get the two volumes which I was entitled to have daily. Conceive what I must have been at fourteen; I was in a continual low fever" (Gillman, 17 and 20). In a revealing letter to Thelwall of 19 November 1796 (*CL*, I, 260), he described himself as "a library cormorant." A devourer of books he remained all his life, so that one must be slow to assume that a book, available at the time, was *not* seen by him. Whether he fully absorbed it or not is another matter, as he himself indicated in the above quoted recollection. But he at least looked into every book he could lay his hands on, whether it was a book of poetry or of philosophy or of science or of politics or of travel, and the things from them which he would come up with later are sometimes amazing, as the magical transformation of travellers' books in *The Ancient Mariner*.

Religion was a favorite topic. "In my friendless wanderings on our *leave-days*," he relates in the *Biographia Literaria* (*BL*, I, 10), "highly was I delighted if any passenger, especially if he were dressed in black, would enter into conversation with me. For I soon found the means of directing it to my favourite subjects

> Of providence, foreknowledge, will and fate,
> Fix'd fate, free will, foreknowledge absolute,
> And found no end in wandering mazes lost."

The range of his reading and of his speculations may be indicated by the fact that it apparently extended to Boehme's *Aurora*, which had been available in an English translation since the seventeenth century. In a letter to the German poet Ludwig Tieck of July 3, 1817, he said: "Before my visit to Germany in September 1798, I had adopted (probably from Behmen's *Aurora*, which I had conjured over at school) the idea, that Sound was = Light under the praepotence of Gravitation, and Colour = Gravitation under the praepotence of Light; and I have never seen reason to change my faith in this respect" (*CL*, IV, 750–51). In view of this remarkable piece of Boehmian hocus-pocus, or *Naturphilosophie*, it is conceivable that "conjured over" did not imply understanding, but some kind of rapt repetition.

If Coleridge read religious and mystical books at school, he also read the contemporary sceptics or "infidels" and went himself through a phase of incredulity. Voltaire was then one of his authors; Helvetius is also mentioned in this connection, but without a definite date (*CL*, I, 78). "After I read Voltaire's *Philosophical Dictionary*," he said in an autobiographical narrative made much later to Dr. Gillman, "I sported infidel" (Gillman, 23)—i.e., he proclaimed his infidelity openly at school. His authoritarian schoolmaster, Dr. Bowyer, made short shrift of it and gave him a severe flogging, which Coleridge later piously declared was the only just flogging he ever received (Gillman, 24).

Hanson, speaking of this episode, says: "He named Voltaire's *Philosophical Dictionary* as the originator of his doubts[48]; but Erasmus Darwin's arguments against the existence of God and criticism of the evidence of revealed religion, played their part" (p. 21).

The text referred to in the note (i.e., Gillman, 23) does not cite Darwin. Indeed, the mention of Darwin in this connection seems to arise out of a misunderstanding. Coleridge met Erasmus Darwin himself years later, in 1796, and had a number of lively discussions with him, according to Coleridge's own account. "He bantered me on the subject of religion. I heard all his arguments, and told him that it was infinitely consoling to me, to find that the arguments which so great a man adduced against the existence of a God and the evidences of revealed religion were such as had startled me at fifteen, but became the objects of my smile at twenty" (*CL*, I, 177).

Therefore Darwin's arguments were not *those*, but only *such as those*, as had impressed Coleridge at fifteen, in 1787 (e.g., Voltaire's). In that year it was impossible for Coleridge to have received an impression from Erasmus Darwin's famous *Botanical Garden*, since that poem was published two years later, in 1789.[2]

But Coleridge did not want to become a clergyman like his father. At the age of thirteen, he wanted to become a doctor, influenced by the fact that his brother Luke was studying at London Hospital to become a surgeon (Hanford, 120). Characteristically, he then read every book on medicine that he could lay his hands on, "English, Latin, yes, Greek" (Gillman, 23). Rather than become a clergyman, he at one time was ready to become a cobbler and tried to be apprenticed to one: that, too, was stopped by his headmaster's vigorous measures.

In addition to this omnivorous reading habit, there was in Coleridge a powerful imagination, the native gift of a great poet, but also an imagination (or fancy, as he might have called it) that worked in the most unusual and most bizarre fashions, as evidenced in his *Notebooks*. In time, it was to give the world some immortal poems; but it could also operate as a disturbing factor. We have seen in the letter to Tieck on Boehme quoted above what strange flights this imaginative faculty, when applied to purely scientific subjects, could take. Yet Coleridge added to his other gifts a deep interest in philosophy in its most abstruse and technical forms, in philosophy as a science, and a love of clarity, of rigor in statement and due regard for distinctions and for complexities, which produced one of the most sinuous prose styles in modern English.

The combination of these three gifts—philosophy, learning and imagination—might have under favorable circumstances produced a poet who was also a deep thinker and an original philosopher. Unfortunately a negative element from the character of Coleridge came into play. Its outward symptom, and the affliction of his mature years, was his addiction to drugs, which contributed to his intellectual and practical instability, so that very few of his great works were carried to completion and many projects were left inchoate.[3]

The roots of that addiction lay deep in his emotional nature, in a certain unaccountable and even morbid element in his personality which may also have been the cause of those serious errors of judgment and fatal decisions, such as his marriage, which marred his whole life. They cast a shadow on almost all that he did or that he wrote, except his greatest poetry; there his dark urges were transformed into the crystal clarity of the perfect image. But for the history of his intellect these negative factors make most of his later statements on chronology and other matters of fact subject to caution.

Add to this that, like many others, Coleridge in his later years was fond of projecting into the past his mature convictions and attributing to his early youth his later accomplishments. As we shall see more fully in Chapter 8, there was also a regrettable tendency to claim priority for valuable ideas found in other writers. True, he speculated early and long, and many ideas or germs of ideas lay fallow in the depths of his memory or in the jottings of his *Notebooks*, now being brought to light by the immense industry of Professor Coburn. But he did not always distinguish between the germ of an idea and its complete development in a finished work. So he would claim that a work, existing only as an idea, was already fully worked out, put into writing, and even "printing in Bristol" (*CL*, III, 533). It is not the aim of this book to explore the depths of Coleridge's complex and unique personality, nor to account for all his shortcomings or all his achievements, but only to ascertain according to the available evidence what books he read on transcendental philosophy and what ideas he got from them.

Coleridge himself claimed an almost incredible precocity: he often spoke of philosophical studies undertaken "before my fifteenth year" (*BL*, I, 9 and 170), i.e., before 1787. But the evidence for this period consists mainly of his own later statements, which must be taken with caution. In particular, there is no independent corroboration of Coleridge's claims to a very early familiarity with the Neoplatonic philosophers. It may at first appear that we have such an independent witness in Charles Lamb, who was a fellow student at Christ's Hospital. In his famous description of Coleridge as a Blue-coat boy, a description which takes the form of an address to his friend, Lamb said that at the Hospital the passer-by might have heard Coleridge "in the day-spring of thy fancies, with hope like a fiery column before thee, . . . unfold, in thy deep and sweet intonations, the mysteries of Jamblichus and Plotinus (for even in those days thou waxedst not pale at such philosophical draughts), or reciting Homer in his Greek, or Pindar." [4]

In regard to this famous testimony, it should be noted, first of all, that Coleridge is said to quote the *poets* in the original Greek, not the philosophers. This knowledge of Greek poetry, while a really remarkable feat for the student of a modern

American college, was something quite possible in the nineteenth century for a bright student in a classical school of the English type, like Christ's Hospital. But Plotinus and Iamblichus are another matter.

Secondly, it turns out that this description was not Lamb's spontaneous and unaided recollection, but was supplied by Coleridge himself. In 1820 the poet stated that Lamb had told him that his essay was "chiefly compiled from his recollections of what he had heard from me" [5]—a typically roundabout situation, which takes us back to our starting point: Coleridge himself. Lamb's description has the same status, neither more nor less, as Coleridge's own recollections, which we will now examine in more detail.

In the *Biographia Literaria* he says: "At a very premature age, even before my fifteenth year, I had bewildered myself in metaphysics and in theological controversy. Nothing else pleased me. History, and particular facts, lost all interest in my mind" (*BL*, Ch. 1; I, 9). Besides the characteristic phrase "bewildered in metaphysics" and the significant admission about "particular facts," this statement gives a definite date: the year 1787, when he became fifteen; but it does not mention the name of any philosopher. Names are mentioned in a later statement in the same book, but no definite date. This is when he speaks of "the early study of Plato and Plotinus, with the commentaries and the THEOLOGIA PLATONICA of the illustrious Florentine; of Proclus, and Gemistius Pletho; and at a later period, . . . of the philosopher of Nola" (i.e., Giordano Bruno; Ch. IX, I, 94). The "illustrious Florentine" is of course Marsilio Ficino. Now, if we join this statement to the previous one (for which there is no support in the text), we can make this acquaintance with the Platonists go back to "before my fifteenth year"; but this is pure conjecture. Ficinus is not mentioned in the *Notebooks* until 1805, and then only for his "prefaces to the Medici" (*NB*, II, # 2746). In that year we know that Coleridge purchased a copy of the *Theologia Platonica*, which he inscribed with unusual precision "Messina 9 Oct. 1805" (Haven, 490). None of the authors mentioned above appears in the list of borrowings from the Bristol Library in 1794–97.[6] "And nowhere (before 1800) do we find mention of Pletho or Ficino, 'the illustrious Florentine' " (Haven, 490).

However, in 1796 Coleridge obtained through a friend a copy of a small collection of ancient Neoplatonists translated in Latin by Marsilio Ficino, and printed at Lyons in 1570, which included a work of Iamblichus and selections from Proclus, Porphyrius, Psellus and the Hermetic writings (i.e., the *Pimander* and *Asclepius; CL,* I, 262 and *NB,* Notes, I, # 180). This tells us what Neoplatonists Coleridge could have read in 1796 and following years, but not what he was reading in 1787, when he was fifteen.

Still another account of the beginning of his philosophical studies was given by Coleridge in 1812. Crabb Robinson reports that on May 3 of that year Coleridge told him that: "when many years ago he began to think on philosophy he set out from a passage in Proclus at the point where Schelling appears to be. And where, with modifications he, Coleridge, has remained." [7]

This conjunction of Proclus with Schelling may perhaps be rendered clearer by a statement that Coleridge made in a letter a little earlier, in 1810: "The most beautiful and orderly development of this philosophy, which endeavours to explain all things by an analysis of consciousness, and builds up a world in the mind out of materials furnished by the mind itself, is to be found in the *Platonic Theology* by Proclus" (*CL,* III, 279).

This is definite evidence that in 1810 Coleridge gave an eminently subjectivist interpretation of Proclus, which would indeed place the latter close to Schelling (at least the Schelling of the Fichte period). Did Coleridge hold that interpretation from his earliest reading of Proclus? and from what works of Proclus, in the original or in translation, did he derive it?

The work mentioned in the 1810 statement is not to be confused with Proclus' *Elements of Theology,* which was translated by T. Taylor in 1792 and later read and annotated by Coleridge (*Notebooks,* I, 1626, 1727, 1728 and 1740; Notes, I, pp. 455–59). This might suggest an early and lasting influence of Proclus, who is undoubtedly the strongest Neoplatonic philosopher after

Plotinus. However, the earliest reference to Proclus in the *Note-books* invalidates this hypothesis. In April 1801 Coleridge was reading, or trying to read, Giordano Bruno: "The work de Monade.—It is far too numeral, lineal and Pythagorean for my comprehension—It read (sic) very much like Thomas Taylor & Proclus &c. I by no means think it certain that there is nothing in these Works, nor do I presume even to suppose that the meaning is of no value" (*NB*, I, 928 fol. 27).

Then follows Coleridge's often repeated maxim about "understanding the ignorance" of an author (*BL*, Ch. XII, I, 160), which has no direct reference to Proclus. Now, if in 1801 Proclus was like Bruno and Taylor still beyond Coleridge's "comprehension," it is rather unlikely that it was Proclus who sparked Coleridge's original interest in philosophy when he was a youth. Hence the statement as set down by Robinson cannot be considered correct.

There is a way of reconciling it with the evidence of the *Notebooks*, if we make the assumption that Robinson omitted to record some words of Coleridge's. In one of the entries on Proclus made in 1803 (# 1728) Coleridge wrote: "The 50th Prop. of the El. Theol. contains totidem verbis my etymology of Natura, without referring either to it or φύσις." The 50th Proposition of the *Elements of Theology* the reader may find in the Notes to # 1728. It may be conjecturally suggested that what Coleridge said to Robinson in 1812 was something like this: "Many years ago, when I began to think on philosophy, I set out from *a definition of Natura, which is to be found totidem verbis in* Proclus and which is also the point where Schelling appears to be," etc. The italicized words may have been forgotten by Robinson when he set down his recollections. This would harmonize all the known facts, with only a slight sacrifice of Robinson's accuracy, which is usually beyond question. But whether it was Robinson's memory which was at fault, or Coleridge's, there is no solid evidence that Proclus was the original source of Coleridge's interest in philosophy.

Nor is there any real evidence for the hypothesis, recently advanced,[8] that Coleridge at an early age (circa 1787) was strongly influenced by the philosophy of Plotinus. "Until 1789," it is claimed (p. 109), "Coleridge's thinking is thoroughly Plotinian." To be indeed "thoroughly Plotinian" it would have to be grounded on a belief in the absolute One, with all that that involves, such as the doctrine of emanation, or the return to the One, of the different spheres of Being, etc. There is no trace of these in Coleridge's earliest effusions. At best, we may find later the echo of a principle derived from Plotinus' aesthetics.

This hypothesis of the influence of Plotinus is based upon another unfounded hypothesis, namely that Coleridge at the age of fourteen was intensely afflicted by a feeling of remorse arising out of "the awful fact of guilt," for what sin we are not told. To this feeling Coleridge is then supposed to have found alleviation and comfort in the philosophy of Plotinus (*op. cit.*, pp. 106–7).[9]

The only evidence in support of the first hypothesis, that of remorse for guilt, is a statement in a letter of 1802 (sixteen years after the supposed access of remorse) that "sickness & some other & worse afflictions, first forced me into downright metaphysics" (*CL*, II, 814; to Sotheby, July 19, 1802). But from this letter it is clear that Coleridge was referring to his recent period of "dejection" which had occurred in the previous spring, when he wrote his famous "Ode" on the subject (cf. Griggs' note, *op. cit.*, p. 815). Coleridge then proceeds in the letter to quote from this very Ode, in the text first printed in the *Morning Post* of 1802. So there is no reason to believe that the words "first forced me" refer back to his early years. It is, rather, the unhappy passion for Asra that is likely to be referred to by "worse afflictions." This passion might conceivably have aroused then some feeling of guilt, but not when he was fourteen. So the first hypothesis does not stand.

The evidence adduced for the second hypothesis, that Coleridge resorted to Plotinus for comfort, is the trivial and conventional verse composed by the very young Coleridge, which is repeatedly declared "thoroughly Plotinian" (pp. 109 and 112) but bears no such metaphysical load, and two school themes in prose of 1790 and 1791 respectively (Hanson, 424–26), which

merely develop in schoolboy manner (though with one Cole-
ridgion touch) trite platitudes. These commonplace moraliza-
tions can hardly be called " 'metaphysical,' " even between inverted commas (Werkmeister, *op. cit.*, p. 115). Similarly, there
is no real evidence for the hypothesis, advanced by the same
scholar,[10] that Coleridge was influenced by Burke as early as
1791.

There are two general difficulties that make it very improbable that Coleridge had already studied Plotinus before he was
fifteen, or even before he was eighteen: first, the difficulty of
finding a copy of the *Enneads*, even in a Latin translation, in a
"circulating library in King Street" [11] at that time, when Plotinus,
as Coleridge himself said later, was "known only as a name to
the majority even of our most learned scholars" (*Essays on . . .
Genial Criticism*, III, *BL*, II, 239). Secondly, the unlikelihood
of even an exceptionally gifted youngster, like Coleridge, being
able to understand Plotinus, an author whom Coleridge in his
full maturity, when he quoted freely from the *Enneads*, considered "abstruse," "obscure" and "difficult indeed" (*BL*, I, 201
and II, 239; Ch. XII and *Genial Criticism*, III). Even the Latin
translation of Ficinus was considered difficult by eminent scholars
of that age: "His version is in many places obscure and intricate,
so as to be intelligible to those alone who are conversant with the
discipline and diction of the Platonists." [12]

The only English translation of a book by Plotinus that was
available to Coleridge as a youth was Taylor's translation of the
Sixth Book of the First Ennead, on the Beautiful (1787). This
Coleridge may have read. It is even possible that he may have
received from that reading a lasting acquisition: the concept of
organic unity in aesthetics, one of his most deep-rooted ideas.
This is how he formulated it in 1814: "The safest definition,
then, of Beauty, as well as the oldest, is that of Pythagoras: THE
REDUCTION OF THE MANY TO ONE—or, as finely ex-
pressed by the sublime disciple of Ammonius τὸ ἄμερες ὄν, ἐν πολλοῖς
φανταζόμενον, of which the following may be considered both a
paraphrase and a corollary. *The sense of beauty subsists, in the
simultaneous intuition of the relation of parts, each to each, and
of all to a whole: exciting an immediate and absolute com-*

placency, without intervenience, therefore, of any interest, sensual or intellectual" (*BL*, II, 238–39; *Genial Criticism*, III).

In this luminous definition Coleridge characteristically merges theories from different sources. Setting aside for the moment Pythagoras as of doubtful authenticity, we will consider the "sublime disciple of Ammonius," who is of course Plotinus, and who is directly quoted. The Greek quotation is from the very same book on Beauty which was translated by Taylor, and may be rendered more literally as "(the inner form)[13] manifesting its indivisible being in the many" (*Enneads*, I, VI, 3). Taylor translates an earlier sentence (I, VI, 2) as "Beauty is established in multitude when the many is reduced into one; and in this case it communicates itself both to the parts and to the whole."[14]

This may be said to correspond to the first part of Coleridge's italicized definition of Beauty. The second part of the definition introduces the concept of "complacency," i.e., pleasure "without interest," which is clearly the Kantian concept of *Gefallen*, as we shall see in Chapter 6. We may consider that the "paraphrase" of Plotinus ended with the previous part, and the second part is what Coleridge called "corollary," although it is not so much a direct consequence as the introduction of a new concept from a later thinker.

Without going now into the Kantian source, let us consider the formula to which Coleridge has given all the dignity of capital type: "THE REDUCTION OF MANY INTO ONE." This is very close to Taylor's "the many is reduced into one." It is perhaps not a wild guess—certainly not the wildest that has been made in this field—to surmise that the phrase in the *Biographia* may be a recollection of Taylor's translation, read in the days of his youth and never forgotten? This aesthetic proposition was surely not beyond the grasp of a gifted youth who had been trained by his master, Dr. Bowyer, to scrutinise closely every detail of a poem: "In the truly great poets, he would say, there is a reason assignable, not only for every word, but for the position of every word; and I well remember that . . . he made an attempt to show . . . *wherein* consisted the peculiar fitness of the word in the original text" (*BL*, Ch. I; I, 4–5).

No better object lesson could be given of the organic relation of the parts, each to each and to the whole. This hypothesis would support the idea that the Plotinus that Coleridge read as a Blue-coat boy was Taylor's translation, then limited to the book on Beauty[15]—a small part of the whole, but a basic book for a future aesthetician and upholder of the doctrine of "multeity in unity," "*il più nell'uno*," etc.[16]

Finally, we can account for the reference to Pythagoras in the quoted passage. It points to another Neoplatonic belief that Coleridge may have originally obtained from Taylor's translation of Plotinus on Beauty; it is not a philosophical belief but an historical hypothesis, and a dubious one: the idea of the "Platonic tradition." This Neoplatonic theory, interwoven with myths, was thus expounded by Taylor in his introduction: "that sublime wisdom which first arose in the colleges of the Egyptian priests, and flourished afterwards in Greece. Which was there cultivated by Pythagoras, under the mysterious veil of numbers; by Plato, in the graceful dress of poetry; and was systematised by Aristotle, as far as it could be reduced to systematic order. Which, after becoming in a manner extinct, shone again with its pristine splendour among the philosophers of the Alexandrian school; was learnedly illustrated with Asiatic luxuriancy of style by Proclus; was divinely explained by Iamblichus; and profoundly delivered in the writings of Plotinus" (p. ix–x).

Not only the Egyptian priests, but also Orpheus and Moses are included in other versions of this tradition, which Coleridge on the whole accepted: particularly the notion that Pythagoras taught a secret doctrine which was passed on to Plato and by him concealed in his writings, but later revealed to the Neoplatonists (cf. *AP*, 231). Coleridge's view of Plato was essentially Neoplatonic, and he may have had his first taste of it in the above quoted passage by Taylor.[17] This passage mentions the name of Iamblichus, and young Coleridge may have picked up from it that name, with which, according to the Lamb story, he dazzled his schoolfellows. This was certainly not beyond his capacity.

However, there does not seem to be serious reason to reject

another statement by Coleridge in the *Biographia Literaria,* although the evidence is as usual contradictory: "I had translated the eight Hymns of Synesius from the Greek into English anacreontics before my 15th year" (I, 170*n*, Ch. XII). Synesius was a Neoplatonist of the fifth century A.D., a disciple of Hypatia, the famous woman Neoplatonist martyred by a Christian mob in Alexandria. Synesius was luckier. During a period of great external danger, the Christian community of Ptolemais made Synesius its Bishop, although he was not even baptized, but had a Christian wife. This most unusual combination of circumstances resulted in Synesius writing a set of Hymns in Greek, in which Christian formulas were combined with Neoplatonic philosophy. Doubtless it was this combination that made him attractive to Coleridge. In the *Biographia* he declares that Synesius' pantheism was not of the atheistic kind which Coleridge found objectionable in Spinoza, and he quotes from the Hymns repeatedly in that book (*BL*, I, 166*n*, 169–70, 188 and 195).

But unfortunately nothing remains of Coleridge's adolescent feat of translating the Hymns into English anacreontics, and the whole story is somewhat shaken by a letter dated March 26, 1794, when Coleridge was twenty-two and nearer the age of his supposed translation. In it, Coleridge tells his brother George how he sold some books during the period of his enlistment in the army at Reading, and how he would like to buy them back. Among them was the Neo-Latin poet Casimir and "a Synesius by Canterus," i.e., the edition by G. Canterus, 1576; those two "I mean to translate" (*CL*, I, 77). The possession of this rare edition, which not only gives the Greek text of the poet but also a convenient translation into Latin, would tend to support a still earlier acquaintance with that author. But if Coleridge had actually translated Synesius in his fourteenth year, why does he tell his brother that he still means to translate him? Two years later, Coleridge seems to have undergone one of his not infrequent changes of opinion, and calls Synesius "the hyper-Platonic Jargonist" (*NB*, # 200, dated 1795).

In his later years Coleridge gave still another account of his first awakening to philosophy, an entirely unimpeachable one in itself, but one that invalidates all the other accounts. Coleridge told Dr. Gillman that his interest in philosophy was originally aroused when he was a schoolboy by reading the essays on Liberty and Necessity in a little known eighteenth-century book, *Cato's Letters* (Gillman, 23). This once popular work, published in 1724 and often reprinted, was written by Thomas Trenchard and Thomas Gordon. Trenchard was an active political controversialist, who wrote pamphlets against standing armies and established religion. Intellectually, he was typical of the English Enlightenment. He believed in Reason but also in God, the God of natural religion. The essays in *Cato's Letters* (Cato is merely a pseudonym) are mainly on contemporary political issues, such as the Monarchy and its powers, Church and State, Jacobites and Quakers, etc. Like the American Founding Fathers, Trenchard believed that "All men are born free" (II, 43) and that "Men are naturally born equal" (II, 275), as well as that "there ought to be no inequality in Society, but for the sake of Society" (II, 277). Toward the end of the book he becomes philosophical: he expounds a theory of knowledge in Lockian terms (IV, 196–206) and discusses also the problem of the Will (IV, 175–84 and 185–96), arguing in favor of Necessitarianism and consequently denying Free Will. These must be the "essays on Liberty and Necessity" that Coleridge referred to. Needless to say, there is nothing Platonic or Neoplatonic in them. They are, however, both lucidly and logically argued, and might well have turned an intelligent youngster toward philosophical pursuits.

There is even one reference to a Neoplatonic doctrine in Trenchard in which the concept of the *Anima Mundi* "or Universal Spirit" is mentioned, but without any sympathy (IV, 209). The same doctrine is mentioned again later (IV, 213). Two pages earlier, Trenchard referred to the idea of the body as the prison of the soul and to the doctrine of reincarnation (IV, 211–12), both of which are Platonic. But no clue is given to the names of the philosophers who maintained these doctrines, or even to the school of thought to which they belonged.[18]

The conclusion of this discussion of Coleridge's earliest intellectual ventures is that he was an omnivorous reader, took a lively interest in philosophy and in religion, underwent the usual religious crisis of adolescence, may have read Plotinus *On Beauty* then available in an English translation, and found in it the idea of organic unity in the aesthetic object; but there is no firm evidence that he had read any main Neoplatonic philosophical text "before my fifteenth year." Neoplatonism cannot therefore be considered a guiding influence on Coleridge's thought from his earliest years.

As for other philosophers read in his teens, there is evidence for writers in English philosophy, particularly of the eighteenth century, and some Continental writers, ranging from Boehme to Voltaire, both available in English.

Unquestionably Coleridge in his teens may have read other philosophers besides those named, but these are the only ones for which so far we have definite evidence.

ii

THE EVIDENCE for Coleridge's philosophical interests becomes more definite and more abundant as times goes on, and certain facts stand out clearly for the period of his twenties. First, he became a disciple of the associationist David Hartley, whose *Observations on Man* were published in two volumes in 1749 and reprinted more than once in the eighteenth century.[19]

In spite of its contemporary vogue, Hartley's philosophy has been considered "antiquated" by historians of philosophy: "He does not mention Berkeley; he seems never to have heard of David Hume." [20]

Hartley's first volume builds up, proposition by proposition, a comprehensive theory of all human faculties and emotions, based upon a purely sensationalist epistemology, and proceeding on the theory of association of ideas by succession and contiguity. This leads logically to a necessitarian view of the human will: freedom does not exist. But the second volume goes into metaphysics and builds up the traditional Christian view of the existence of God, the immortality of the soul, the inspiration of Scripture and "the Truth of the Christian Religion" (see especially Ch. 2). He even expatiates on "Theopathy" or the love of God (I, 497 etc.). As all modern critics observe, there is a basic contradiction between the assumptions of Volume I and those of Volume II, but it was not visible to many in eighteenth-century England, where Hartley had a disciple like Priestley. Coleridge became aware of the contradiction only later; in the *Biographia Literaria* he said: "the whole of the second volume is, with the fewest possible exceptions, independent of his peculiar system" (*BL*, Ch. VII, I, 84). But in 1797 Coleridge extolled Hartley for having "demonstrated" that God was "all in all" (*PW*, note to *Religious Musings*, l. 43).

This "peculiar system" centered in the doctrine of "miniature vibrations" or *vibratiunculae:* "sensory vibrations" in the body cause a tendency to "diminutive vibrations" in the brain, thus determining "ideas" in the mind (Proposition IX, I, 58 ff.) and ideas include all mental phenomena. These ideas then become associated by succession and contiguity (Proposition X, I, 65), and so generate all emotions, and all general ideas, culminating in Theopathy.

There is no record of when Coleridge first read Hartley. But in a letter to his brother George on November 6, 1794, Coleridge says that he had "made an intense study of Locke, Hartley and others" by that date (*CL*, I, 126). Hartley's book had many qualities that could appeal to a philosophical Englishman of the eighteenth century: it was based on Locke's epistemology and did not contradict Locke's own faith in God; it was closely reasoned, step by step, and provided a comprehensive system of psychology. It has the same formal qualities as Trenchard, who as we have seen influenced Coleridge as a youth, and is written in a similar style. To the modern reader, perhaps the most interesting discussion is that on words and ideas (I, 267–89). Coleridge's enthusiasm for Hartley manifested itself not only in his writings of the time, such as the poem *Religious Musings* (1794–96) and its notes, added in 1797, but also in the fact that he gave his first-born son the name of Hartley (1796).

A still more important intellectual consequence has recently been claimed for Hartley by Richard Haven. He recognizes that Hartley was a sensationalist and an empiricist, and that for him the only connection between "ideas" was provided by mechanical association. But he argues that, since Hartley's "ideas" were "necessarily determined" by experience, they were therefore necessarily true and provided reliable knowledge of the external world (Haven, 480).

This of course raises a number of questions. For one thing, the data of sensation are entirely contingent and do not carry with them any kind of logical necessity. Association of ideas, being casual, is contingent and affords neither necessity nor universality. It is true that Hartley slips in the word "necessity" or "necessarily" in his second volume, when he expounds his theological system, as in II, 6, 11, 12, etc.; and also when drawing conclusions he uses the word "must," implying logical necessity (II, 13, 14, 15 and passim). But he never proves this necessity.

For instance, he introduces the word in the very first Proposition of Volume II: "Something must have existed from all eternity" (II, 5), which is a traditional proposition of metaphysics, and as such (as metaphysical, and not as Hartley's) was the object of destructive criticism by Kant in his Dialectic of Pure Reason (A 427, B 455). This Proposition is followed by others no less metaphysical, on the existence of God and the immortality of the soul, also to be criticized by Kant. Now what proof is brought forward by Hartley? The very first Proposition receives its proof from the "fact" that we give to it "an instantaneous, necessary assent" and that we cannot deny it (II, 6). But no reason is given for its necessity, except the purely psychological "fact" (if it is a fact) of our assent. All the ensuing propositions, which depend logically on the first one, are also for Hartley necessary truths, and inevitably share this lack of logical foundation.

Incidentally, there seems to be still an echo of this "First Proposition" in Coleridge's later book, *The Friend*. Hartley describes the reaction of a thinking man to the proposition that there was "a Time when Nothing existed" as follows: "we find an instantaneous and irresistible check put to the conception, and we are compelled at once to resist the supposition" (II, 5). Even after reading Kant, Coleridge said: "The very words, There is nothing! or, there was a time when there was nothing! are self-contradictory. There is that within us which repels the proposition with as full and instantaneous a light, as if it bore evidence against the fact in the light of its own eternity" (*F*, 340).

Furthermore, in Volume I Hartley had argued, in keeping with his sensationalist premises, that all assent, even "rational assent," is founded merely on association, "proceeding from a close association of the ideas suggested by the proposition, with the idea, or internal feeling, belonging to the word truth, or of the terms of the proposition with the word truth" (I, 324). Now this makes even rational consent a matter of contingency and not of necessity and universality. So Coleridge could not have found in Hartley a logical foundation for such a sensationalist theology, and the allusion (if it be such) in *The Friend* to the first Proposition of Hartley's Volume II is only a reminiscence, a mere verbal echo. If Hartley had actually argued in the way attributed to him by Haven, he would simply have been juggling with the word "necessary." In Volume I the word hardly ever appears.

Furthermore, if Coleridge had been deceived by verbal juggling through which the contingent is magically transformed into the necessary, then it would only go toward showing Coleridge's philosophical immaturity: he would have fallen into the "gross confusion of probability with absolute certainty, of contingency with necessity" which he later criticized in Petvin (Brinkley, 287). But there is not much evidence for this. Haven himself concludes: "it is impossible to say whether Coleridge ever found Hartley's psychological theories wholly adequate. Certainly he did not long continue to do so" (Haven, 487). And he proceeds to show how Coleridge began to turn away from Hartley after writing the poem *Religious Musings* in which Hartley is eulogized as

> He of mortal kind
> Wisest, he first who marked the ideal tribes
> Up the fine fibres of the sentient brain. (368–70)

Four years afterwards Coleridge in a letter to Godwin of September 22, 1800, which discusses epistemology and semantics, coolly brushed aside Hartley's theory: "all the nonsense of vibrations etc. you would of course dismiss" (*CL*, I, 626). On March 16, 1801, he wrote to Poole an important letter which attests his study of Kant (bracketed by him with Aristotle: *CL*, II, 707): "If I do not greatly delude myself, I have not only completely extricated the notions of Time, and Space; but have overthrown the doctrine of Association, as taught by Hartley, and with it all the irreligious metaphysics of modern Infidels—especially the doctrine of Necessity—This I have done" (*op. cit.*, 706).

Yet in spite of this firm assertion, seven months later, in a letter to Southey of October 21, 1801, he calls Hartley "a *deep* metaphysician" (the italics are Coleridge's) and ranks him with "Zeno, St. Paul, Spinoza" as well as with "Kant and Fichte" (*CL*, II, 768). Two years afterwards he proposed to "defecate" Hartley: in a letter to Godwin, of June 4, 1803, he declares his intention to write "an Essay containing the whole substance of the first volume of Hartley, entirely defecated from all the corpuscular hypotheses—with new illustrations" (*op. cit.*, 949). Nor are these all the oscillations that Coleridge went through in regard to Hartley. About Coleridge's final position there can be no doubt: he formally refuted Hartley and associationism in three successive chapters of the *Biographia*, V, VI, and VII. He summed up his whole critique in one pregnant sentence: "Association in philosophy is like the term stimulus in medicine; explaining everything, it explains nothing; and above all, leaves itself unexplained" (*BL*, II, 222, *Genial Criticism*, I). But during his formative years, 1794–1803, we find him shifting backwards and forwards in his attitude to Hartley, and apparently returning to him after he had "completely . . . overthrown" him.

A similar vacillation, on an even larger scale, is found in Coleridge's attitude to Spinoza, occurring practically all his life.

The uncertainty extends to the date of his first contact with Spinoza. In a letter to Southey of September 30, 1799, he states very definitely that he is "sunk in Spinoza": "I however sunk in Spinoza remain as undisturbed as a Toad on a Rock" (*CL*, I, 534). Three months later he still speaks jocularly of his "Spinosism"; in a letter to the same of December 21, he writes: "My Spinosism (if Spinosism it be and i' faith 'tis very like it) disposed me to consider this big City as that part of the Supreme *One*—which the prophet Moses was allowed to see" (*CL*, I, 551). Yet a year after, on June 7, 1801, he wrote to Humphry Davy: "as soon as possible, I shall read Spinoza & Leibnitz" (*CL*, I, 590). So apparently he had not yet read Spinoza, and could not have been "sunk" in him the year before! [21]

Coleridge's oscillations in his allegiance to this or that philosopher have been noted by his most detailed biographer, Hanson, in his criticism of Southey's well-know enumeration of them. "The suggestion of certain streams of thought being turned on and off like a series of taps—a suggestion palpably false of any thoughtful being and particularly of one such as Coleridge, who relinquished nothing that his mind had once made his own —can be harmful, can leave an impression the reverse of true in the mind. Coleridge did not so much discard a thought as transform it, fit it into place in the jig-saw of his mind" (p. 295).

Psychologically this is true enough. But it is not necessary to go beyond Coleridge's own statements to underline the philosophical impossibility of holding contradictory assumptions at the same time: see for instance what Coleridge himself had said about Hartley's Volume I and Volume II. To speak of a jigsaw in such a case may be psychologically appropriate, but philosophically it is derogatory. If the thought is really "transformed" and "fitted into place," then the result is not a jigsaw but a synthesis, not a mere juxtaposition of pieces but a logical relation of ideas. Even less than a jigsaw, Coleridge's mind at times resembled a whirlpool of thoughts, images, and emotions. He would follow an advance with a pause and possibly a retreat, before making another advance which would take him beyond his starting point.

Indeed, Coleridge's reading habits have received even more

derogatory descriptions from some critics, particularly from J. H. Stirling, the greatest Victorian student of Hegel. According to him Coleridge was in the habit, not of reading philosophers, but of reading "in" philosophers: "The truth probably is, that Coleridge was not properly a student of philosophy, but rather a reader *carptim* [piecemeal]." [22] There is some confirmation of this in Coleridge's own statements about his "lazy reading": "I would not give up the Country, & the lazy reading of Old Folios for two Thousand Times two Thousand Pound" (to Poole, March 21, 1800; *CL*, I, 328), and in his schoolfellow's, C. V. Le Grice's, recollections: "He was very studious, but his reading was desultory and capricious." [23] In 1801 Coleridge admitted that he "had really never *read*, but only *looked thro'* " Locke's *Essay*, which he was then criticising (*CL*, II, 679). And from a statement of 1820 it might even appear that he had read only the Prefaces to Kant's systematic works (*UL*, II, 265); but that would be an unfair reading of that letter.

Stirling's most severe judgment was: "it is difficult to believe that there is any single philosopher in the world whom he either thoroughly studied or thoroughly understood." [24] While admittedly Coleridge was not very methodical and worked by fits and starts, he had an intelligence which often made up for these shortcomings. And while admittedly some of his interpretations will not stand today, we shall see in the following chapters more than one philosopher that Coleridge studied and understood.

From the year 1794 onwards we can follow with much more assurance Coleridge's studies in philosophy. The record of the *Notebooks* begins in 1794 and is abundantly supplemented by the growing volume of his extant letters, in which Coleridge tirelessly expounds to his friends his philosophical ventures, perplexities, and doubts, sometimes at the rate of two or three long letters in a single day. For the years 1795–98 we have the record of Coleridge's and Southey's borrowings from the Bristol Library and we can follow from month to month his readings through this record, complemented by the occasional evidence of the marginal notes, which, when available, are usually significant.

Among the earlier borrowings from the Bristol Library one of the most important was Cudworth. In 1795 and 1796 Coleridge borrowed Ralph Cudworth's *True Intellectual System of the Universe* (1678) in the edition of 1743, and he also took notes from it (*NB*, I, # 200, 201, 203, 204, and 208; cf. 246, 247). Among the Coleridge MSS preserved at the British Museum there is a set of notes from Cudworth, apparently in Coleridge's youthful handwriting, which may well be the original notes he took at the time (Egerton 2801, foll. 212–15). They attempt a summary of Cudworth's argument following the text very closely (but not for long), as a beginner might do.

Cudworth's temper is that of a theological controversialist of the seventeenth century. He loads his page with invectives against the wretched and ridiculous atheists and overwhelms the reader with masses of fantastic and uncritical learning. This no doubt contributed to the almost complete oblivion in which he fell in the following centuries. In the nineteenth century Isaac D'Israeli dedicated to him a chapter of his book on *The Amenities of Literature* (1840), almost compassionate in its Victorian condescension to an eccentric of the past, but accurate in its details.

However, in spite of this, Cudworth presented substantial philosophical theories in his work, which, while interrupted by many digressions, are yet expressed in lucid and forcible language. His metaphysical and epistemological theories are worth disentangling from his theological diatribes—not to speak of his ethical theories, which have been only recently discovered in MS.[25]

Cudworth belonged to the group of Cambridge Platonists. He held a Neoplatonic conception of the existence of "one original mind," i.e., God's, in which all individual minds "participate."[26] This universal mind thinks the eternal Ideas of Plato, and we all think the same Ideas because we participate in the same mind. So that "truths are not multiplied by the diversity of minds which apprehend them; because they are all but ectypal [= derivative] participations of the one and the same original or archetypal mind and truth" (III, 71).[27]

As is evident from the above, Cudworth relies heavily upon the concept of "participation," which of course goes back to Plato: it is one of the latter's formulas for the relation between the Ideas and particulars. But this concept, in this connection, had already been the object of radical criticism by Plato himself, in the *Parmenides* (130 E—132 B), that perplexing dialogue in which Plato presents a thoroughgoing criticism of the theory of Ideas. Aristotle, stepping up the attack, had flatly called "participation" nonsense in the *Metaphysics* (A, 9, 992 a 29). Nevertheless, Neoplatonists still held to the formula, and Cudworth in particular.

More important for epistemology is a shorter work of Cudworth's, *A Treatise Concerning Eternal and Immutable Morality*, published posthumously in 1731 and not included in the edition of 1743 [28] read by Coleridge at Bristol, and not cited in the *Notebooks* of the time. Like all philosophers of the rationalist school, Cudworth asserted very strongly the a priori element in knowledge, and in this shorter work gave a fuller account of the operation of an a priori factor in sense perception. Perception involves for him first of all the sense datum or "phantasm," as he calls it. He gives as an instance the perception of a white triangle. First sense receives the phantasm, or "an appearance of an individual thing, as existing without it, white and irregular, triangular, without any distinction concretely and confusedly together." Then the intellect formulates a judgment upon it, exerting "its own native vigour and activity," and analyses the phantasm into two objects, "the one white, the other triangular. . . . And then . . . it concludes . . . that here is something as a common substratum, 'subject,' to both these affections or modifications, which it calls a corporeal substance; which being one and the same thing, is both white and triangular." Then Cudworth points out that "whiteness," "triangularity," and "substance" are all universal, a priori notions: hence a priori thinking operates even in the perception of a sensuous object (III, 603-4).

However this analysis might lead to the conclusion that we do not perceive white triangles but only the whiteness of triangularity. True, substance, white and triangular are said to be "all individual" (III, 604), but on Cudworth's showing it is hard to see in what their individuality consists.

Cudworth certainly stressed the "self-active" character of the human mind.[29] No doubt, as Professor Coburn observes, this "helped to release Coleridge from associationism and necessitarianism" in which Hartley had involved him (*NB*, I, 203*n*). However, the notes Coleridge took at the time from Cudworth in his notebooks consist only of short quotations or bare references to Greek philosophers in the original language, i.e., from Plato, Aristotle and Plotinus, and Cudworth abounds in such quotations.[30] It seems as if Coleridge then used Cudworth's *True System* mainly as a quarry for useful quotations from Greek thinkers, although the Egerton fragment shows that he also took note of Cudworth's general argument.

To Cudworth Coleridge may owe a firmer grasp of the general philosophy of Plotinus, with which Coleridge seems better acquainted after 1796. Cudworth may also have strengthened in Coleridge's mind the idea of the so-called "Platonic tradition," or continuous transmission of one and the same esoteric doctrine from Pythagoras to Plato and from Plato to the Neoplatonists, which we saw he could have got originally from Taylor. Certainly that theory remained basic in the mind of Coleridge, and it reappears even in the Lectures on the History of Philosophy (*PhL*, 107–8, 115, 165, 237, etc.).

Interesting indications of the effect of Cudworth on the mind of Coleridge are the single words and technical terms which pass from Cudworth's into Coleridge's prose, and sometimes verse. The most distinctive is "plastic," which derives from Cudworth's peculiar theory of "plastic Nature." The latter is a creature intermediate between God and the world, that looks after, and provides for, all organic life, thus sparing the Almighty the bother of looking after every sparrow that falls. "Plastic" is often used by Coleridge in the sense of "creative," as in the early poem, *The Eolian Harp*, in a passage which we shall quote later (l. 48).[31] And one of the several terms of Coleridge's for the mental act of synthesis which brings together the many into one, is "unitive": and that was a favorite term of another Cambridge Platonist, Henry More, but is also to be found in Cudworth. A striking phrase in a letter, "to counterfeit infinity," to which we will come later in this chapter, has also been traced to Cudworth.[32]

It has been claimed that Cudworth anticipated the conclusions of Kant's *Critique of Pure Reason*, so that Coleridge was already in possession of those conclusions when he came to read Kant and therefore did not have much to learn from him.

The claim that Cudworth had anticipated Kant, although made by some contemporary scholars, is not a new one. According to James Martineau, who wrote in 1885, it was first advanced by a German contemporary of Kant, Christopher Meiners,[33] and later repeated by Dugald Stewart (1815; *W*, 43–45). Martineau then proceeded to refute that claim, in a passage to be quoted in full in Chapter 5. In 1898 appeared a rather light-hearted address by William James advising philosophers to "outflank" the troublesome Kant by the simple method of ignoring him. This was justified by the fact that Kant's philosophy had been anticipated in what James called "the older English lines," particularly Cudworth's.[34] James did not realize he had already been refuted by Martineau. Ten years later the same claim was repeated, on the strength of James' statement, by A. O. Lovejoy, again with no reference to Martineau.[35]

In 1924 the claim was extended by Claude Howard to the problem of the genesis of Coleridge's philosophy,[36] an extension which was considered exaggerated by Muirhead (p. 38, *n.* 3). In a succeeding work[37] Muirhead did full justice to Cudworth as a philosopher in the Platonic tradition, but rejected Stewart's claim, showing that it was based on an indirect and insufficient acquaintance with Kant. Stewart's claim was even more strongly criticized by Wellek in 1931 (*W*, 43–45). In his later review of Coleridge studies[38] Wellek dismissed Howard's thesis that "all of Kant is contained in the English Neoplatonists" as merely an "unfounded claim." Yet in 1949 F. L. Brett in an interesting paper on "Coleridge's Theory of the Imagination"[39] repeated once again that claim, but gave an otherwise accurate exposition of Cudworth's epistemology in *Eternal and Immutable Morality*. The later supporters of the claim were equally ignorant of Martineau's refutation of it.

The full refutation of the claim, however, must wait until we have seen what Kant's philosophy actually was. The subject will be taken up again at the end of Chapter 5.

Coleridge also read Berkeley in 1796, borrowing his works in the 1784 edition from the Bristol Library. But the question of Berkeley's influence on Coleridge is more complicated than appears at first sight, for Berkeley had more than one philosophy. Most people, especially literary students of Coleridge, associate the name Berkeley with the paradoxical "immaterialism" of his early years; but in later years he developed another philosophy, which is closer to the Neoplatonic philosophy of the Cambridge thinkers whom Coleridge favored at this time. The "immaterialist" system, called also subjective idealism, and crystallized in the formula *"esse est percipi,"* was expounded in his first works, the *Principles of Human Knowledge* (1710) and the *Dialogues between Hylas and Philonous* (1713), written when the author was respectively twenty-five and twenty-eight. But when he was fifty-nine he wrote the *Siris, a Chain of Philosophical Reflections and Inquiries Concerning the Virtues of Tar-Water* (1744), in which he expounds Platonism of the Cambridge type, quoting abundantly from Cudworth and from Cudworth's authorities, like Plotinus and Themistius.

In his writings of 1796–97 Coleridge makes several enthusiastic references to Berkeley, but few in which definite doctrines are mentioned (see *CL*, I, 245 and 335). In the letter to Thelwall of December 17, 1796, Coleridge probably refers to Berkeley's early immaterialism: he rejects a body-soul theory, "not that I am a Materialist; but because I am a Berkeleyan" (*CL*, I, 278); but there is no discussion of the *esse est percipi*. The most emphatic assertion, perhaps, is to be found in the Gutch Notebook (1795–96), where the plan of a projected poem includes the intention of making "a bold avowal of Berkeley's system! ! ! !" (*NB*, I, 174.6). The poem was never written, so we do not know the terms of that intended "bold avowal." The only specific reference in the notebook is to Berkeley's *Maxims on Patriotism* (*NB*, I, 174.21). In a poem completed in 1796, *Religious Musings*, there is a footnote added in 1797 which again praises Berkeley highly: "This paragraph is intelligible to those who, like the author, believe and feel the sublime system of Berkeley; and the doctrine of the final happiness of all men" (?) (*PW*, 124). The passage to which this note is appended will be quoted fully later in this chapter; but it is so vague that, as Piper says (p. 49), one reader "might well take (it) for Platonic," while another, well qualified, reader, Charles Lamb, "welcomed (it) as necessitarian, though this did not deter Coleridge from claiming it was Berkeleyan a year later after he had adopted that philosophy." So much for the evidence afforded by that note.

It has therefore been reasonably conjectured by Muirhead (p. 46) that Coleridge by this time (1798) had become aware of the "later Platonic (Berkeley) to whom *esse* is *concipi*"—i.e., the Berkeley of the *Siris*, a work in which Coleridge, after reading Cudworth, would have found himself in familiar company. Some support for this conjecture is to be found in a later letter of Coleridge, not quoted by Muirhead. On January 14, 1820, Coleridge wrote to J. Gooden making his oft-repeated division of all philosophers into two schools, which he calls the Platonic (really the Neoplatonic) and the Aristotelian (really the empirical). To the former belonged "Bacon and Leibnitz and in his riper and better years Berkeley—and to this I profess myself an adherent" (*UL*, II, 265). Here Coleridge shows clear awareness of the difference between Berkeley's earlier philosophy and the Neoplatonism "in his riper and better years."

Even before that, there are criticisms of the earlier Berkeley in Coleridge's writings. In his first attempt to construct a Logic, made in 1803, Coleridge described "the *Hylas and Philonous* of Bishop Berkeley as a masterpiece of the Eristic art" (Snyder, 62). This is not as bad as it might sound; by Eristic, Coleridge meant the art of "detecting the imperfections of our apprehensions and of the language adopted as the exponent of them." So *Hylas and Philonous* "is a work which can never be confuted but by a real improvement in our intellectual apprehensions and philosophical language" (*ibid.*). Presumably this improvement had occurred for Coleridge in 1803: he had seen the *Critique of Pure Reason*, where there is a whole section dedicated to the refutation of the "dogmatic" idealism of "the good Berkeley" (B 274–79; cf. B 71).

There is also a minute criticism of a passage in the *Principles of Human Knowledge* in a Notebook of 1804 (# 1842), and a neutral reference to Berkeley in a letter of the same year (*CL*, II, 1032). In the *Biographia Literaria*, the *esse est percipi* is considered valid in the case of the perception of harmony in music (*BL*, I, 81, Ch. VII). Being quoted without the name of the author, it was not identified by any of the commentators. A later reference (I, 92, Ch. VIII) is critical of Berkeley's subjective idealism. In the MS. "Logic," written still later, Coleridge describes Berkeley's early works, the *Principles* and the *Hylas*, with a remarkable phrase: "crude, yet racy" (II, 287)— i.e., immature yet lively. It would seem that Coleridge's criticism of the immaterialist theory eventually took the form that sensation is the beginning of the cognition of an external world, a thesis variously developed in "Logic," II, 163–65 (quoted by Boulger, 112*n*), in a Notebook of 1828 quoted by Muirhead (76–77) and *NB* 27 quoted by Boulger (111–12), and in marginalium on Schelling quoted by Sara Coleridge (*BL2*, 391–92).

I cannot either see "a bold avowal of Berkeley's system" in another MS. note referred to by Professor Coburn (*NB*, I, note to 174.16), and already published in the nineteenth century. It consists of a remark on the *Siris*, praising Berkeley as a pioneer of modern chemistry (!) but makes no reference to his philosophical system or systems. It does quote from the *Siris* a passage on Plato's and Aristotle's idea of God, without comment thereon and with no profession of faith in any theory of Berkeley's.[40]

A much larger claim for Berkeley's influence on the early Coleridge has been made by Appleyard. Coleridge is supposed to have derived from Berkeley a belief in "the unity of man with the natural world and with God" which he then expressed in his early poems (p. 46). This is one of those vague general ideas which purely literary students are prone to claim as "philosophy" but which have very little philosophical content. When Appleyard speaks specifically of Berkeley's early philosophy, he rightly terms it "the theistic immaterialism of Berkeley" (p. 48). But this theistic immaterialism does not involve the "emphatic identification of mind with Nature" (p. 48): for the immaterialist Berkeley "Nature" does not exist. Nor does it by any means involve the identification of God with man.

Certainly Coleridge in this period makes in his poems statements concerning the unity of God with man and with Nature, but, as we shall see later (# iii) when we consider these poems, the doctrine is never philosophically formulated or argued. Devoid of philosophic content, and tossed around in the shifting currents of Coleridge's verse, it becomes little more than a form of words which assumes what meaning it may have from the mood or the fancy of the moment. As Piper observes, the theories on the nature of the world outlined in these early poems are essentially "for poetical purposes": when it comes to a definite doctrine, "he did not commit himself to the idea" (p. 48). Appleyard himself says: "the possibility that Coleridge was attracted to a doctrine because of its poetic utility as a means of professing a meaning or insight cannot be ignored" (p. 52).

A more convincing case is made out by Appleyard for another doctrine of Berkeley's which he has traced in these early poems of Coleridge's. It is the idea of the "Divine Visual Language": God communicates his will to man through the various phenomena of nature, which function as a series of signs for God's thoughts. Coleridge calls it "one mighty alphabet" (*Destiny of Nations*, l. 19 f.), "that eternal language, which thy God / Utters, who from eternity doth teach / Himself in all" (*Frost at Midnight*, 60–62). For it Appleyard (p. 49) points to *Alciphron, or the Minute Philosopher*, Dialogue IV, paragraph 8–15. This work of Berkeley's is dated 1732, and thus does not belong to the early group, but it comes before the *Siris*. The derivation may be accepted, unless someone finds the idea of the Divine Alphabet in another thinker, say a Neoplatonist or Boehme. *The Minute Philosopher* is also quoted in a late MS. by Coleridge preserved at the Huntington Library and known as "The Divine Ideas" (Z, 295).[41]

In conclusion, while it is a fact that Coleridge went through a Berkeleyan phase in his thinking between the years 1796–98, when he christened his second son (born in 1798) with the name of the philosopher, there is not much trace of Berkeley's philosophy in his writings of the time, with the exception of the idea of Divine Visual Language. Later he showed a definite preference for the later, Neoplatonic Berkeley over the early subjective idealist. All this goes to show that there is not much in the claim of some purely literary students of Coleridge that he got from Berkeley what he was later to receive from Kant, as if the two philosophies were identical.

iii

THROUGHOUT all these intellectual vicissitudes Coleridge appears to have maintained a basic faith in traditional religion, though its actual dogmatic content tended to vary. It seems that he remained a Christian even during the time when he was converted, temporarily, to a much more earthy faith, that in the French Revolution.[42] He then left the University without taking a degree and embarked upon his ill-fated attempt to set up an absolute Democracy, or Pantisocracy, on American soil, the only concrete result of which was an ill-assorted marriage. For a time he was a Unitarian.[43] "He preached frequently at the Unitarian chapels of Taunton and Bridgewater" (Hanson, 150). It was in this guise that Hazlitt first met him, as he relates in his famous description. One of the earliest entries in the *Notebooks* consists of an outline of a "Sermon on Faith" (1794, NB, I, # 6), of which he wrote in 1812, quite justly, that it showed "proofs of an original and self-thinking mind" (*ibid.*). In February, 1796, Coleridge delivered in Bristol six Theological Lectures,[44] inspired by his early radicalism, both in religion and in politics, which is also in evidence in the contemporary *Watchman*.

The *Notebooks* for this period contain relevant references: in # 161, a list of projected works, the first of many such lists of castles in Spain; # 64, an entry dated 1795–96, contains a reaction against a materialist who disbelieved in the existence of the soul, Thomas Cooper (1789);[45] # 174.16 contains an attack on Godwin in 1796 for his denial of Free Will. By this time Coleridge had become convinced that Necessitarianism made men, as he says picturesquely, "outcasts of a blind ideot called Nature / ruled by a fatal Necessity" (*loc. cit.*).

In 1796 he also met Wordsworth. Their friendship ripened in 1797, and resulted in the great productive season of the summer when the *Lyrical Ballads* were planned and composed. The *Biographia Literaria* now takes up the narrative: "I retired to a cottage in Somersetshire at the foot of the Quantocks and devoted my thoughts and studies to the foundations of religion and morals" (*BL*, I, 132, Ch. X). An account of his philosophical reflections follows. But he injects in them a quotation from Kant, just when he is about to claim that "a guiding light" had dawned upon him "even before I had met with the Critique of the Pure Reason" (I, 134). Let us look a little more closely at this record.

"I began then to ask myself, what proof I had of the outward *existence* of anything?" (I, 133). The same question had of course been raised by Descartes and by others after him, and Berkeley, read in 1796, had built his immaterialism upon a negative answer to it. As Descartes ended by basing his belief in external reality upon the goodness of God, so Coleridge turned to speculate on "the existence of a Being, the ground of all existence." This is followed by the quotation from Kant's *Only possible proof of the existence of God*, a precritical writing (1763) in which Kant argues that this proof is to be found in the idea of necessary Being, i.e. of a Being whose idea necessarily implies existence: this was Kant's early version of the ontological argument, which he was to reject totally in the

Critique of Pure Reason. In the passage quoted by Coleridge, Kant argues that God should also be endowed with intelligence and will (I, 133–34), and not be an impersonal entity as in pantheism. This was indeed a constant theme of Coleridge's thinking, but there is no reason to believe that in 1797 he had read Kant, so he is simply anticipating on his narrative and illustrating his thoughts at a certain stage by means of his later reading, rather than recollecting their exact genesis.

The rest of this narrative, referring to the period immediately preceding his departure for Germany, relates that he had found a "guiding light" in the argument that, while religion could not be discovered by the intellect, neither could its falsity be demonstrated by reasoning (*BL*, I, 134). This too is a Kantian argument, to be found in the conclusion of the Transcendental Dialectic: "the objective reality [of God] cannot be proved, but also cannot be disproved" (A 641, B 699). But taken by itself, this is not a distinctively Kantian argument, and it can well have occurred to other thinkers (Pascal's wager, for instance, is a variant of it), including Coleridge before he went to Germany.

"Religion," he concludes, "must have a *moral* origin" and its doctrines cannot "be wholly independent of the will" (I, 135). Again, if the argument is that faith in religion depends upon the *reality* of the moral will, this is the argument of the *Critique of Practical Reason.* There may be here a hint of Coleridge's later development of the theory of the will which we shall see in Chapter 9. The discussion which follows involves such basic Kantian concepts as the distinction of the Reason from the Understanding (I, 135–36). Kantian is also "the sacred distinction between things and persons" (I, 137). This whole narrative is saturated with later acquisitions, among which is also the passage from Job, translated from the German paraphrase by Jacobi (*BL3*, 113*n*). However, there is little reason to doubt its conclusion: "A more thorough revolution in my philosophic principles, and a deeper insight into my heart, were yet wanting" (*ibid.*).

His *Notebooks* of the period contain some hint of speculations on Space and Time (# 334). Two entries (# 248–49) have been noted by Prof. Coburn as possibly referring to some second-hand account of Kant which he could have received in England before going to Germany; but they seem too vague and indefinite, and their terminology is more British and empirical than Kantian. The first one however seems to confirm the account in the *Biographia* of his questioning external reality: "Similarity of sensation the cause of our common error in supporting external [properties / prototypes]."

To these years belong also Coleridge's first essays in autobiography, the letters to Poole, which are also essays in self-analysis. Coleridge, needless to say, was his own greatest analyst. His keen interest in all psychological phenomena, particularly the abnormal, made him observe with almost clinical objectivity in his letters and notebooks all the meanderings, the strange twists, the odd associations of thoughts which occurred in his ever-active mind, asleep or awake. In one of the letters to Thomas Poole, written in the fall of 1797, Colerige related how the *Arabian Nights* made such a deep impression upon him as a child "that I was haunted by spectres, whenever I was in the dark" (*CL*, I, 347). In the letter dated October 6, 1797, there is a well-known passage in which Coleridge's mind glides almost insensibly from the imaginative into the philosophical: "For from my early reading of Faery Tales, & Genii &c &c—my mind had been habituated *to the Vast*—and I never regarded *my senses* in any way as the criteria of my belief. I regulated my creeds by my conceptions—even at that age" (*CL*, I, 354).

In the same letter he rejects a view of the universe as "a mass of *little* things" (*loc. cit.*). A "mass of little things" was something entirely abhorrent to Coleridge. In a letter to Thelwall of October 13, 1797, he said that at times the universe itself appeared to him "what but an immense heap of little things? I can contemplate nothing but parts, & parts are all little—!—My mind feels as if it ached to behold and know something *great*—something *one* and *indivisible*" (*CL*, I, 349).

Here again one sees the imaginative gliding into the philosophical, but he does not remain in the latter long enough to give it precision and definition. "Something one and indivisible" either Plato or Plotinus could provide, but which of them? Their philosophies are not interchangeable. Instead of pursuing this search, Coleridge immediately slips back into the aesthetic, a vision of natural beauty: "and it is only in the faith of this that rocks or waterfalls, mountains or caverns give me the sense of sublimity or majesty!—But in this faith *all things* counterfeit infinity!" (*ibid.*).

To weave a single narrative out of these bits of confession and self-analysis in verse and prose, scattered in essays and letters, notebooks and marginalia, may lead to valuable studies of Coleridge's psychology, such as House's or more recently Deschamps'. However it is not the aim of this book to portray the man Coleridge, but to study the sources of his philosophy, and to study them in the prose writings of Coleridge that have a definite philosophical content, and in the thinkers that have a definite place in the history of philosophy, such as Kant and Hume, Cudworth and Schelling. The fate that particular philosophic ideas undergo in Coleridge's poems (apart from prose notes and introductions) is a question best left to students of his poetry.

But since the connection between Coleridge's philosophy and his poetry is a matter which frequently arouses interest, I will now proceed to make three observations upon it, especially concerning the early period which we are now discussing. These observations are 1) on general grounds, 2) on the variety of interpretations of these poems, and 3) on some particular passages.

1) Poetry in general, and good poetry in particular, does not provide an appropriate vehicle for philosophy. Philosophical thinking requires rigor of statement and no deviation from the rational level, whereas poetry proceeds in a way that Coleridge once defined as "opposite" to that of philosophy, since poetry has beauty for its goal and not truth. Its expression is concrete and imaginative, not abstract and logical. The end result of philosophical thinking is a concept; of poetic composition, a lyrical image. Hence the evidence to ideas that poems may occasionally

afford is at best indirect and uncertain, hard to pin down and full of inconsistencies. So good poetry is poor philosophy, just as poor philosophy may turn into good poetry, as Coleridge himself said in 1796: the doctrine of the pre-existence of the soul "may be very wild philosophy; but it is very intelligible poetry, inasmuch as soul is an orthodox word in all our poets" (*CL*, I, 278). "Nature" and "God" are also orthodox words in poetry, and poetic statements that include these words do not have to convey a philosophic meaning. The ultimate foundation for these views will appear in Chapter 6.

Coleridge himself oscillated in his statements on the relationship of poetry and philosophy. Many times he affirmed the union or harmony of poetry and philosophy (in 1802, *CL*, II, 810; *BL*, I, 19, Ch. XV, and II, 129, Ch. XXII; *PhL*, 395; etc.). But in his most formal definition of poetry in his most deliberate critical book he said: "A poem is that species of composition, which is opposed to works of science, by proposing for its immediate object pleasure, not truth" (*BL*, II, 10, Ch. XIV). If philosophical ideas enter into a poem, they cease to be philosophy and become poetry. This is unreservedly true of all good poetry; but even Coleridge's early reflective poems, not usually ranked as great poetry, do not carry clear and unequivocal evidence of philosophical ideas.

2) This is confirmed by the variety of philosophical interpretations which are given to them. Take for instance the often quoted passage in the *Eolian Harp* (1795):

> And what if all of animated nature
> Be but organic Harps diversely fram'd,
> That tremble into thought, as o'er them sweeps
> Plastic and vast, one intellectual breeze,
> At once the soul of each, and God of all?

These lines suggested Plotinus to Mrs. Powell (p. 86, n. 3) and a "Neoplatonist" to House (p. 76), a recollection of Hartley's "vibrations" to Deschamps (p. 409, n. 12), while Stallknecht found a possible source for them in Boehme, and now Piper (p. 46) finds a more prosaic source for them in Priestley. But

Coleridge himself connected them with medical speculations by "Monro" on "a plastic immaterial nature" (*CL*, I, 294–95), as noted by Schrickx.[46]

The lines in *Religious Musings* (35–45) culminating in "God all in all! / We and our Father one!" may sound mystical or Spinozistic, or even "Christian Platonism" (whatever that may mean), but Coleridge himself went out of his way in a footnote to tell us that they are *"demonstrated* by Hartley . . . and freed from the charge of Mysticism" by Hartley's learned commentator, Pistorius.

Even imaginative phrases from Coleridge's prose may puzzle the interpreters. Take the striking phrase "counterfeit infinity" found in *NB*, I, 273 and in the letter of 1797 quoted above. It was attributed by Abrams to the effects of opium. Gérard dedicated to the phrase one of his sensitive and erudite papers and interpreted "counterfeiting infinity" as a rejection of pantheism, in the fragment (not in the letter). Now Schrickx has shown conclusively that the phrase derives from Cudworth.[47] In Cudworth it means that the arithmetical infinite is not the philosophical infinite, but a fake infinity, very much like Hegel's later concept of the "false infinite" (*Encyclopaedia of the Philosophical Sciences*, # 104, Zus.), of which Croce made good use in arguing against scientism.[48] All this may be very well; but if we go back to Coleridge's fragment, we can see why Lowes said that "it looks like a modern impressionistic poem" (p. 191):

> inward desolations
> an horror of great darkness
> great things that are on the ocean
> counterfeit infinity

and find it hard to assign it to any definite idea.

3) There are certainly passages in the two long poems of this period (1796), *Religious Musings* and *The Destiny of Nations*, which rise to a higher level than the trite moralizings of Coleridge's teens, and apparently convey a pantheistic philosophy. Take for instance the following passage:

> Infinite myriads of self-conscious minds
> Are one self-conscious Spirit, which informs
> With absolute ubiquity of thought
> (His one eternal self-affirming act!)
> All his involved Monads, that yet seem
> With various province and rapt agency
> Each to pursue his own self-centering ends.
> *(The Destiny of Nations,* 43–49)

However this is not presented as the poet's philosophy, but as something that bolder speculators may maintain:

> Others boldlier think
> That as one body seems the aggregate
> Of atoms numberless, each organised;
> So by a strange and dim similitude
> Infinite myriads of self-conscious minds, *etc.*

Note also "seems," "strange," "dim," and "similitude."

A similar noncommittal phrase is used in the passage already quoted from the *Eolian Harp,* line 44: "And what if all of animated nature. . . ." What indeed. The same phrase occurs again in *The Destiny of Nations,* line 60, before another series of speculations: "And what if some rebellious, o'er dark realms / Arrogate power?" "What if" is a useful device for a poet to avoid commitment.

Similarly *Religious Musings* has several passages that may sound pantheistic (e.g., ll. 43–44, 105–6, 130–31). But do they represent a stable conviction, or are they only poetic ornament, a flash of fancy playing for a moment with "the One" because Unity is poetically grand and magnificent?

Here is the verse paragraph which Coleridge in another note refers to "the sublime system of Berkeley":

> Behold thou, o my soul,
> Life is a vision shadowy of Truth;
> And vice, and anguish, and the wormy grave,
> Shapes of a dream! The veiling clouds retire,
> And lo! the Throne of the redeeming God

Forth flashing unimaginable day
Wraps in one blaze earth, heaven, and deepest hell. (395–401)

These lines can be applied to almost any religious philosophy of the time; they have no specific reference to Berkeley's views.

Another note (to line 33) quotes a Greek philosopher, apparently of the Neoplatonic school, to the effect that "Men have split up the Intelligible One into the peculiar attributes of Gods many," as E. H. Coleridge translates the Greek. But the reference ("DAMAS. DE MYSTER. AEGYPT.") is unidentifiable, and Beer suspects it is one of Coleridge's learned jokes (pp. 118 and 335).

In *The Destiny of Nations* there is a clear echo of Plato's allegory of the cave in the *Republic*:

> we in this low world
> Placed with our backs to bright Reality,
> That we may learn with one unwounded ken
> The substance from the shadow . . . (*ibid.*, ll. 20–23)

So Coleridge was thinking of Plato. But we are not told what "Reality" is or what "the substance" is, nor is there anything about what Coleridge thought at this time of the Platonic Ideas.

Perhaps the most interesting philosophic references are those to something like a Vichian theory of the rise of morality and of civilization, "unsensualized" by Fancy or by the arts (*Destiny*, 80–87; *Musings*, 208–10). But Coleridge had not yet read Vico, and the theoretical implications of the lines are not clear.[49] Furthermore, "Fancy" and "Imagination" had not yet been desynonymized: see "Fancy" above, and in *Musings*, line 155. Both Fancy and Imagination occur, apparently undiscriminated, in *Effusion at Evening* (1792), lines 1 and 22.

Another way of finding ideas in Coleridge's early poems, followed by some contemporary critics, is to interpret them in terms of Coleridge's later philosophical writings, using the concepts of "subjectivity" and "objectivity," or of "unity in multeity," to describe their contents, and then to claim that

they "confirm obliquely his contention that he found in Kant
and Schelling what his own predilections had already led him
to." [50] We are going to see what Kant and Schelling taught
Coleridge and that will be enough to show how very "obliquely"
this deduction is made.

Coleridge's great poems, like *Kubla Khan* and *The Rime of
the Ancient Mariner*, call for a purely aesthetic interpretation,
and no system of philosophy can be derived from them, or is
adequate to them.

We may conclude that Coleridge's philosophical reading in
his youth touched at several points of ancient and of modern
philosophy. Apparently he encountered at a fairly early age the
speculations of Neoplatonists, and this was perhaps his sole
early contact with ancient thought. The philosophy of Neoplatonism ultimately merges all differences in the all-embracing
One, as Plotinus conceived him. It also asserts a concept of
spirituality, both cosmic and human, but in an indeterminate
form, at least as far as Coleridge's mind was concerned. It is
in a most vague and indeterminate form that, as we saw, it
makes an appearance in early poems.

Later Coleridge was to study Plato. By 1801 he had apparently read the *Theaetetus*, the *Phaedo* and the *Menon*. In the
winter of 1801–2 he read the *Parmenides* and the *Timaeus*
(*CL*, II, 680 and 866), and there are other references later.[51]
But he never seems to have been able to disentangle Plato's
philosophical theories from Neoplatonic beliefs. This seems to
be due to his faith in the so-called "Platonic tradition." Since
the metaphysical doctrines of this tradition, which are mainly
Neoplatonist, do not appear in the *Dialogues*, he asserted that
"the proper system of Platonism" is not to be found "in the
writings of Plato" (*PhL*, 164–65). Where is it to be found,
then? In the writings of his "immediate successors . . . and
. . . likewise more in the writings of the Neoplatonists, in the
Roman empire," provided allowance is made for the latters'
anti-Christian bias (*ibid.*). Plato's dialogues are mere dialectical
exercises (*TT*, 64).

One of the basic differences between Plato's philosophy and

the Neoplatonists lies in the status of the Ideas. According to Plato, the Ideas exist outside the mind of God and independently of God: they are, according to the convenient term invented by Professor Wolfson, "extradeical." According to the Neoplatonists, the Ideas are the thoughts of God and subsist within his Mind: they are "intradeical." Coleridge firmly adheres to the latter view: "But the thoughts of God, in the strict nomenclature of Plato, are all IDEAS, archetypal, and anterior to all but himself alone" (*CL*, II, 1195). That is in the strict nomenclature, not of Plato, but of Philo, with whom the theory seems to have originated, or of the Neoplatonists. That theory was carried forwards through Christianity and the Neoplatonic revival of Florence, and even later.

This raises the still unsettled historical question: when was the "intradeical" doctrine of the Ideas discredited, and replaced by the historically correct one, and by whom? Some scholars believe that it happened only in the nineteenth century, some would put it in the late eighteenth century. But through the kindness of Professor Eugenio Garin of the University of Florence, I was referred to Jacob Brucker's little book on the *Ideas* (1723), where the extradeical theory is correctly attributed to Plato, and the Neoplatonists are criticized as poor judges. Coleridge knew Brucker's large history of philosophy, but apparently never came across the book on the Ideas. While Coleridge was later well aware of the difference between "Platonism" and "Plotinism" (see Ch. V, end), and one of the first to use the terms "neo-Platonists" and "neo-Platonic," at least in England, in the matter of the historical interpretation of Plato he was behind the times.[52]

iv

WE NOW COME to Coleridge's fateful visit to Germany, September 1798 to July 1799.

The idea of the trip had been maturing for some time. German literature was then attracting attention in England for the first time and publications on German books and writers began to appear. The first disciple of Kant to come to England arrived in 1794 and lectured on Kant in London and in other cities. Books on Kant began to be published, and so did translations, or attempts at translation (*W*, 5–15). Kant's fame reached Bristol when Coleridge was living there; in 1796 a physician of the town, Dr. Thomas Beddoes, wrote an enthusiastic article on Kant, particularly on the third *Critique*, and Beddoes was a friend of Coleridge. "Coleridge saw much of Beddoes in Bristol in 1795–98 . . . Beddoes is the most likely personal source— i.e., in addition to all the articles and translations from German literature appearing then in reviews—of the Coleridge-Wordsworth plan to go to Germany" (*NB*, I, Notes, # 246).

Coleridge was caught up by the tide of the German vogue.[53] On May 5, 1796, he wrote to Thomas Poole that he proposed to translate "all the works" of Schiller, and immediately afterwards mentioned plans for a trip to Germany: he was intending to live upon advances from a publisher on his future earnings for the Schiller translation, and thought of residing in "Jena, a cheap German University where Schiller resides"; and also to make a study of the works of "Kant, the great German metaphysician" (*CL*, I, 209). This appears to be Coleridge's first mention of Kant. The next mention is in a letter of December 17 of the same year to John Thelwall, in which he also names the philosopher Moses Mendelssohn (grandfather of the musician): "Germany deems him her profoundest Metaphysician, with the exception of the most unintelligible Emanuel Kant" (*CL*, I, 284). This almost sounds as if he had already been trying to read Kant, but is probably only an echo of the discussions on Kant then going on in England.

Late in 1797 Coleridge writing to a friend said: "I am transslating the *Oberon* of Wieland—it is a difficult language. . . . I pray you, as soon as possible, procure for me a German-English Grammar" (*CL*, I, 357). It sounds paradoxical, but not uncharacteristic, that Coleridge should be translating from the German before he had learnt the grammar of that language.

Finally in 1798 Coleridge found a patron who financed the

voyage, and he left for Germany in September with the Words-worths, William and his sister Dorothy. He stayed for some time at Ratzeburg near Hamburg to learn the language, before going on to the University of Göttingen in 1799.

As soon as he landed, Coleridge began to acquire German books. He then bought Luther's Bible, Lessing's *Fables,* Herder's *Folk Songs,* and works of Klopstock and other German poets (*NB,* I, # 340, 345, and 346). He set himself to study the Ger-man language at times very intensely, as his notebooks attest (# 353 ff.) and became sufficiently familiar with it to be able to read both scientific and literary works. But his knowledge of German grammar was never perfect, and his pronunciation he himself called "hideous" (*NB,* I, Notes, 451). The "Life of Les-sing" which he then projected never went beyond a few notes from an abridgment of the standard life of that writer (*NB,* I, 377).[54]

Even before reaching Göttingen, Coleridge had heard Ger-mans speak of Kant and been present at a discussion about him. On September 21, 1798, he paid a visit to the German poet Klop-stock in Hamburg, and wrote an account of it to Thomas Poole —a vivid and amusing account which he rewrote and published later, not once but two times, as part of his *Satyrane's Letters* (i.e., satirical letters from Germany). We will take first his earliest account as providing the most immediate recollection and less likely to be colored by afterthoughts. It is written in an English (university?) slang now obsolete, but not too hard to follow. "Of Kant he said, that he was a Mountebank & the dis-grace of Germany—an unintelligible Jargonist.—And that his New Lights were going out very fast in Germany. (N.B. *I* meet everywhere tho', with some SNUFFS that have a live spark in them—& fume over your nose in every company.—All are Kant-ians whom I have met with)" (*CL,* I, 444).

The "N.B." within parentheses was rewritten in 1809 in more formal language. "Throughout the Universities of Germany, there is not a single Professor, who is not either a Kantean, or a disciple of Fichte . . . or lastly who, though an antagonist of Kant for his theoretical work, has not embraced wholly or in part his moral system, and adopts part of his nomenclature" (*The Friend*, 1809, pp. 283–84).

This passage was reproduced, practically unaltered, in the appendix to the *Biographia* (*BL*, II, 174–75, Letter III). But even in its first racy version it testifies remarkably how much Coleridge had already heard about Kant—"all are Kantians whom I have met with"—and the impression this made upon him, confirmed by all his later experience.

We hear less of Kant when Coleridge is at Göttingen, except some anecdotes from sources perhaps not entirely reliable (*W*, 70 and Hanson, pp. 352 and 500, n. 73). But it seems very unlikely that he did not hear more of Kant in a university where no less than three courses were being offered on his philosophy, and one disciple, Bouterwek, was giving a course on aesthetics (Winkelmann, 39). This was the great age of Kantianism in Germany. The old philosopher was still alive and publishing, and his last great *Critique* had appeared in 1790, only nine years earlier. Coleridge, it is true, took none of the courses offered on Kant, but preferred to take Natural History and Physiology from Professor Blumenbach (his medical interests were not dead), the New Testament from Professor Eichhorn, and the Gothic language from Professor Tychsen (*BL*, I, 139, Ch. X)—a typically Coleridgian mixture of science, religion, and philology. But he certainly associated with other students, both English and German (one was the son of Blumenbach), and the English later reported that Coleridge's talk was abundant, as always, and largely devoted to metaphysics, as always too. So it is highly unlikely that he did not hear discussions of Kant's philosophy from his associates. Recently a note has been found that shows a definite understanding of Kant's philosophy. In Göttingen Coleridge was making a survey of English medical works mentioned in German periodicals, and there he found a review of a book by the English physician Dr. John Brown, whose medical theories ("the Brunonian system," not to be confused with that of Giordano Bruno) were then attracting much attention. Coleridge notes that the German reviewer "blames Brown for attributing Necessity & Universality to theses built on Analogy & Induction." Coleridge's retort was: "Answer—Brown was no Kantian,

& probably held nothing but high degrees of Probability possible" (*NB*, I, 389 Fol. 29).

The significance of this entry was noted by Chinol (p. 28), and more fully brought out by Wilkinson. "The notebooks make it clear that as early as 1799 he not only knew Kant well enough, whether at first or at second hand, to spot a Kantian bias in the critic of a medical work, but that his philosophical powers were already so highly developed that he could make, en passant but with complete sureness, the kind of inference only possible to someone familiar with the fundamental issues involved" (*NB*, I, Notes, 452).

When he returned to England in July 1799, Coleridge brought back with him a boxful of German books on metaphysics for the value of £30 (*CL*, I, 519 and 599), among which it is reasonable to assume were works of Kant, possibly some of those which we know were later in his possession, dated as early as 1787 and 1794 (*PhL*, 459): e.g., he owned a copy of the second edition of the first Critique (1799), now in the British Museum (signature C. 126 i. 9), enriched with his marginalia.

However, the most philosophical entry in his German notebook comes from his reading an account of Platonism: the distinction of Unity from Entity (*NB*, I, 374 Fol. 3–4), and the Averroists' conception of the collective soul of humanity (*ibid.*), which he was later to compare to the *Ich* of German philosophy (see this volume, Ch. 4).

Finally, it should be said that these years were the heyday of the (first) German Romantic school, when the Schlegels Schelling, Novalis, Tieck, and Steffens met in Jena. Apparently Coleridge had no contact at the time with them or with the "cheap German university" where he had once planned to study. Later in life he was to meet L. Tieck and A. W. Schlegel.

v

IT IS USUALLY believed that Coleridge began a serious study of Kant not long after his return to England, and precisely in the early months of 1801. On March 16, 1801, he wrote the famous letter to T. Poole which has been quoted above and in which he spoke of his "most intense study of philosophy" at that time, involving "an attentive perusal of the works of all my Predecessors from Aristotle to Kant." As a result, he had "completely extricated the notions of Time and Space" and "overthrown the doctrine of Association, as taught by Hartley, and . . . the doctrine of Necessity" (*CL*, II, 706–7).

This has been taken to mean that Coleridge by then had mastered at least the Transcendental Analysis of Space and Time in Kant's first *Critique*. But it has been objected to this that in the same period (actually a month earlier than the quoted letter) Coleridge showed no signs of being acquainted with German philosophy in the philosophical letters which he wrote to his patron, J. Wedgwood, in February, 1801 (*CL*, II, 677 ff.). These letters consist of an attack on Locke's originality, not on his philosophy; they make no reference to Kant and seem to be based still on Hartley.[55] Incidentally, it is ironical to see Coleridge, who was later to suffer so much because of charges of plagiarism against himself, should begin with an (unsubstantiated) charge of plagiarism against another philosopher. This certainly supports the criticism, made more recently, that Coleridge "was always unfair to Locke." [56]

These letters, four in number, seem to have been somewhat overrated by some modern scholars. In any case, the conclusions based on them of Coleridge's ignorance of Kant and persisting empiricism at that period have been rejected by more recent scholars (Chinol, 32–34; cf. Griggs in *CL*, II, 678). Indeed it is possible to discern some traces of Kantism even in those letters, where Coleridge gives another rather unhistorical interpretation, that of Plato's Ideas as the "original Faculties and Tendencies of the Mind" or "Laws of human Thinking, and the word should be translated 'Moulds' and not Forms" (*CL*, II, 682). Coleridge is here describing Plato's Ideas in terms which are more appropriate to Kant's Categories. The word "Moulds" is used for Kant's categories in the *Friend* in the MS. "Logic" (II, 176) and elsewhere.[57]

There are also two references to Kant in a letter of February

13, 1801, which also proudly refers to the letters on Locke (*CL*, II, 675–76). From now on references to Kant become more frequent in the letters and in the *Notebooks*, and we will no longer follow them chronologically. Coleridge was then reading Kant, if not all the time, at repeated intervals. Miss Coburn notes more intensive study in 1803, then again after 1810, "and more still after 1817 i.e., between the composition of the *Biographia* and the 1818 *Friend*" (note to # 1517). In 1804 he read the minor works of Kant (see # 2151 and 2316; the first of these will be discussed later in this chapter). There are other references to Kant in that year (# 2375, and probably 2057) and in 1805 (e.g., # 2598, 2663, and 2666). In the *Biographia*, Chapter IX, Coleridge made his most solemn and most famous statement about Kant: "The writings of the illustrious sage of Königsberg, the founder of the Critical Philosophy, more than any other work, at once invigorated and disciplined my understanding. The originality, the depth, and the compression of the thoughts; the novelty and subtlety, yet solidity and importance of the distinctions; the adamantine chain of the logic; and I will venture to add (paradox as it will appear to those who have taken their notion of IMMANUEL KANT from Reviewers and Frenchmen) the *clearness* and *evidence*, of the 'CRITIQUE OF PURE REASON'; of the 'JUDGMENT'; of the 'METAPHYSICAL ELEMENTS OF NATURAL PHILOSOPHY'; and of his 'RELIGION WITHIN THE BOUNDS OF PURE REASON,' took possession of me as with a giant's hand. After fifteen years' familiarity with them, I still read these and all his other productions with undiminished delight and increasing admiration" (*BL*, I, 99).

No other thinker won a similar tribute from Coleridge. Shorter tributes to Kant, no less emphatic, abound in other writings. In 1804 Coleridge asked: "what is there in Kant that is not admirable?" (# 2316). Some fifteen years later he asked: "what since Kant is not in Kant in germ at least?" And in 1820 he wrote to a friend: "In him is contained all that can be *learnt*." [58] Still more tributes are to be found in the unpublished writings, to be quoted in part in Chapter 11.

While recognizing (as any student of philosophy must) the overwhelming importance of Kant, Coleridge did not subscribe to all his doctrines, and made a number of criticisms, sometimes quite drastic, to be seen in later chapters. If one were to enumerate the works of Coleridge in which ideas of Kant are adopted or discussed, one would have to list all the prose works of Coleridge published by him in the nineteenth century, plus his letters and notebooks, only now being published in their entirety. The unpublished dissertations are also being brought out now, and they afford much Kantian material. There remain to be considered the marginalia, also to be edited in their entirety.

However, when dealing with the marginalia as evidence for some belief of Coleridge, and particularly for the chronology of his ideas, certain facts should be kept in mind. First of all, Coleridge like most people jotted notes on the margin while he was reading the book, and not necessarily after completing the reading of the book as a whole, so that his notes represent, as he once called them himself, "Doubts during a first perusal, i.e., struggles felt, not arguments objected." [59] This heading occurs over marginalia to Kant and shows that Coleridge did not erase the doubts he felt during his first perusal, even if they were cleared by his later reading, but left them intact, as evidence of the stages his thinking had gone through.

Another important set of Marginalia is that on Schelling, and there are plenty of doubts, objections, and criticisms in them. But there is also this important note: "A book I value, I reason and quarrel with *as* with myself when I am reasoning" (BL2, 394; italics mine).[60] So Coleridge's notes must be taken for what they are, valid for the moment he wrote them, but not necessarily his final opinion on the subject.

Since they are rarely dated, the moment for which they were valid is generally hard to determine. Some of the dates that actually occur on marginalia are very revealing. Take the ones on Kant's *Metaphysische Anfangsgrunde der Naturwissenschaft*, published by Professor Schrickx.[61] They exhibit something like strata, each expressing a later opinion contrary to the preceding. The earliest are undated, but were made "some years" before

1811. The second note is dated "July, 1811" and the third "August, 1819." How many other notes may have a similar stratification which, not being dated by the author, may be to-day completely obliterated?

A remarkable warning was given by Coleridge himself in what is the most massive set of marginalia in all his writings. That is the set of marginalia on the works of Boehme in William Hall's English translation. Coleridge's copy is now in the British Museum, and on the flyleaf there is an appeal to the reader not to take the marginalia in the body of the book as Coleridge's final and considered opinion, and indeed repudiating the "Errors" of Boehme which he had previously followed.[62] This warning is dated August 27, 1818, so that the notes in the body of the book, which express agreement with Boehme, must be considered anterior. How many other marginalia were tacitly repudiated by Coleridge in later reflections, without warning to the reader? For all these reasons the marginalia, valuable and fascinating as they are, must be used with caution.

Then there is also the external evidence to Coleridge's philo-sophical ideas, viz., the accounts of his conversations with friends and acquaintances. The most valuable among these are the conversations with Henry Crabb Robinson, to which we have already made reference. Robinson kept a voluminous diary in which he recorded many conversations with the Romantic writers. He was a friend and an admirer of Coleridge, but a candid and sometimes critical friend, who could see the short-comings of a genius and criticize him when he thought him wrong. Furthermore he had studied at Jena for four years (1802–5) and acquired a sound knowledge of German phi-losophy: he had no axes to grind, and for all these reasons his testimony to Coleridge's philosophical utterings are of the greatest value.[63] There are occasional statements by other friends, but less abundant and of lesser importance.

While ideas from Kant are liable to turn up in Coleridge's writings at any time after 1800, they are sometimes so strangely attired that they escape the ordinary reader. Here are two strik-ing examples.

In the *Notebooks* there is a vision of the creation of the solar system, which sounds very imaginative and therefore very Coleridgean, especially since it ends with the direction, added later, "For my own Life—written as an inspired Prophet,—*throughout*": "Saw in early youth as in a Dream the Birth of the Planets; and my eyes beheld as *one* what the Understanding afterwards divided into 1. the origin of the masses, 2. the origin of their motions, and 3. the site or position of their Circles & Ellipses—all the deviations too were *seen* in one intuition of one, the self-same, necessity—& this necessity was a Law of Spirit." (*NB*, II, # 2151; dated July—August 1804).

However, Miss Snyder found the following passage in Kant's *General Theory of the Heavens* (1755, translated into English as *Kant's Cosmogony* in 1900): "The view of the formation of the planets in this system [Kant's] has the advantage over every other possible theory in holding that 1) the origin of the masses gives 2) the origin of the movements, and 3) the position of the orbits as arising at the same point of time; nay, more, in showing that even the deviations from the greatest possible exactness in these determinations, as well as the accordances themselves, becomes clear at a glance." [64]

There is no better comment on this than Miss Snyder's: "Such a comparison, in fact, raises serious doubt as to whether Coleridge 'saw in early youth, as in a dream,' anything of the sort here described, or whether the whole may not have been conceived in the year 1804, when he had had ample opportunity to familiarize himself with Kant's 'Cosmogony' " (p. 621).

The entry in the *Notebooks* concludes with some characteristic expressions of Coleridgean theism: "in this unity I worshipped. . . . God is the one, the *Good*," but the vision of the cosmos is Kant's.

The other example we owe to Professor J. W. Beach.[65] In the second section of *The Friend*, Essay V, Coleridge discusses the fundamental principles of Method in reasoning, and takes occasion to sum up the philosophy of Plato in one sentence: "The grand problem, the solution of which forms, according to Plato, the final object and distinctive character of philosophy, is this: for all that exists conditionally (that is, the existence of which is inconceivable except under the condition of its dependency on some other as its antecedent) to find a ground that is unconditional and absolute, and thereby to reduce the aggregate of human knowledge to a system." (p. 307, Lect. 2, Ess. 5).

Professor Beach comments: "In attributing the above formula to Plato, Coleridge gives no reference." And indeed the formula, as it stands, is most suspicious: such terms as "ground," "conditional" and "unconditional" smack of German philosophy. Beach reveals that "the formula appears, almost literally, in Kant's *Critique of Pure Reason*, as follows . . . in Smith's translation": "Obviously the principle peculiar to reason in general, in its logical employment, is:—to find for the conditioned knowledge obtained through the understanding the unconditioned whereby its unity is brought to completion" (A 307, B 364).[66]

This surprising attribution of a thought of Kant to Plato, *sic et simpliciter*, throws a lot of light not only on Coleridge's Kantianism, but also on his so-called Platonism. It is a commonplace of literary students of Coleridge when they talk of his philosophy to call it Platonic and leave it at that, as if that explained everything; but the writer who could cheerfully attribute to Plato a thought from the *Critique of Pure Reason* does not seem to have had a very clear or a very historical idea of Plato. It is unquestionable that Coleridge had a great admiration for Plato, so I suspect that his reasoning at this point was something like this: "Plato, being the greatest of all philosophers, must have been acquainted with all the basic truths of philosophy; this proposition of Kant's on the conditioned and the unconditioned is a basic truth of philosophy; therefore it must also have been Plato's."

The origin of Coleridge's projection of Kant into Plato may perhaps be found in his marginalia to Taylor's Proclus of 1792, published by Professor Coburn in her appendix to the *Notebooks*, Notes, I, 455 ff. These notes are not dated, but they belong to a time when Coleridge was already acquainted with

Schelling, perhaps after 1812—1813 being the date of the earliest reference to Schelling in the letters (*CL*, III, 461), although Schelling is mentioned in a Notebook entry of 1806 (II, # 2784).

In these notes Coleridge at first expressed himself with due caution, well aware, and even regretful, that he is reading Proclus in translation and not in the original: "This enunciation appears (as far as I can *guess* from Taylor's strange English) to approach more nearly to the great discovery of the mediation between the Intellect and the Sense by the 'Intuitus puri' or 'Formae Universales Representationis', i.e., Space and Time. . . . than any passage that has occurred in my reading before the De Mund. Int. et Sens. of Immanuel Kant" (pp. 456–57).

Here Coleridge cautiously ("*guess*," underlined by him) draws a parallel ("appears . . . to approach more nearly") with Kant's theory of Space and Time as pure intuitions or forms of representation, as presented in the Dissertation of 1770 (and of course in the Transcendental Aesthetic in the *Critique of Pure Reason*). He then becomes bolder and speaks critically (and cryptically) of Plato's "fiction of intelligible Aspections, Ideas," but adding as a cautious afterthought: "I by no means suppose Proclus to have *mastered* the truth contained in this passage; yet it is educible from the words" (p. 457).

After another dozen pages of the text, Coleridge throws all caution to the winds. He considers what he had called his 'guess' as a firmly established truth, and his 'supposition' about Proclus turns into the positive: Proclus does anticipate Kant's transcendental aesthetic and Kant *is* identified with both Platonism and Neoplatonism. "It seems clear, that the Critical Philosophy, as contained in the works of Immanuel Kantius, is a Junction of the Stoic *Moral* with the Platonic *Dialectic:* which Kant has unfairly confounded with the *Sophistic* (Logik der *Schein*)[67] but which is in truth the same with his own transcendental Logic: even as the Mathesis of Plato, so finely determined in this chapter by Proclus, is Kant's transcendental *Aesthetic* (intuitus puri)."[68]

He then proceeds to project also Fichte and Schelling into "the Alexandrine Philosophy," but that need not detain us here.

We may ask, however, was there anything in the text of

Taylor that Coleridge was annotating—anything besides the passages quoted by Coburn—that might account for Coleridge's astonishing projection of Kant into Proclus?

It may be that Taylor's footnote (I, 45–46), expounding Plato's epistemology in the *Republic*, "concluding part of the sixth book," may have recalled Kant's to Coleridge. Taylor speaks of the three cognitive faculties: sense, "cogitation" and Intellect, and this may have recalled Kant's famous trichotomy of sense, understanding and reason.

However, the resemblance ends when we come to Proclus' theory of mathematical essences, in which Coleridge mistakenly sees the Kantian foundation of the truth of mathematics upon the a priori forms of intuition, or *intuitus puri*. Proclus-Taylor speaks of the Soul "educing" mathematical "species" from itself "and from the intellect combined" (I, 57). But Proclus here is speaking of the second and third hypostases in Plotinus's system of emanation from the One, and "eduction" is part of a cosmic process, not a psychological act. There is possibly a distant parallel with later transcendental theories, but Kant's is subjective, whereas Proclus-Taylor's is metaphysical and objective. Later Coleridge became aware of the metaphysical character of these speculations and asked: "Besides, amid all these fine flights concerning the Soul, the Intellect, and the One, what becomes of the poor 'I'—of the Self of each person? Whence comes, whence goes, the personality?" (458).

Then Coleridge surprisingly turned back to assail Plato for "his fiction of intelligible Aspection, Ideas, *kata Plat.*" (457). The last is in all likelihood *katà Plátona*, according to Plato. Surprisingly, for Coleridge usually defends Plato's theory of Ideas, even when he misrepresents it. Here he seems to be either attacking the Ideas from an empiricist viewpoint, as fictions, or criticizing them from a Neoplatonic point of view as extradeical (for the Neoplatonists, Ideas are intradeical).[69] At this point of Coleridge's development the latter hypothesis is more likely than the former; but it runs against another difficulty: it would imply that Coleridge had a clear idea of the difference between Platonism and Neoplatonism, which he does not always have.[70]

Whatever the reasoning that led Coleridge to this projection of Kant into ancient thought, it will now be clear that ideas of Kant's may appear in Coleridge disguised (with no intention to deceive) in the most unexpected ways.

We will now cease to follow the chronological development of Coleridge's philosophical thought, and turn to Kant to take stock of Coleridge's references to him. We will attempt to expound Kant's three *Critiques* and show Coleridge's reaction (when there was one) to Kant's various doctrines. The chronological sequence will now be the development of German philosophy, and Coleridge will take second place. There will be no attempt to present Coleridge's various reactions chronologically, nor to evaluate the German influence in terms of the phases of Coleridge's intellectual development. This development we shall not neglect completely; but it is a long and complicated story, as may be seen from the samples we have given of it in this chapter, with much material still to be published and several points still to be clarified. The task of giving a complete history of Coleridge's intellectual development, important as it is, must be left to others. Our aim will be reached if we make the philosophers that Coleridge was responding to somewhat less forbidding, and to show the reader what there is in them that Coleridge saw in them.

CHAPTER 2

Kant I—The Critique of Pure Reason

K ANT[1] FORMULATED IN the *Critique of Pure Reason* (1781) a new philosophical point of view, the transcendentalist, involving a new theory of knowledge or epistemology. In the *Critique of Practical Reason* (1788) Kant showed how from this point of view an ethical theory could be constructed that would support the traditional beliefs in God, freedom of the will and immortality. In the *Critique of Judgment* (1790) he showed the possibility of still further developments, throwing light both on aesthetics and on the theory of life. His successors went even further: they developed out of transcendentalism a new metaphysics, no longer traditional but idealistic and historistic, the metaphysics of Mind, or of Spirit as actualized in world history.

We have seen that Coleridge's basic beliefs, in spite of some oscillations, remained fundamentally those of Anglican Christianity, supported by the framework of traditional metaphysics. But acquaintance with Kant and with his successors, particularly Schelling, produced a deep impression upon him, and he made a serious attempt to base orthodoxy upon the foundations of the new epistemology—an attempt which may be hopeless but which he was not the only one to make. How far in making this attempt he progressed in the direction of absolute idealism will be discussed later, especially in Chapter 8. But on the whole it seems that he tended to remain faithful to Christian orthodoxy and to traditional philosophy. So the question arises: what was there in Kant to attract him so strongly?

First of all, Coleridge found in the *Critique of Pure Reason* a solution to the conflict between the two opposing schools of philosophy prevalent up to his time, presenting a synthesis of them in a third doctrine that was substantially new. These two schools are known as the empirical and the rationalist, the first believing that truth could be reached only from experience, and the other believing that it could be reached by deduction from a priori principles. Kant criticized both schools, and maintained that, while all knowledge of nature and of man comes to us from experience, experience itself is governed by the a priori functions of the mind. To understand his argument we must first see something more about the tenets of the two opposing schools, between which Coleridge himself had somewhat oscillated in his youth, as we saw in the previous chapter. Our exposition of the two schools will be summary and partial, since it will be directed toward Coleridge and adjusted so as to account for his views, which we will illustrate by quotations from his works.

We will begin with their purely epistemological views, or the theory of knowledge. This will lead us to Hume, when it will become apparent that the theory of knowledge has an increasingly important bearing upon metaphysics, or the general view of the world and man's place in it. Then we will turn to their metaphysics proper.

i

EMPIRICISM, as developed by a succession of British thinkers in the seventeenth and eighteenth centuries—Hobbes, Locke, Berkeley (in part) and Hume—is the view that all our knowledge derives from the data received through our senses or from what Coleridge called "notices of the senses" (*Aids*, 154). Sense data (to call them by a more modern name) are preserved in the memory and elaborated by our minds. The result of this elaboration is what are known as empirical concepts, or ideas derived from experience. Empirical concepts thus relate to all our knowledge of such things as trees, stars, animals, minerals, men, etc.

At first sight this seems a perfectly obvious commonsense view. From what source do we derive our knowledge of the world outside us other than from what we see, hear, smell, taste, and touch? Even if our senses' range is increased by means of special instruments, it is ultimately upon our senses that we rely. However, there is another factor to be considered. It was said in the definition given above that sense data are subject to a process of elaboration by the mind, and result in concepts or general ideas. This is the foundation upon which the whole vast structure of scientific knowledge in all its branches is built up. A single sense datum does not give us much knowledge, and a mere accumulation of sense data does not constitute knowledge: the data must be systematically collected, compared and classified, and inferences must be drawn from them according to the principles of scientific method.

The philosophical question is, what are the intellectual processes by which sense data are elaborated? Do they involve principles which are not themselves derived from sense data? A principle is something very different from a sense datum. The latter is limited to a single sensation, or group of sensations, experienced at one time and in one place. But a principle goes well beyond a single datum or group of data; it extends to phenomena which occur at other times and other places, and some principles may be said to apply to all times and to all places. For instance, take the principle upon which almost all scientific reasoning is based, the principle of causality, which may be formulated: "every event must have a cause," or more simply "every change of condition has a cause." We cannot take a step in any direction, undertake any investigation in any field of nature, without assuming its truth. And yet it is not a sense datum, nor a generalization from a limited number of sense data, for its validity goes beyond our experience and everybody else's. By means of it we can infer causes of which we have no experience, and predict effects which we have yet to experience. It stretches backwards into the past without restriction, and forwards into the illimitable future.

By means of principles like that of causality we are able to make generalizations upon the causes of phenomena and account for any number of instances, which are brought under it and explained by it. There is of course danger in excessive generalization, as there is in any excess. But practically all philosophers, including empiricists, admit the validity of generalizations. Obviously, they could not formulate a single theory (including empiricism) without them, since theories are generalizations.

But the question still remains for the philosopher: are *all* generalizations derived from experience? In particular, are universal principles, such as the law of causality, derived *only* from sense data? Since Plato at least, there have been philosophers who believed that the real nature of things can be discerned only by the intellect or the reason. Plato himself went further and argued that there are Ideas, as he called them, that exist in themselves and for themselves, eternal and unchangeable, independently of all human thought, and even independently of all divine thought (= extradeical). They are absolute and eternal as God himself, and stand as it were in front of God, who built the world using them as a model, as the *Timaeus* says.

Plato also believed that the supreme Idea was the moral principle, or the Good. In other words, a standard of ethics cannot be considered valid unless it is universal. Once it is limited to a single group of facts circumscribed in time and space, it ceases to be valid for other places and other times. Once we begin whittling down space and time, we end by being reduced to a single spot and a single moment, the Here and Now. Or, as Coleridge put it, "He, who begins by loving Christianity better than Truth, will proceed by loving his own Sect or Church better than Christianity, and in loving himself better than all" (*Aids*, 66). To ensure this universality, Plato placed the Ideas in a heaven beyond the reach of this world.

But other philosophers reject this supramundane view. They want to remain within the world of human experience, and therefore reject the eternal and immutable Ideas as figments of the imagination. Knowledge they limit to sense data and to ideas (with a small I) derived from sense data. This view received a classic statement in the formula *"Nihil est in intellectu quod non fuerit prius in sensu."* Or as Coleridge put it, they "presume, with Mr. Locke, that the mind contained only the reliques of the senses" (*S&C*, 300). In the *Biographia* (I, 163, Ch. XII) he ridicules the philosophy whose aim is "to explain the *omne scibile* by reducing all things to impressions, ideas and sensations."

The empiricists carry their theory to the extent of maintaining that all general ideas are derived solely from the senses. Even the most abstract ideas are for them reducible to sense data, or a posteriori. Locke argued that all general ideas were simply ideas of particular objects, obtained through the senses and generalized by a process of progressive abstraction and of name-giving. Even Berkeley, who on this point was a complete empiricist, derived general ideas from particular ideas drawn from experience, and Hume was the most radical of all empiricists.

This is how Coleridge in later life (1825) represented satirically the empiricists and their rejection of Ideas. "Dr. Holofernes, in a lecture on metaphysics, delivered at one of the Mechanics' Institutions, exploded all ideas but those of sensation; and his friend, Deputy Costard, has no idea of a better flavored haunch of venison than he dined off at the London Tavern last week. He admits (for the Deputy has travelled) that the French have an excellent idea of cooking in general; but holds that their most accomplished *maîtres de cuisine* have no more idea of dressing a turtle than the Parisian *gourmands* themselves have any real idea of the true taste and colour of the fat" (*C&S*, 68–69).

In this little bit of ridicule, Coleridge shows to what a low level an idea is reduced when it is made purely empirical. Are haunches of venison and the like the only things we can have an idea of?

The opposite view to empiricism in the seventeenth and eighteenth centuries is usually called rationalism. It held that our reason can obtain direct insight into truth by a process of logical thinking which does not depend on sense experience but on pure logic and absolute rationality. In this way we are able to know a number of universal truths which are so evident or so primary that they do not require proof. We know by pure reason that two contradictory statements cannot be true, that an effect must always precede its cause, that the sum of the angles of a triangle is equal to two right angles, etc. Some of these are the truths of logic, and some the truths of mathematics; but the rationalists, such as Descartes, Spinoza, and Leibniz, believed that the basic truths about reality and the nature of the universe, as well as the truths of ethics and of the nature of mind, could also be reached by that way, which was called a priori, meaning that its truths do not depend upon experience but are logically prior to it. Truth itself is an a priori idea, although experience may provide us with instances of particular and limited truths.[2]

Obviously, the a priori ideas—truth in itself, good in itself, beauty in itself—are historically derived from Plato's Ideas. But for Plato the Ideas existed independently of our minds, whereas for the rationalists they are concepts of reason. This naturally raises a number of questions as to the place of reason in the universe.

Belief in a priori knowledge sometimes took the form of belief in so-called "innate ideas." It was thought that a priori ideas, not being derived from experience, must be inborn in us, and so even chronologically anterior to all individual experience. It was believed that this would ensure their logical *a priority*, which actually does not require any such extrinsic prop. Innatism is a psychological hypothesis, claiming to be a matter of fact; but it does not stand the test of fact, as the main empiricists, Hobbes and Locke, conclusively proved.

The empiricism of Hobbes called forth in England an answer from the rationalist group usually called the Cambridge Platonists, although some of them taught at Oxford, and their philosophy was rather Neoplatonic than Platonic. Coleridge called them: "Plotinists rather than Platonists" (*LR*, III, 415). We have already seen how Coleridge read one of them, Cudworth, in 1796, and took notes from him. Now the Cambridge Platonists were rationalists in the sense that they believed in a priori knowledge, but they eschewed the term "innate Ideas" altogether.[3] Cudworth, for instance, could state the doctrine of the a priori without ever using it: "our human mind hath other cogitations or conceptions in it, the ideas of intelligible natures and essences of things, which are universals, and by and under which it understands singulars." [4]

Furthermore the empiricists, in keeping with their main premise, also maintained that the mind of man was entirely passive and inert, and incapable of producing anything of its own. Otherwise there would be something in it which does not come from the outside. So the mind was likened to a blank sheet upon which nothing is written to begin with, and upon which experience, coming from the outside, inscribes the data of sense, thus producing knowledge. This blank sheet is the "tabula rasa" of the Ancient Stoics and the "white paper" of Locke (*Essay*, II, 1, ii).

Cudworth on the contrary affirmed, indeed stressed, the active character of the human mind, in opposition to the empiricism of Hobbes: "the mind," Cudworth said more than once, is "not a mere passive thing, but must needs have a self-active power of its own." Still more important, he did not conceive even ideas as inert objects, but as motions of the mind: "even the rationes and essences of things are not dead things, like so many statues, images, or pictures hung up somewhere by themselves alone in a world: neither are truths mere sentences and propositions written down with ink upon a book, but they are living things, and nothing but modifications of mind and intellect" [5]—modifications, or better still, acts of the mind. However these flashes of philosophical insight in Cudworth are buried in a heap of antiquated erudition and interminable diatribes against atheism and atheists.

Coleridge also has some effective attacks on the doctrine of the passive mind. Already in 1801 he rejected the idea that the mind was "a lazy looker-on on an external world" (*CL*, II, 709), or, as he put it later, "a mirror reflecting the landscape, or as blank canvas upon which some unknown hand paints it" (*BL*, I, 66, Ch. V), or "the mere quicksilver plating behind a looking-glass!" (*op. cit.*, 82, Ch. VII).

However, in spite of their speculative vigor and of their active polemics, the Cambridge Platonists were followed by a tidal wave of empiricist philosophy in the eighteenth century that practically submerged them. Empirical epistemology led the way with Locke, followed by Berkeley and by Hume (both empiricists, though going in opposite directions theologically) and so prevailed in England. But rationalism continued to flourish on the Continent, where Descartes was followed by Spinoza in Holland and both were followed by Leibniz in Germany, with his numerous disciples. Most of these thinkers, with the exception of Spinoza, were supporters of the traditional beliefs in God, Freedom, and Immortality.

Skirmishes between the two opposing schools begin with Descartes: in his answers to objectors, we find a section (the 3rd) dedicated to answers to Hobbes' objections, not to speak of the answers to the objections by the French empiricist and materialist Gassendi (the 5th). Locke, as we mentioned, devoted himself to refuting the theory of innate ideas.

Finally, Leibniz gave an answer to the empiricists in a single sentence, indeed in a single clause. To the empiricist maxim that "there is nothing in the mind that does not come through the senses," he affixed in 1765 the clause "with the exception of the mind itself" (*excipe, nisi intellectus ipse*),[6] a clause which Coleridge was fond of repeating,[7] and which was fully developed and worked out in Kant's *Critique of Pure Reason*.

ii

DURING ALL this discussion of the a priori and a posteriori theories of human knowledge it may well have seemed to the non-philosophic reader that the whole question was a purely academic one. What does it matter whether our ideas are derived from experience or from reason? As long as we have ideas, they are there and we can use them. But it is just here that the difficulties begin. How can we use them, if they are only debilitated sensations? How far can we trust them, if they are the mere shavings of experience? What general view of man and of life can we build, if our bricks are made of straw, or merely of dreams and wishes?

The fact is that the conclusions of epistemology, purely technical or theoretical as they may seem, have a direct bearing on problems of the world-view, or metaphysics as they are usually called. This will become apparent when we consider more carefully empiricism in the radical form it took with Hume, the thinker that Kant said "first awakened me from my dogmatic slumber and gave an entirely different direction to my investigations in speculative philosophy." [8] This "slumber" of Kant involved nothing less than the whole view of the universe and of man that had prevailed in European thought for centuries.

Ever since the triumph of Christianity traditional philosophy in Western Europe maintained the view of a universe ruled by law, created by a benevolent deity who endowed man with an immortal soul and gave him a code of ethics to obey. So the existence of God, the spirituality of man and the rationality of the universe had been tied up together in a single system, and to reject one of these doctrines was to imperil all the others. The problem of proving the existence of God and the immortality of the soul, as well as the freedom of the will and the validity of the moral code, was met in Christian philosophy by resort to the logic of the great systems of ancient thought, mainly Platonism and Aristotelianism, with their theories of Ideas, Universals, and Concepts, and so the great scholastic systems were built up. However, even in the Middle Ages the classical logical theories were challenged by the Nominalist school.

Ancient thought became known even more fully since the Renaissance, with the effect that doubts and problems which had been kept in the background came to the fore. Nature was then conceived to be governed by laws of its own, different from those of Christian teleology and discoverable by a logic different from that of the schools. On the other hand, the idea of subjectivity, fitfully glimpsed in ancient thought,[9] became the cornerstone of modern philosophy through the Cartesian *cogito*. Subjectivity was still considered essentially as rationality, and through the full use of reason working with the instruments of logic and of mathematics it was thought possible to capture wild nature and put her behind the bars, as it were, of natural laws discovered by science and expressed as far as possible in mathematical formulae. On the foundation of this rationality, metaphysics became a science again, and the systems of Descartes and his successors, of Leibniz[10] and his school in Germany, were constructed.

But empiricism renewed the old battle of the Sophists against the rule of law and of the medieval nominalists against the realists, and reduced all knowledge to sensation: "consciousness considered as a result," as Coleridge put it (*BL*, I, 81). Hume, following these principles to their logical conclusion, caused the collapse of the entire traditional system of thought. This once proud edifice, consisting of a rational universe, a world of monads and substances, souls and bodies, working together in pre-established harmony, was torn down by Hume and reduced to a chaos of single sensations and impressions, casually occurring as disconnected phenomena, and held together only by accidental associations. Instead of substances, there were only sensations; instead of universals, there were only faint traces of impressions; instead of the soul, there was only a mere stream of sense-data, with no objects to arouse them and no mind to perceive them. Obviously it was absurd to attribute such a thing as freedom of will and of choice to the swirls of jumbled impressions to which the soul was reduced. This was also a serious blow to the validity of the sciences, whose operation involves at every step the validity of the notions of cause and effect, and the stability and uniformity of a universe of law. To meet this requirement, an entirely new concept of natural events was needed, different both from mechanism and from providential theism; but Hume did not provide it. In his view, everything happened as it happened, and no cause could be assigned to its happening, even if it could be said to happen.

Hume carried his scepticism to the point of denying personal identity, quite consistently with his general view. As there are no substances outside us, so within us there is no identity: no soul, no mind, no self. In a famous passage he said: "For my part, when I enter most intimately into what I call *myself*, I always stumble upon some particular perception or other. . . .

I never can catch *myself* at any time without a perception, and can never observe anything but the perception" (p. 252). We will take up this point again in Chapter 4.

For the rationalist school, and for Coleridge too, the most pernicious consequences of empiricism were atheism and all the other forms of "infidelity." Coleridge put it in a nutshell in 1801: Hobbes and Gassendi taught that "all knowledge and rational belief were derived from experience—we had no experience of God, or of a future state—therefore there could be no rational Belief" (*CL*, II, 701). Empiricism brought also disbelief in the free will of man and consequently in all moral obligation. If such a view were universally accepted, all morality would crumble and complete license would prevail.

Here, for instance, is how Coleridge envisaged the catastrophic results of what he called "the mechanico-corpuscular theory . . . espoused as a revolution in philosophy": "Consequences exemplified. A state of nature, or the Ouran Outang theology of the origin of the human race, substituted for the first ten chapters of the Book of Genesis; rights of nature for the duties and privileges of citizens; idealess facts, misnamed proofs from history, grounds of experience and the like, for the principles and the insight derived from them. Gin consumed by paupers to the value of about eighteen millions yearly. . . . lastly, crimes quadrupled for the whole country, and in some countries decupled" (*C&S*, 68–71).

While Coleridge's fear of evolutionism (not Charles Darwin's, of course, which was yet to come)[11] sounds very much dated to-day, most of the other consequences appear disastrous enough.

Indeed the progress of the revolution in France seemed to confirm the worst fears of men who thought like Coleridge. There empiricism had led to the most radical rejection of all religion. But in England things went otherwise. The English empiricists, whose principles logically should have led them to assert materialism and deny supernaturalism, usually did not reject the basic doctrines of religion. We have already seen an example of this in David Hartley, who was virtually a materialist as well as a necessitarian, but who still believed in God and even preached the love of God. Earlier, in 1729, Anthony Collins maintained an empirical epistemology and denied free will, but accepted the deistic view of God. Another example was Joseph Priestley, who supported the materialism of Hartley, but who surprised his fellow-materialists in France by calmly asserting that he was a believer. At a famous dinner in Paris in 1774, he was told by another guest that "the two gentlemen opposite me were the Bishop of Aix and the Archbishop of Toulouse, 'but,' said he, 'they are no more believers than you or I.' I assured him that I was a believer; but he would not believe me." [12]

This makes it easier to understand how Coleridge in his youth could maintain necessitarianism and yet retain some kind of religious faith. But outside England empiricism led to materialism, materialism led to atheism. In Britain Hume rejected supernaturalism and as we saw seriously endangered the traditional concept of a universe of law and order.

iii

AGAINST the destructive conclusions of Hume's scepticism Kant slowly, methodically and comprehensively proceeded to rebuild upon new foundations the edifice of science and of philosophy, the universe of law and order and the rationality of man. This he accomplished by means of a more profound analysis of the knowing process than any other philosopher, perhaps, had ever effected before him. He did this in the *Critique of Pure Reason* (1781), which therefore may be classed as epistemology.

It is the very thoroughness of Kant's analyses that makes his book so laborious and hard to follow. The reader new to Kant must not expect a simple statement of problems or a quick resolution of doubts. He must be prepared instead for a minute dissection that heaps distinctions upon distinctions, establishes territories and provinces the existence of which he had never

heard of before, and then christens them by means of an out-landish terminology entirely different from that of any other philosophy. As the most recent commentator says, "despite the appearance of great order and structure, the text is filled with repetitions, contradictions, and not a few sentences which seem utterly incomprehensible" (Wolff, 42). Kant himself admitted that the book was "dry, obscure, unfamiliar, and long drawn out." [13] Other causes of obscurity are Kant's involved prose style and his frequent use of Latin scholastic terms, which he said he introduced because they would be known to the educated reader of his day (B 403) and which today only make for greater difficulty. But perhaps the greatest cause of obscurity is Kant's extreme care to balance his conclusions, which makes him terminate an elaborate argument in one direction with a sudden turn to the opposite direction, so that when the reader thinks he has finally nailed Kant down to one side of a question, out he comes with a qualifying clause that sets everything again in doubt. Basically this may be due to the fact that, while arguing against the sceptical results of empiricism, Kant did not wish to fall back into the "dogmatic slumber" of previous meta-physics, as he called it, and he required for his own conclusions a basis as solid and as open to control as the empirical position claimed to be. Yet all these obstacles are worth facing and struggling with because, as the recent interpreter just quoted says, "Kant is the focal point of all modern philosophy" (Wolff, 21).

The fact that Coleridge, who was after all a contemporary of Kant, saw at once the greatness and the importance of Kant's philosophy, at a time in which there were no lucid expositions, no historical and textual commentaries, nor the perspectives of later philosophy to go by, is greatly to Coleridge's credit as a student of philosophy, and it is the aim of this book to show this in detail. However, this task does not involve an exhaustive analysis of Kant. Here we are concerned mainly with what there is in Kant that Coleridge adopted or adapted, so we need not go into all the intricacies of the three *Critiques*, but only into those sections which are necessary for understanding Coleridge.

Now before Kant, an answer to Hume had already been attempted by the so-called Scottish school of philosophy. Reid and his followers (among whom was also the James Beattie criticized by Coleridge in *BL*, I, 182, Ch. XII) had argued that belief in the existence of external objects and in personal identity (both challenged by Hume's scepticism) are just matters of common sense, and no sensible man would deny them. Kant however was not satisfied with this appeal to mere common sense. He did not feel that knowledge of external reality was a matter beyond possible doubt. To this alleged knowledge, and to all other alleged knowledge, he asks the question: *"How do we know it?"*, which may be called the "critical" question also in the sense that it is the basic question of the *Critiques*: How do we obtain knowledge of things which exist independently of ourselves? And how can we be sure that our knowledge of those things corresponds exactly to those things themselves? The common sense answer to the last question is: we test the correctness of our knowledge by comparing our concept with the thing itself. For instance, our concept of iron combines the properties of weight and of impenetrability. To see whether this is true, we refer to the object itself, iron, and check whether it is heavy and impenetrable. If it is, then our knowledge of iron is correct: we have compared our knowledge with its object (cf. Wolff, 137). But to do that, Kant answers in his *Logic*, is to have knowledge of the thing, and then we are only comparing one knowledge with another knowledge: "My knowledge, in order to be true, must agree with the object. Now I can compare the object with my knowledge only by this means, namely by having knowledge of it. My knowledge, then, is to be verified by itself, which is far from being sufficient for truth." [14]

Or, as he put it in the *Critique* in connection with a particular object, "outside our knowledge, we have nothing which we can set over against this knowledge as corresponding to it" (A 104). This is the dilemma propounded in the *Critique of Pure Reason,* and it constitutes the basic problem of epistemology since Kant.

If we try to meet this dilemma by assuming that everybody

possesses in his mind an inborn standard of truth which enables him to distinguish true knowledge from error, we are slipping back into the theory of "innate ideas" of pre-Kantian rationalism which had been refuted by the empiricists. Here Kant takes his stand on their side: there are no innate ideas, no truths that we possess before having any experience: "That all knowledge begins with experience is beyond doubt. For by what else should our mental powers be awakened, were it not by objects which affect our senses? We possess no knowledge which precedes experience in time and with it everything begins" (B 1).

What then is experience? Kant again agrees with empiricists in thinking that it consists in receiving sensations which come to us from external objects. These sensations affect what Kant calls our "sensibility" (*Sinnlichkeit*) or "sense" (*Sinn*), i.e., the capacity for receiving sense data, and sensibility is purely receptive, mere receptivity (*Rezeptivität*, A 19, B 34). We find this terminology also in Coleridge: "in philosophical Language *Sense* means the *Faculty*, of which the different *Senses* are *organs*" (letter of 1817, *CL*, IV, 790). In the MS. "Logic" he speaks of "receptivity," although he attributes the term to "elder writers": "the capability of acquiring representations which our elder logical and metaphysical writers entitled receptivity, is what we call Sensibility or Sensuous Nature" (II, 219–20). And again in *The Friend* he had said: "Under the term sense I comprise whatever is passive in our being . . . sensations . . . impressions . . . This, in the language of the schools, was called *vis receptiva*, or recipient property of the soul, from the original constitution of which we perceive and imagine all things under the forms of space and time" (*Friend*, 110n, Sec. I, Ess. 3). In spite of the pet reference to the elder writers, this definition reveals itself as Kantian by the inclusion of the "forms of space and time" which as we shall see later in this chapter are for Kant the "pure forms" of perception (e.g., A 22, B 36).

Kant agrees with the empiricists in attributing sensations to external things, so that what we know in experience are only the impressions that they produce in us, not things as they are in themselves. This is one of the key terms of Kant: "things in themselves," *Dinge an sich* (e.g., B xxviii), things as they exist independently of ourselves. But their appearance to us is all we know of them according to Kant (*ibid.*). For what I have called here "appearance," Kant uses often the term *phenomenon*, and for "things in themselves" the corresponding term is *noumenon*.[15] This dichotomy was adopted by Coleridge, already in 1805 (*NB*, II, # 2666 fol. 3 and Note) and later in *The Friend* (p. 291; Sec. II, Ess. 3). In keeping with Kant, he contrasts the *phenomenon* with the "thing in itself" (*BL*, I, 133, Ch. X). In an unpublished note he even proposed to shorten the two terms to *phenomen* and *noumen*, while referring them explicitly to Kant: "The great founder of the Critical Philosophy has expressed his regret at the disuse of the distinction so familiar in the old philosophy of Phaenomena and Noumena" (Egerton MS. 2801, fol. 96). I do not know to what passage of Kant he is referring, unless it is the following from the *Prolegomena*: "Since the oldest days of philosophy, inquirers into pure reason have conceived, besides the things of sense or appearances (*phenomena*), which make up the sensible world, certain things of the understanding (*Noumena*), which should constitute an intelligible world" (par. 32, Beck, p. 64; Wolff, p. 14).

Coleridge even uses the word "phenomenology," which was brought up by Kant in a letter to Lambert, available to Coleridge (as it was to Hegel, who made important use of it) in the collection of the minor works of Kant.[16] In *The Friend*, phenomenology is defined as the "doctrine concerning material nature" (p. 310*n.*, Sec. II, Ess. 6). In the MS. "Logic" (I, 84) it is classified among the sciences but not defined; in another MS. it is defined as the science of "perception" (Egerton MS. 2801, fol. 147).

While according to Kant phenomena are what we are acquainted with all the time, noumena are entirely beyond the reach of our knowledge (at least in the *Critique of Pure Reason*). Yet Kant always affirmed that beyond phenomena, noumena do exist (e.g., A 249–50, B 306); not only they exist, but they are the source of our sensations. A doctrine of this kind, which asserts that we can only know phenomena, not things in themselves, is usually called phenomenalism. Kant would be an absolute phenomenalist if he did not believe in the existence of things in themselves beyond phenomena.

Since we cannot go beyond our knowledge of phenomena to compare them with the noumena, how is Kant to proceed in the theory of knowledge which is the aim of his work? On his premises there is only one way: the mind must turn back on itself and proceed to a thorough selfanalysis. It should scrutinize its own operations, see how far they can go, and at what point they stop and can go no further. The limits they ultimately reach are the boundaries of our knowledge.

This is what Kant means by a "critique" of Reasons: an inquiry into how far our Reason can really go, in order to test the validity of philosophies based upon Reason alone. We must decide "what we can know" before we can decide "what is," and the question of being is made dependent upon the subjective conditions of knowledge: epistemology is thus given absolute priority over all other philosophical inquiries (Wolff, 96–97).

Coleridge considered this so important that he turned the *Critique* into a special discipline for which he invented, as usual, a name: "philocrisy." In an unpublished note, he defined it "the pre-ponderative inquisition of the strength and measures of the human mind" (Notebook 30, Additional MS. 47,527, fol. 38). "Pre-ponderative" means "preliminary to weighing"; the metaphor is expanded and explained in another note: "that logical *propaideía dokimastiké,* that critique of the human intellect, which, previously to the weighing or measuring this or that, begins by assaying the weights, measures, and scales themselves" (*LR*, III, 157). And *propaideía* is another Greek term derived from Kant who speaks repeatedly of *Propaideutik* (A 841, B 869).

The inquiry into the processes of human knowledge and its limitations was also one of the goals of empiricism, but in Locke this analysis of the mind turned into a purely psychological investigation, i.e., an inquiry into matters of fact: what are our faculties and in what way do they operate. Thus he came to formulate some of the basic laws of psychology, such as the law of association of ideas. The law shows that our ideas associate by means of contiguity, succession or resemblance, and diverse sensations become associated either because they come together or follow immediately after each other or because they resemble each other. We saw what use Hartley made of this law.

From it the empiricists believe they can derive all the other laws of the mind. Now Kant agreed that association of ideas was a matter of fact; but his aim was not factual, it was epistemological. Kant wants to know not only what mental processes are, but what their validity is in relation to truth. We have just seen this question asked in regard to sensations. Do they give us knowledge of real objects? Kant answers No, they only give us knowledge of appearances. But they are not delusions, being produced by the action of real objects upon our sensibility.

Similarly the question to be asked about the association of ideas is: What do we learn from their laws as to the validity of the connections thus established between ideas? And the answer is: Nothing. Because one idea comes next to another or together with another, it does not mean that the things they refer to are necessarily connected. As everybody knows, *post hoc, ergo propter hoc* is a fallacy. Nor are phenomena necessarily connected because they resemble each other.

We have introduced in the last paragraph two ideas which are basic for epistemology and indeed for philosophy: the idea of "necessarily connected" and the idea of "cause" with its correlative, "effect." Kant believed that truth is both universal and necessary (e.g., B 4). In a true statement, the connection asserted is necessary and not casual or accidental, and it must be so at all times, i.e., it must be universal.

The difference between Kant's inquiry and the investigations of psychology is fundamental, and it must be stressed. It may indeed appear at first sight that Kant's object is psychological, i.e., factual and empirical, for he is continually dealing with mental processes, such as sensation, memory, imagination and other so-called faculties, describing their operation and defining their laws. But this would be a basic misunderstanding, which Kant sought to ward off from the very beginning (A xvii). Kant's inquiry is not on the factual side of these operations, but on their truth-bearing value, on the universality and necessity of their results. It is all the more necessary to stress this difference because Kant himself did not always maintain it. But a psychological interpretation of the *Critique* (as has been sometimes attempted) simply misses its point. Coleridge, too, was at times inclined to fall into this misunderstanding, although usually it was clear to him that Kant's aim and method were not psychological or factual, but, as he put it, "logical," and he praised the *Critique* as a great contribution to this kind of "logic," the transcendental logic (MS. "Logic," II, 210, 326, etc.).

On the other hand, this difference between the critical inquiry and psychology should not be interpreted as a rejection of the science of psychology on the part of Kant, as Coleridge sometimes thought.[17] Kant fully recognized, as we have seen, the claims of psychology as an empirical science, based on observation and descriptive in method. He acknowledged its capacity to formulate empirical laws of mental events, such as the laws of association. He even cultivated it himself and gave a course in it, under the name, then current for it, of "Anthropology."[18] In addition to this empirical psychology, he also discusses "Rational Psychology," but that is the metaphysical theory of the soul, which propounds its unity, simplicity, and immortality, as developed in traditional German metaphysics (e.g., Baumgarten) and later to be criticized by Kant.

Another warning on the psychological approach: what we usually call the "faculties" of the mind are not interpreted by Kant usually in the same sense as traditional psychology, as something which first exists potentially and then becomes actual.[19] They are rather what Kant calls "functions" or activities of the mind, which can be said to exist only in so far as they are actual (cf. Paton, I, 245–48).[20] They are manifestations of what Kant calls the "spontaneity" or autonomous activity of the mind, i.e., not determined from outside but self-determined. Thus

Kant rejects for good the empiricist doctrine of the passivity of mind, the mind as a blank sheet upon which something outside it impresses its data. In doing this Kant was not just making another psychological theory, but stating an epistemological necessity: there are factors in our mind which cannot be accounted for by experience, so they must be generated by the mind itself. They are therefore a priori, or as Kant also calls them, "pure" (cf. B 1, the title of the section). There is also a metaphysical point involved, though Kant does not make it explicitly: a function is a pure activity which does not presuppose a pre-existent Being. That will appear in the post-Kantian idealists.

If we accept this view of truth—viz., that its characteristics are universality and necessity—then for Kant an important consequence follows: truth cannot be stated in terms of data derived only from sense because these data are all limited and contingent, the opposite of universal and necessary. Since however we commonly believe that we know the truth about some things at least, and even act on this belief, then we must have some other source of knowledge besides the senses, and this source must put us in possession of truths known independently of experience, i.e., a priori. This is the point on which Kant agrees with the rationalist school. For him all knowledge begins with experience, but does not end with experience (B 1). "Experience tells us what is, but not that it must necessarily be so and not otherwise" (A 1).

We must again be on guard against the psychological interpretation. A priori for Kant does not mean "previous to experience"; for Kant nothing precedes experience. It means "not derived from experience but from the understanding, and therefore not depending on experience for its validity." It is logically presupposed by experience, not temporally antecedent. No empirical psychological investigation will reveal the a priori or the grounds for its validity; only reflection upon the logical presuppositions of experience.

The very notion of pure a priori thinking arouses hostility in people brought up in the deeply-rooted Anglo-Saxon empirical tradition. Nothing is so suspect, indeed nothing seems to be so much hated and feared, as the a priori, or purely ratiocinative approach: the "high Priory Road," as Pope ridiculed it in the *Dunciad* (IV, 471). Yet Kant, who accepted most of the positive beliefs of the empiricists in reference to experience, though not what they denied, was firmly convinced that there are truths known to us independently of experience (e.g., B 2).

We may ask for some example of these a priori truths. According to Kant, most mathematics are a priori truths. Most of what we know about time is also a priori, since it is independent of experience, time being rather a condition of all experiential facts than a fact observed through our senses. We know that "time is irreversible" independently of all experience; scientists do not conduct experiments to see if time can be found to go backwards, for any experiment is based upon the assumption that certain facts will happen *after* others have been set in motion, and not *before*. Or take the principle of causality, which may be stated in the most general way as "every change of condition must have a cause." Kant points out that the principle of causality is not entirely a priori, because it is through experience that we know that there are changes of condition (B 3 and A 9, B 13). But, on the other hand, its validity does not depend on experience. We do not carry out experiments to prove the principle of causality, for the experiment itself presupposes its validity. An experiment is the introduction of a cause to determine an effect: if the general relation of cause and effect is in doubt, there can be no experiment that validates it. So, according to Kant, the principle of causality refers to something which we know through experience, i.e., events, but it is a priori in its affirmation of cause. We will see later what the basic a priori factor in the concept of cause is according to Kant, i.e., a category, and in this case a very abstract general concept, that of Ground and Consequence. This for Kant is purely a priori.

Another set of notions which may be considered partly a priori and partly a posteriori is numbers. We would not number things unless we experienced them, so number presupposes experience, but number itself according to Kant is a priori, and so are all the laws of arithmetic. We do not waste time carrying out experiments to prove such propositions as $7 + 5 = 12$ (Kant's standard example) or that the square root of 4 is 2. They are truths independent of experience; indeed if experience does not conform with them, we question experience, as when we question someone who has shortchanged us.

Coleridge highly prized the Kantian concept of the a priori, as may be seen from the following marginalium to a book by J. Petvin, whom Coleridge considered making a half-hearted compromise with empiricism (1820): "how much was done by Kant, in strictly appropriating the terms a priori. Had this been fully elucidated, Locke would never have had the suffrage of men like Petvin."[21] However, even Coleridge tends to water down the a priori by making it almost chronologically prior rather than only epistemologically so. In a note to the *Biographia* he begins well but ends speaking of "pre-existence" of a priori: "By knowledge a priori we do not mean that we can know anything previously to experience, which would be a contradiction in terms; but that having once known it by occasion of experience (that is, something acting upon us from without) we then know, that it must have pre-existed, or that experience itself would have been impossible" (*BL*, I, 193, n., Ch. XII).

And here is a similar statement from *The Friend*: "a priori (that is from those necessities of the mind or forms of thinking, which, though first revealed to us by experience, must yet have pre-existed to make experience itself possible)" (*F*, 111*n*, Sec. I, Ess. 3).

Included in the above definitions of the a priori is the concept of "necessary conditions of experience." These are designated by Kant by means of the key-term "transcendental," which has been rightly extended to cover all of his philosophy.

Let us now tackle one of the most important pairs of terms in the Kantian philosophy: "transcendent" and "transcendental." They are similar in appearance but their meaning is so different that they are practically opposite. "Transcendent" means something completely beyond human experience, something inaccessible and unapproachable, hence revealed only to initiates and by special dispensation. Instances are Plato's hyperuranium with its world of absolute and eternal ideas, and the God of traditional theology, whom we cannot see or touch or imagine or even think, since his spiritual essence is so much beyond anything we can experience in this life.

"Transcendental," on the contrary, is something that is a *condition* of our actual experience—not a *cause* of experience, but a factor without which our experience could not take place. Experience is a fact, or an event, which takes place continually, every minute of our lives, and like every event there must be some conditions under which it is possible, as well as others under which it is not. Kant's object is to bring to light those conditions which are required to make experience possible. This phrase, the reader will have noted, is already in the last quotation we made from Coleridge.

A sentence that brings out the contradiction between the two terms has been aptly coined by Wolff (35*n*): "*Transcendental* philosophy demonstrates the impossibility of *transcendent* philosophy."

Far from being "transcendent," anything "transcendental" has to do with a fact which is always with us, experience. Experience is the stuff and substance of our everyday life, and its conditions must be within reach of any one's reflection. Hence when Kant speaks of transcendental functions of the mind, he does not mean supernatural functions or extrasensory perceptions, but only mental acts which are in use in every common perception, such as seeing the table in front of us or hearing the dog bark in the yard. Hence Kant's "transcendentalism" is not a philosophy which aims at going beyond experience into a transcendent world, but on the contrary stays as close to experience as possible, seeking only the factors which condition it.

Having grasped this, let us take the next step, which is essential for the Kantian philosophy, and will take us at one bound out of empiricism. Anything transcendental in the above sense does not derive from experience. On the contrary, to borrow the Kantian terms used by Coleridge in the last quotation from him, it is that which makes experience itself possible. As Max Müller put it, when asked to sum up the *Critique of Pure Reason* in one sentence, "that without which experience is impossible, cannot be the result of experience." [22] Since without it no experience could take place, it must have a source other than experience, but not *beyond* experience. In other words, the transcendental is a priori, and the conditions of experience are sought by Kant in the a priori functions of the knowing mind. [23]

This basic Kantian distinction between transcendent and transcendental impressed itself upon Coleridge's mind, and he repeatedly affirms it, although sometimes a little loosely, as in the *Biographia Literaria*, Chapter XII, where he says that we may "divide all the objects of human knowledge into those on this side, and those on the other side, of the spontaneous consciousness (. . . *conscientiam communem*). The latter is exclusively the domain of PURE philosophy, which is therefore properly entitled *transcendental*, in order to discriminate it at once, both from mere reflection and *re*-presentation on the one hand, and on the other from those flights of lawless speculation which, abandoned by all distinct consciousness, because transgressing the bounds and purposes of our intellectual faculties, are justly condemned, as *transcendent*."

The following note is appended to this passage: "The distinction between transcendental and transcendent is observed by our elder divines and philosophers, whenever they express themselves *scholastically*. Dr. Johnson indeed has confounded the two words; but his own authorities do not bear him out" (I, 164).

This is one of Coleridge's amateur attempts at etymology and does not agree with the *New English Dictionary*. The two words *transcendent* and *transcendental* were indeed used by the Scholastic philosophers, but without any difference in meaning; the distinction was made by Kant. As for Dr. Johnson, he indeed shows no awareness either of the Scholastic meaning or of the meaning that Kant was to assign to those words. *Tran-*

scendent for him means only "excellent; supremely excellent; passing others," and all his examples bear him out. *Transcendental* means for him "1) General; pervading many particulars. 2) Supereminent; passing others," and his one example again bears him out.

In any case, this is neither the Kantian nor the Scholastic concept, which is "applied by the Schoolmen to predicates which by their universal application were considered to transcend the Aristotelian categories or predicaments" (*NED*). Coleridge's incursion in the history of terminology betrays a tendency to find recent ideas already in the English divines of the seventeenth century, which has its fullest expression in *Aids to Reflection*.

Closer to Kant is the formulation in the MS. "Logic": "All knowledge is excited or occasioned by experience, but all knowledge is not derived from experience, such for instance as the knowledge of the condition that renders experience itself possible, and which therefore must be supposed to exist previous to the act of seeing: though without the act of seeing we should never have learnt that we possess eyes" (II, 107).

The last simile is a favorite with Coleridge. It is to be found in the passage on the a priori quoted above (*BL*, I, 193) and in *Table-Talk* (II, 384n).[24]

The "Logic" also expounds the distinction between transcendent and transcendental: "Transcendental knowledge is that by which we endeavour to climb above our experience into its sources by an analysis of our intellectual faculties. . . . while transcendent philosophy would consist in an attempt to master a knowledge that is beyond our faculties" (II, 208).

In the "Logic" Coleridge adopts the Kantian concepts of Transcendental Aesthetic and Transcendental Logic, thus justifying them: "We have deemed it expedient not to leave unnoticed or unexplained the terms which the most profound of modern Logicians and the proper Inventor and Founder of the Transcendental Analysis had adopted" (II, 210).

In this same passage he adds a supplementary note vigorously rejecting the idea that "Kant stole the transcendental analysis and was not the founder of the Critical Philosophy" (II, 209ᵛ–211ᵛ). This charge against Kant, as Wellek points out (*W*, 75), was put forward at the time by Dugald Stewart (*W*, 40–49).

To sum up: Kant's transcendental functions of the mind are not innate ideas, or objects that pre-exist in the mind and that are to be found there ready-made. They are instead part of the necessary structure of the mind which must be presupposed to account for the fact of experience, hence verifiable through the process of reflection upon our own mental processes, and not by deduction from general principles. Furthermore they are activities of the mind that operate upon the manifold of sense-data, and therefore come into action only in connection with experience and have no significance outside that connection. In a famous statement Kant said that sensation without thought is blind, but thought without sensation is empty (A 51, B 75, *Co* 80, n. 1). (Strangely enough, I have found no mention of it in Coleridge.) This means that in actual knowledge the a priori is always found mingled with the empirical, and the difference is revealed only through analysis. While empirical philosophers assume "experience" dogmatically, always referring to it but never analysing it, Kant may be said to have analysed experience as a synthesis of a priori and a posteriori, and to have distinguished its form from its matter: the form is a priori and "spontaneous," or originating spontaneously in the mind, and the matter is a posteriori, the data of the sensibility which as we have seen are purely receptive (*ibid.*). The data of sensibility are in turn distinguished into a) the data of the *external* senses such as the sight, data which appear contiguously in space, and b) the data of what Kant, following Locke, calls "inner sense," i.e., psychological data (feelings, emotions, desires, etc.), which appear to us ordered successively in time. Time is the "form of inner sense" as space is the "form of outer sense." Sensations, when considered as mental events, also come under the form of inner sense, as we experience them one before and one after the other. All thoughts, feelings, emotions, desires, and other mental phenomena are therefore perceived by us under the form of inner sense or time. This involves a distinction between mental phenomena which occur in time, the flux of shifting experiences, the "stream of consciousness," on one side, and the self that perceives all this on the other, the knowing subject which unifies these phenomena and arranges them within the frames of space and time.

One more word on Kant's terminology. We have seen that the transcendent means that which is beyond experience, such as the noumena. Now the opposite to that is "what is entirely within the limits of possible experience," and this Kant calls "immanent" (A 295, B 352). Both empiricism and transcendentalism (his own philosophy) are considered "immanent" by Kant (e.g., A 296, B 353, and A 846, B 353). These two terms, transcendent and immanent, will become prominent in post-Kantian metaphysics, which will aim at being purely immanent and reject all the transcendent side of earlier metaphysics. That aim is one of the permanent legacies that Kant made to philosophy.

We will continue to follow Kant's exposition of the Transcendental Analytic according to his arrangement, which he called "the Architectonic of Pure Reason" (A 832, B 860 ff.). Upon this architectonic, scorn has been poured by later critics; but even if we were to share it, we must acknowledge that this arrangement was followed by Coleridge himself in his main exposition of Kant's Analytic, i.e., the MS. *Logic*, and this is a good reason for following it here.

A fundamental point of the Architectonic is the classification of the three mental functions: sensibility, understanding and reason.[25] Sensibility as we have seen is the capacity to receive impressions. The understanding (*Verstand*) is the capacity to conceive concepts, or general ideas. Concepts are in turn subdivided into 1) "pure concepts of the understanding," i.e., a priori ideas by means of which we organize experience and make it intelligible, such as the idea of causality, as defined above;—"pure" meaning a priori, and 2) "empirical concepts," i.e., generalizations from the data of experience, made a posteriori, to be further discussed in Chapter 4.

There is still a third cognitive faculty, the Reason (*Vernunft*), which has for its object what Kant calls "Ideas," i.e., concepts which transcend experience, such as the concepts of metaphysics. The distinction between Understanding and Reason, as is well known, lies behind many of Coleridge's later arguments, but he gave it a different turn from Kant. It is arguable that these three "faculties" or functions really represent different philosophies, and are more intelligible when taken as such than as parallel powers of cognition: Sensibility stands for empiricism, Understanding for transcendentalism or Kant's own point of view, and Reason stands for traditional metaphysics. Only the second is valid, and covers a process of cognition which is both intelligible and efficient.[26]

The cognitive activity resulting in pure concepts is asserted by Kant in contradiction to empiricism, which reduces concepts to sensations or impressions. That general ideas exist, as acts of the mind, is implicitly admitted by all empiricists, since without generalizations there could be no theory, not even empiricism. For instance, Hume's analysis of knowledge proceeds by means of such general ideas as "impressions," "sensations," "perceptions," "passions," "emotions," "images," and "ideas," including such abstract terms as "all," "general," "kind," and even "universal" which he uses once together with "permanent" (*Treatise*, I, IV, iv; ed. Selby-Bigge, p. 225). His argument depends entirely upon the validity of these terms for all the particulars subsumed under them. If each term were limited to one impression of one person, there would be no argument and no empirical philosophy.

Kant firmly believed that if concepts were reducible to empirical impressions they would have no validity. As Paton puts it in regard to the general ideas of Unity, Multiplicity, Causality, etc., which Kant calls categories and to which Chapter 3 will be dedicated: "We acquire knowledge of the categories, that is, we bring them into clear consciousness, by generalization or abstraction from experience; but they possess a claim to universal and necessary validity which cannot be *derived* from experience, but must, according to Kant, be due to their origin in the nature of the mind" (I, 336n).

From all this we can begin to see Kant's position in relation to the two great schools of thought, rationalism and empiricism. While he agrees with rationalism on some points (such as the a priori, though on different grounds), he agrees with empiricism on others (such as that of immanence, though with a difference). His own position appears already as not merely a compromise between the two, but as a new theory with features of its own.

The reader who is already familiar with the subject will expect here or hereabouts some mention of Kant's dichotomy of analytical and synthetic judgments, which, combined with his distinction of a priori and a posteriori, produces the concept of the "synthetic judgment a priori," by which new truths are known a priori. This doctrine was taken up by Coleridge in his MS. "Logic" and given considerable attention (II, 265–396). Here Coleridge follows faithfully the *Critique*; for details, see Chinol (61–62).

However, more will not be said about it here, except that the present writer is inclined to agree with the idealistic critics of Kant that reject all this classification as unfruitful and leading to the dreary waste of formal logic. In the nineteenth century Caird rejected it and stated bluntly that "Judgment is never analytic" (*Kant*, I, 336). In the twentieth De Ruggiero said: "there is no such thing as a division into two kinds of judgments, analytical and synthetical; synthesis is a primary act, forming the presupposition of all analysis." [27] We will therefore speak only of a priori concepts, leaving the judgments aside.

iv

WE ARE NOW able to present the general plan of the *Critique of Pure Reason*. The book is divided into two main sections: I, "The Transcendental Doctrine of Elements" (i.e., the elements of knowledge), which is the one we will concentrate on, and II, a shorter and less important section, called "The Transcendental Doctrine of Method," with which we will not deal.

In turn, the first section is thus subdivided:

Part I, Transcendental Aesthetic.
Part II, Transcendental Logic.
   1st Division, Transcendental Analytic.
   2nd Division, Transcendental Dialectic.[28]

As the reader sees, the term "transcendental" occurs everywhere, and its precise meaning in each case will appear as we expound the different parts of the book. The first part of Kant's task is the analysis of the knowing process, and that he calls, understandably, "Analytic." It is "transcendental" because it deals with the necessary conditions of experience, which as we have seen are a priori.

And here is how Coleridge adopts Kant's subdivision: "the science of *Transcendental* Analysis, so called from the character of its aim and object, which is to rise from the *knowledge* or *matter* of consciousness, to the faculty by which it is known or presented. . . . Transcendental Analysis is comprised under two heads, Transcendental Aesthetic, or the Analysis of the pure Sense, or *Faculty* of Intuition, and Transcendental Logic, or the analysis of the Understanding, or discursive faculty" ("Logic," II, 412–14).

The stress on the concept of "faculty" is basically un-Kantian, as we have seen above; but the rest of the subdivision is Kantian, with only slight differences.

The second part of Kant's task is to show the limits that the knowing process cannot go beyond without error, and in particular the limitations of "Pure Reason," i.e., human reason when it tries to go outside the limits of experience and to set up a priori demonstrations of the existence of God, of the rationality of the universe and of the immortality of the soul. None of these arguments is legitimate according to Kant, and in the last part of the *Critique of Pure Reason* (the meaning of the title will now be apparent) he makes an unsparing criticism of all these arguments, and concludes against the possibility of any metaphysics.

Now this destructive task Kant calls by the name of

"Dialectic," a term which in Kant is purely negative and designates the refutation of error and the unmasking of sophisms, or, as he calls it himself, "the logic of illusion" (A 61, B 86). So, while the Analytic is mainly positive, the Dialectic is mainly negative. These divisions will be used by Kant also in the other *Critiques*.

We now come to the heart of Kant's critique of empiricism. For empiricism, simple and straightforward as it may appear at first sight, actually involves a number of underlying assumptions, which only gradually become apparent and which are open to criticism. One of these is called "psychological atomism" and it has been found particularly active in the philosophy of Hume.[29] It was this atomism which aroused the criticism of Coleridge, so it is worth further examination.

Psychological atomism—or epistemological atomism, as I prefer to call it—is the doctrine that our knowledge is ultimately made up of sensations, which are single units and separate like atoms. This view is in turn based on another assumption, which is that to construct a theory of knowledge we must break up knowledge and find its smallest constituent, and then derive all mental operations from it. This is the method of analysis, formulated long ago by Aristotle: "a compound should be resolved into the simple elements or parts of the whole" (*Politics*, I, 1252 A). It is instructive to observe the ancient philosophical foundations of empiricism below its plain, commonsense appearance.

When the empiricists apply this method to knowledge, they find that sensations are the ultimate constituents and therefore they conclude that all mental activity is reducible to sensations, and that there is nothing in the mind which is not so reducible. But the method of analysis can be applied only with certain safeguards. In particular, the parts of the compound should not be so completely separated in the analysis that they cannot be brought together again. This may seem obvious, but in practice it means that in the analysis the unifying principle that keeps the parts together should be explicitly brought out and defined. Now the analysis of empiricism fails to do just that. It was acknowledged by Hume himself, when with almost unparallelled candor for a systematic philosopher, he admitted that his system led to an insoluble dilemma. This he did in an appendix to the *Treatise of Human Nature*: "There are two principles which I cannot render consistent, nor is it in my power to renounce either of them, viz., *that all our distinct perceptions are distinct existences*, and *that the mind never perceives any real connection among distinct existences*" (p. 636). He had fallen into the trap of separating components so completely, that they could not be united again.

No philosopher rejected epistemological atomism more completely than Kant, though he did not write a formal refutation of it. He believed, as one of his interpreters put it, that "nothing absolutely simple can be apprehended in sense-experience" (*Co*, 84). Sense experience may be apparently analyzed into single sensations, but we can never grasp a single sensation: when we try to, we find that there are always other sensations connected with it, and that it forms part of a cluster or *Gestalt* of sensations. Hence sensations are always plural and Kant always speaks of them as such, using the phrase "the sensuous manifold." This manifold itself cannot be grasped, according to Kant, except through the unifying mental activities, which are purely spontaneous or self-originated, in other words a priori.

Having seen Kant's answer to Hume's atomism, we can appreciate the importance of a critical remark by Coleridge on Hume—a remark entirely in agreement with Kant. In 1804 Coleridge wrote in one of his notebooks (II, # 2370): "How opposite to nature and the fact to talk of the one *moment* of Hume; of our whole being an aggregate of successive sensations. Who ever *felt* a *single* sensation? Is not every one at the same moment conscious that there co-exist a thousand others in a darker shade, or less light; even as when I affix my attention on a white House on a grey bare Hill or rather long ridge that runs out of my sight each way . . . the pretended single sensation is it anything more than the *Light*-point in every good picture either of nature or a good painter; & again subordinately in every component part of the picture?"

Coleridge goes straight to the heart of Hume's atomism with that simple question: "who ever *felt* a *single* sensation?" The single, isolated sensation has been recognized as a myth by later philosophy, and even by psychologists.[30] Yet the single sensation is a necessary assumption of empiricism: if all the connections provided by thought are excluded, because a priori, then we are left only with the isolated atoms of sensation. The rejection of the self as the coordinating and unifying centre of consciousness, which as we saw Hume carried out, leads to a world of chaotic sensa, which relate to each other only by accidental proximity. In challenging this basic assumption of empiricism, Coleridge refutes the whole system and destroys all the castle of inferences built upon it.

We will return to that interesting phrase "the *Light*-point"; but first let us see the continuation of the paragraph:

"And what is a moment? Succession with *interspace?*"

Here I take "interspace" to mean "interval," [31] i.e., "is there ever any interval between a moment and its successor?" To this Coleridge himself replies:

"Here it is evidently only the *Licht-punkt*, the Sparkle in the indivisible undivided Duration. Christmas Day, 1804."

In other words, just as Time is "indivisible undivided Duration"(this would have pleased Bergson), so the world of sensuous experience cannot be divided or dissected into single sensations. "Atomism" is rejected.

Let us now see what Coleridge meant by "Light-point" and its German equivalent *"Licht-punkt."* German dictionaries define the latter as "bright, illuminated point, focus." It is *not*, as perhaps some one might think, the vanishing point of perspective, called in German *"Fluchtpunkt"* or *"Augenpunkt."* We must turn to the English phrase for illumination. "Light point" is explained by the N. E. Dictionary through a quotation from Coleridge's contemporary, the painter Henry Fuseli.[32] In his *Lectures on Painting*, written *circa* 1816, he says that in a painting "one point is the brightest in the eye, as on the object, this is the point of light. From it, in all directions, the existent parts advance or recede, by, before, behind each other; the two extremes of light and shade make a whole, which the local or essential colour defines." [33]

This makes Coleridge's criticism of Hume's atomism fully justified in the case of sight sensations, where there is no separate sensation. What is taken to be such is simply the most vivid patch of light in the visual field, which acquires its vividness against a background of lesser light.

Now, both Kant and Coleridge seem to have suffered under the same handicap in connection with Hume: they both knew his *Enquiry concerning Human Understanding* (1748), but not the earlier and more radical *Treatise of Human Nature* (1740). The reasons for the existence of these two different versions of the same work are well known. Hume put all his philosophy in the *Treatise*, but it fell dead from the press. So he later wrote the *Enquiry*, which is a popular exposition of his views, considerably reduced in scope: it does not present his "atomism," nor his denial of personal identity, nor his theory of mathematics. It was commonly included among Hume's *Essays*.

But it is now known that some quotations from the *Treatise* reached Kant in the book of James Beattie against Hume, *Essay on the Nature and Immutability of Truth* (1770), translated into German in 1772 (Wolff, 24–25). In Coleridge I have not found any clear reference to the *Treatise*. In the passage on Hume in the *Notebooks*, II, 2370 (1804), no reference is given. Hume is not among the Bristol readings. In the *Philosophical* Lectures he refers to Hume's "Essay on Cause and Effect" (*PhL*, 381) and to "Mr. Hume in the Essays" (*PhL*, 373). Professor Coburn refers the first to the *Treatise*, but it could just as well be the *Enquiry*. In the *Statesman's Manual* he refers to "Hume's *Essays*" for the argument against causality (*C&S*, 233).

Yet both Kant and Coleridge seized upon essential points of Hume's theory and criticized them effectively. For Kant, perception occurs only when the "sensuous manifold" has been unified in the awareness of a single, well-defined unit. So for him the most elementary form of knowledge is not the chaos of unconnected sensa of the empiricists, but the consciousness of an individual object. For this act he uses the term *Anschauung*, which creates problems in translation. Kant himself gave the

Latin *intuitio* as its equivalent, and it has often been translated in English as *intuition*. Recent translators think that its meaning would be better rendered by *perception*,[34] since *intuition* usually means "immediate knowledge," particularly immediate knowledge of some truth which is grasped directly and without any intermediate process of ratiocination. But "immediate" is often taken to mean "instantaneous," like "a flash of intuition," whereas speed has nothing to do with Kant's *Anschauung*, while the individuality of the object does. D. G. James' description of the work of the imagination provides a good definition of *Anschauung*: "the apprehension of individual wholes." [35]

Kant's own definition of the term is somewhat more complicated than the one given above. It will be found in the passage of the *Critique* where he gives a list of his terms, with explanations (A 320, B 377). From the classification which he there gives of the cognitive faculties or acts, we obtain the following definition of *Anschauung*: "a conscious representation which relates to a single object, immediately known."

Coleridge had perfectly grasped the significance of *Anschauung* and he strove to find a satisfactory English equivalent for it. In his MS. *Logic* he says: "it is to be regretted that we have not a correspondent verb, as the Latin *intueri* and the German *anschauen*" (II, 215; cf. *BL*, I, 190*n*, Ch. XII; to be quoted later, in Ch. VIII). He generally used "intuition" as a translation, but with repeated warnings to the reader that he was not giving it its ordinary meaning but a different one, which Coleridge also found in seventeenth century writers (it actually goes back to Scholasticism). In 1814 he wrote: "I have restored the words, *intuition* and *intuitive*, to their original sense—'an intuition,' says Hooker, that is, a direct and immediate beholding or presentation of an object to the mind through the senses or the imagination'" (*Genial Criticism*, III, *BL*, II, 230). The last clause, "or the imagination," shows where "perception" falls short: it indicates only cognition of a real object, whereas *Anschauung* indicates a mental picture regardless of the real existence of its object, and is therefore good also for imaginary pictures, and hence for aesthetic analysis.[36]

Coleridge repeatedly attempted to invent an English word

for *Anschauung*. In 1807 he suggested "Onlook" (*NB*, II, # 3113), very much as a century afterwards an American philosopher suggested "Atsight" for the same purpose.[37] Later Coleridge proposed the word "Aspicience" for *Anschauung*, recording it in an unpublished note on Kant (Add. MS. 34, 225, Fol. 144). The word is a perfect etymological mould for the German term: *as*-corresponds to *An*- and -*spicience* to -*schauung*; there is even a similarity in the sounds. But the word, being buried in Coleridge's MSS., has enjoyed no currency, although it deserves it. Its very novelty would warn the reader that it is a technical term, with a special meaning, and all the confusions of "intuition" would be avoided.

If the most elementary form of knowledge be that of the individual object, the *Anschauung*, and we are inquiring into its necessary conditions, what about space and time? They seem to be the two great coordinates of all perception: every object appears to us in a certain space and at a certain time. What are they?

The discussion on the nature of the two coordinates has been carried out by philosophers for centuries.[38] With the greater awareness of subjectivity which arose in later antiquity and developed with Christianity, it was natural that some philosophers would conceive one or the other or both coordinates to be subjective in character, as against previous belief in their objective existence. Kant's theory is that they are subjective: they are the transcendental forms of perception (*Anschauung*), functions of the mind that organizes the data of experience into an ordered whole. This is argued in the part of the *Critique* called the Transcendental Aesthetic. It is transcendental because it deals with what Kant thinks are the necessary conditions of experience; it is aesthetic because it deals with the conditions of sensation, *aísthesis* in Greek. Kant here explicitly rejects the new meaning that had been given to Aesthetic by his predecessor Baumgarten (i.e., the study of the Beautiful, of Art and of Taste) and reverts to its etymological meaning (A 21, B 35, *n.*). Without these forms of intuition, which are like hooks or frames in our minds, into which sensations are, so to speak, caught and placed one after the other or one next to the other, we could not experience anything.

Yet common sense is very strong in its conviction that space at least is an objective reality. Real things exist in space, so space must be real too. Common sense imagines space like an immense receptacle into which things are placed in juxtaposition to each other. But Kant believed that our perceptions of objects are based on our subjective sensations, framed by our intuitions of space and time, and so arranged according to the constitution of our mind. Apart from our mental organization, sensations would be a vast amorphous confusion (A 165, B 195, and A 201, B 247), a mere buzzing and pushing,[39] or simply "chaos," as Coleridge was fond of saying: "the instruments of sensation . . . furnish only the chaos, the shapeless elements of sense" (*F*, 340, Sec. II, Ess. 11) and "without it (the understanding), man's representative powers would be a delirium, a chaos, a scudding cloudage of vapors" (*Aids*, 346, from the *Essay on Faith*). They become instead the orderly picture of the universe that we are familiar with by means of the action of our perceptive (or as Coleridge calls them, "representative") faculties, together with the understanding and the reason. These faculties "lie prepared," as Kant once went so far as to say (A 66, B 61), in our minds, independently of all experience since they condition experience. They are in fact what Kant calls the *form* of our experience, while sensations are its *matter* (A 20, B 34).

Coleridge supported repeatedly Kant's doctrine of the ideality of Space and Time. In one of his published works he had spoken of "my conviction that space was not itself a *thing*, but a *mode* or *form* of perceiving, or the inward ground and condition in the percipient, in consequence of which things are seen as outward and coexisting" (*Aids*, "Aphorisms on Spiritual Religion," II, p. 117*n*).

In the MS. "Logic" he gives in full Kant's arguments in support of this doctrine, in a chapter entitled "Judicial Logic including the Pure Aesthetic" (II, 212–43).[40] He follows Kant's "Transcendental Aesthetic" (A 22, B 37 to A 32, B 49) and its numbered arguments, one by one: 4 for Space, 5 for Time. He then turns to Kant's *Prolegomena* (as Miss Snyder had indicated, p. 91), and there he takes over as an "Illustration" (II, 234) Kant's argument on symmetrical objects, or "incongruous counterparts" as they are also called (*Co*, 161–66), e.g., a pair of gloves, which are identical in every part but as a whole reversed, so that the left hand cannot wear the right glove. If space were objective, the spatial differences of symmetrical bodies could be objectively determined. But since they are distinguished solely by the subjective differentiations "right" and "left," they are something subjective.[41]

Coleridge also illustrated Kant's doctrine of the ideality of space by means of a beautiful simile, that of a kaleidoscope.[42] Looking inside it, we see an immense variety of different patterns produced by the shift of the colored fragments inside the tube, prismatically reflected. Now the quality "common in kind to all the thousand successive figures presented to us" by the instrument is "evidently symmetry." This quality is not a quality of the materials inside the tube: it "subsists wholly in the instrument itself. In the constitution and constituent laws (or modes of action) of the kaleidoscope itself this symmetry originates, and by these it is communicated not to the fragments themselves but to the figure in the beholder's mind resulting from that arrangement; and that they are all so arranged as to fall under one common form, viz., that of symmetry, is the work of the instrument itself" (II, 242).

In the same way, space is a figure in the mind of the beholder and not an objective reality. If it is objected that even a kaleidoscope possesses those material fragments of glass, etc. that become symmetrical when reflected, it can be replied that Kant never denied that our sensations are caused by objective reality, the things in themselves. But "there is nothing in space save what is represented in it" (A 374*n*) and "space itself is in us" (A 370).

This simile brings out Coleridge's brilliant capacities for imaginative illustration of abstract doctrines, even if the germ of it is in Schelling: "Is the soul, like a cylindrical concave mirror, that reflects unformed images as regular figures?" (*SW*, I, 379,

Abhandl. III). We shall see in Chapter 8 Coleridge's familiarity with the work referred to.

Let us now make another simile, to illustrate the condition of the knowing subject according to Kant. The knowing subject becomes rather like a spectator who sits in a cinema and watches the moving picture appearing on the screen before him. Similarly the observer of nature, or of the world in general, sees before him a living pageant of color, sound and other qualities. However, according to Kant, the projector that throws the picture on the screen is not something existing outside the spectator, but it is his own mind, using a film upon which outside impressions have been impressed. The screen itself is not outside the spectator, but it is his own consciousness, on which the film made by the recording apparatus of his own mind is projected. So that everything—the show, the projector, the screen—all, except impressions on the film—exists only in the mind of the spectator, and there is nothing outside it, save the things in themselves, unknowable in their own nature.

It would then appear that according to Kant the whole show or appearance of reality, including nature herself, exists only in the way of an optical illusion inside a cinema, and we can never go out of the theatre and get in touch with things as they really are. To some thinkers, this situation has disturbing affinities with the plight of humanity in Plato's cave.

Faced by the dilemma of declaring nature a complete illusion, or else declaring it a purely subjective reality, Kant was consistent to the main trend of his thought. In the first edition of the *Critique* he said: "save through it [it = our understanding], nature, that is, the synthetic unity of our manifold of appearances according to rules, *would not exist at all*, (for appearances, as such, cannot exist outside us—they exist only for our sensibility)" (A 126–27; italics mine). We may be drenched to the bones by a shower, nevertheless "drops of rain are mere appearances," and "their round shape, and even the space in which they fall, *are nothing in themselves*, but merely modifications or fundamental forms of our perception" (A 46, B 63; italics mine). In the second edition of the *Critique* Kant gave this definition of nature, taken as the totality of beings: "By nature . . . is meant the sum of appearances in so far as they stand . . . in thoroughgoing interconnection" (B 446). In the first edition (which Coleridge may not have known; his copy is of the second) Kant had said: "Nature is not a thing in itself but is merely an aggregate of appearances, so many representations of the mind" (A 114).

Coleridge repeats Kant's definition in his own definitions of nature in this sense (i.e., as totality, not as essence, nor as *natura naturans*): in *The Friend*, "the aggregate of phenomena" (*F*, 310n, Sec. II, Ess. 5); in *Aids*, "the sum total of the facts and phenomena of the senses" (*Aids*, 167n), and in the MS. "Logic," II, 165, and 226.

This taken all together is the doctrine that Kant called "transcendental idealism," and which at the same time was also "empirical realism" (A 369–70). It is distinguished from "transcendental realism" which regards time and space as something real in themselves, independently of our sensibility (A 369) and from "empirical idealism" (i.e., Berkeley's) which "denies the existence of the external objects of the senses" (A 368).

Let us note another point in connection with our simile of the movie theatre. There is at least one strong reason why that simile cannot be accepted as a complete analogy to our conscious life. It omits all reference to action. In our real life, we do not just sit back and watch the pageant of the world roll by. We get up and walk up into the picture and then act in it. We meet with obstacles and resistances, and we counteract them by exerting our will and going into actions of different kinds among the so-called images on the screen. There is no parallel to this in the cinema situation. Kant of course was fully aware of the reality of effort, and after writing the *Critique of Pure Reason* composed the *Critique of the Practical Reason* dealing with the problems of the will. But the post-Kantians felt that he had never really reconciled the theoretical point of view of the first *Critique* with the practical view of the second; we shall find this particularly in Schelling (Chapter 8 of this volume).

Before leaving the topic of the ideality of space and time, let us see one final consequence of this doctrine, which was not noted, as far as I know, by Coleridge, or perhaps by anyone else. This doctrine ultimately means that we, or the knowing subject, are beyond both space and time. Space and time are simply the projection of our perceptive faculties. When we really grasp the idea that every act of thought and of perception springs from a source which is itself beyond space and time, we may well draw back in consternation at the measureless abyss which suddenly gapes at us—and gapes not in front of us (which would be alarming enough) but *inside* ourselves. Certainly this is "discovering ourselves." It is apparently *we*, and not a transcendent being such as the God of traditional theology, who exist beyond the limits of space and time. If this is so, we may well ask in perplexity, *where* are we? or, since "where" can only be applied to space, and we are beyond it, *what* are we? and how do we have our being, how do we exist? what is this innermost self beyond all the limits of space and time? The imagination may well boggle and the understanding feel lost at this prospect. Can we, as Coleridge put it, "dare commune with our very and permanent self" (*The Friend*, Introd. Ess., p. 68)? If so, a whole new view of reality and system of values is required.

The fact is that, through the whole Kantian doctrine, the knowing process, or self-consciousness, gradually acquires ontological status and becomes the proper object of metaphysics, even if Kant did not fully realize it. Through his doctrine a new metaphysic becomes possible, referring no longer to some objective absolute, or to some substance, entity or being outside us, but centering on the subject and on the act of thinking, a metaphysic which is therefore not transcendent but immanent. This is indeed a "Copernican revolution" such as Kant envisaged in the Preface to his book, in which he said that since all philosophies that made the subject depend on the object had failed, it was time to try the other way, and make the object depend on the subject (B xvi). But the complete achievement of this aim was reserved to the post-Kantians.[43]

CHAPTER *3*

Kant II—The Doctrine of the Categories

THROUGH THE DOCTRINE of the ideality of Time and Space Kant had made considerable progress in his Copernican revolution. The object of knowledge was being made more and more to depend upon the knower, instead of subordinating him to itself. However, there still remained what may be called the entire content of the forms of perception, viz., the world of natural law and of the great scientific systems. True, the fact that space and time have been shown to be only subjective forms casts a shadow of uncertainty over all those things, great and substantial as they are; at least, it seems to call for a more elaborate theory to reconcile their objective reality with the subjectivity of the forms of perception. But Kant proceeds to invalidate the objectivity of science by means of an even more radical doctrine, which is expounded in the Transcendental Analytic and which he calls the doctrine of Categories.

"Categories" is a familiar word in philosophy ever since Aristotle. They are classes of qualities, the most general ideas of all; and Kant was well aware of his great predecessor. But he criticizes Aristotle for having picked up his categories casually, without a guiding principle, with the result that even the forms of perception, space and time, and the empirical concept of *motion* are included in them (A 81, B 107). Kant's categories are systematically arranged and they are functions of the knowing process, not classes of things-in-themselves, the unattainable noumena.

Experience, according to Kant, involves something more than sensations arranged in the frames of space and time. It involves certain basic general ideas which do not derive from mere sensations. These general ideas serve to organize the mass of representations into connected wholes, so that we obtain the articulated world of objective reality which we perceive in our daily life. We may combine the various sensations called "yellow, fragrant, sour" into a single temporal series and locate them in space; but we do not get the total idea of "lemon" until we refer all the representations to the same object, *as an object*, and think of it as a fruit, i.e., as something belonging to a certain class of realities existing independently of ourselves. Now the idea of a thing, or of objective reality, is not itself a sensation, even though elicited and verified by sensations; it is not a representation or a set of representations; it is a mental pattern, or frame, into which an unlimited number of representations may be fitted, thus making single objects out of them. It is that which Kant calls a category, i.e., a purely mental formation to which no outside object corresponds as its counterpart, but in virtue of which outside objects exist for us, so that we attribute to them not only shape and dimension, but existence and qualities.[1]

Kant's own list of categories does not include "thing" or "object," nor the correlative notion of "qualities," but it does include, as we shall see, that of "substance and accident," which correspond to what we have called "thing and quality."

Kant believed that it was his duty to make a complete list of categories. This should not be impossible, he pointed out, on the assumption that they are a priori concepts, or functions of our thinking process. The analysis of that process would bring out the truly general ideas involved in it, and these will be the categories. Kant came to the conclusion that there were exactly twelve categories, all comprised. The Table of Categories is the keystone of his "Architectonic" and is applied also in the other *Critiques*, so it is one of the most important parts of his system.

It was also Kant's aim to give a full demonstration of the a priori necessity of the categories, which he calls the Deduction of the Categories. This is one of the most notoriously complicated parts of the *Critique*. Coleridge himself in a note to his own copy of the book wrote that it comprehends "the most difficult and obscure passages of the *Critique*." [2] The difficulty is increased by the division of the Deduction into two parts, a Metaphysical Deduction and a Transcendental. The Transcendental Deduction is further subdivided into the Subjective and Objective Deductions, and the limits between the two are not clearly marked (*Co*, 240, *n.* 3). To increase complications, there are also two different versions of the whole Transcendental Deduction, one in the first edition of the *Critique* (A, 1791) and the other in the second edition (B, 1787), and interpreters differ on their characteristics.[3] Coleridge used the second edition: his copy, with his annotations, is preserved in the British Museum, and apparently he was not aware of the differences between the two editions, which were brought to light by later scholarship, the famous *Kant-Philologie*.

Finally, what may well be considered the most important principle introduced in the whole section is not the Categories or any of their derivations, but something else, which is not mentioned in the title heading of the section, and which will be discussed in our next chapter. Here we will ignore the subdivisions of the Deduction, which apparently were also ignored by Coleridge, and attempt to give the gist of it in simple terms.

What Kant calls the *Metaphysical* Deduction of the Categories is something that most people to-day would call a logical deduction, or a classification of categories based on formal logic. Kant first sets up a classification of all the possible varieties of propositions, called the Table of Judgments (a "judgment" in Kantian terms is a proposition), then he proceeds to abstract from each class the most general idea involved in its definition, and that is the category. For instance, the most common type of proposition is the so-called Universal Proposition, of the kind "All A's are B" or "All men are mortal." From this one abstracts the most general idea involved, i.e., "all" or Totality, and that is the first Category. Similarly from the class of Negative Propositions we obtain the category of Negation, and from the class of Hypothetical Propositions—"If A is true, than B follows"—we obtain, with a little more stretching, the category that Kant sometimes calls Ground and Consequence. This stretching is rather more obvious in the last six categories; but, with some effort, Kant gets all his twelve categories in the way indicated.

The judgments and the corresponding Categories are then classified in groups of three each, and there are four of these groups, making up the total of twelve categories. I give below both tables in parallel columns. I have added for clarity an example of each variety of Judgment; these examples are not to

TABLES

Judgments (A 70, B 75)	*Categories* (A 80, B 106)
1. *Quantity* 　Universal: "All A's are B" 　Particular: "Some A's are B" 　Singular: "This A is B"	1. *Quantity* 　Totality 　Plurality 　Unity
2. *Quality* 　Affirmative: "A is B" 　Negative: "A is-not B" 　Infinite: "A is non-B"	2. *Quality* 　Reality 　Negation 　Limitation
3. *Relation* 　Categorical: "A is B" 　Hypothetical: "If A, B follows" 　Disjunctive: "A is either B or C"	3. *Relation* 　Inherence and Subsistence 　(*substantia et accidens*) 　Causality and Dependence 　(*cause and effect*) 　Community (*reciprocity between agent and patient*)
4. *Modality* 　Problematic: "A may be B" 　Assertoric: "A is B" 　Apodeictic: "A must be B"	4. *Modality* 　Possibility—Impossibility 　Existence—Non-existence 　Necessity—Contingency

be imputed to Kant. I have also taken the liberty of rearranging the three Categories of Quantity so that they correspond exactly to the Judgments of Quantity, following the suggestion of Paton (I, 297, *n.* 2). Coleridge of course followed Kant's original arrangement.

How did Kant arrived at his classification of Judgments? He claims that his classification is the one "ordinarily recognized by logicians" (A 71, B 96), but no logician has recognised it as such. The research conducted by Kant scholars on contemporary logicians and Kant's own development led to the conclusion that Kant first made the Table of Categories, then made a Table of Judgments to fit it.[4] Some of the items in the latter Table might be found here and there, but nothing like Kant's Table was found "in any existing logic," and Kemp Smith concluded that Kant's classifications "were reached only by the freest possible handling of the classifications currently employed" (*Co,* 192–93).

Kant's classification of propositions is in part based on their conceptual content (e.g., those of Quantity), in part upon their verbal form (e.g., those of Quality). The analysis of the verbal form of a statement with the purpose of determining its logical value is a typical process of formal logic, the kind of logic in which Kant was trained. But it is open to criticism. Verbal expression is basically intuitive, affording cognition of particulars, which are then frozen into conventions.[5] Hence speech can convey conceptual thought, which deals with universals and not with particulars, only indirectly, by symbolizing them in images of particular things, and so all abstract terms are originally metaphorical.[6] But the structure and parts of the symbol are not the same as the structure and parts of the concept, so that analysis of the structure of the verbal form will not yield the structure of the thought.[7] For instance, verbal symbols of concepts vary from language to language, but this does not mean that the concept varies from language to language: the concept of unity is expressed by different verbal symbols in different languages—ἑνάς in Greek, *unitas* in Latin, *Einheit* in German, *unity* in English, etc., but this does not mean that they are all different concepts. Not only single words differ from language to language, and even from writer to writer, but also the grammar and syntax of different languages differ from each other, and the style differs from writer to writer, while the thought may remain the same. The differences in languages provide the main problem of the translator, but a good translation will convey the same thought from one language to another.

So a classification of statements according to their verbal form alone may have grammatical or syntactical value (perhaps even rhetorical), but not logical, if logic is the science of thought. Indeed logicians have always denounced the traps which language may present to thought, and dissected the fallacies based on the verbal form of statements. Philosophers basically concerned with thought in itself have given up the attempt to analyze thought by means of its verbal expression.[8] These philosophers have to acknowledge a deep debt to Kant, but they have also to discard some of his logical formalism.

On the other hand, Kant's categories, aside from their more or less arbitrary classification, are of prime importance to philosophy. They may be said to correspond, at least in part, to Plato's Ideas, such as Being, Unity, the Limit, the Unlimited, etc., brought down from the hyperuranium to earth and conceived as functions of the knowing mind. Considering the significance that Kant attributes to the concept of category, its a priori character and its function as the foundation of all knowledge, it has been said that Kant is the modern successor of Plato.[9]

Coleridge's adherence to Kant's theory of the categories has been called by Wellek "slavish acceptance" (*W*, 123). Since Wellek did not reproduce Kant's tables, assuming no doubt that they were well-known, or Coleridge's, because they were the same as Kant's, this judgment may appear too harsh to admirers of Coleridge. Let the reader judge for himself. I have already given Kant's tables in full, now I will give Coleridge's, from the MS. "Logic."

"The Judgments are characterized according to

1

Quantity

Universal
Particular
Single

2   3

Quality   *Relation*

Affirmative   Categorical
Negative   Hypothetical
Limitless   Disjunctive

4

Modality

Problematic
Assertorial
Apodeictic
Remarks.

"One use of this table is that it gives us an opportunity of pointing out certain differences between common Logic or the Canons of the Understanding and the Transcendental Logic or the analysis of the Faculty itself" (II, 431).

"Table of Categories being a register of the primitive
or stock-conceptions of the Understanding

1	2
Conceptions of Quantity	*Conceptions of Quality*
Unity or the one	Reality
Plurality or the many	Negation
Omneity or the all	Limitation

3	4
Conceptions of Relation	*Conceptions of Modality*
Inherence and Subsistence (Substance and accident)	Possibility—Impossibility
Causality and Dependence (Cause and effect)	Entity—Non-entity
Community (reciprocity of action between the agent and the patient) or the equality of Action and Reaction	Necessity—Contingency"

(II, 445)

In elucidation of some of the above it may be said:

1) Kant terms the first two triads "Mathematical" because from them he derives the principles upon which mathematics is built. The term "Dynamic" is applied to triads 3 and 4 because the principles of the science of Dynamics are based upon them (Paton, II, 99). These terms are also used by Coleridge (II, 455–56).

2) Some of the categories are represented by single terms, like "Unity" or "Reality." Others are represented by two terms, like "Substance and Accident," although they constitute a single category. In these, the second term is called by Kant the "correlate" (B 110) and Coleridge follows suit (II, 45–56).

3) The terms with a correlate belong to the Dynamic group. They all deal with the existence of objects of intuition, "in their relation either to each other or to the understanding" (B 110). So also Coleridge (II, 455–56).

4) One classification which is rather troublesome is that of

the Quality of Judgments. Aristotle had recognized Universal, Particular, and Infinite Judgments; but Kant places the first two classes under Quantity, and the last under Quality. However, Aristotle's "infinite" proposition is merely indefinite in quantity; it refers to "some" and not to "all," which would be Universal. For instance, "some pleasure is evil" would be for Aristotle an infinite proposition, because we are not told how much pleasure, or what pleasure, is evil, while "all pleasure is evil" would be a universal proposition.

Coleridge following Kant (A 71–73, B 97–98) tried to explain "infinite" judgments in a special paragraph (II, 433–34). In a Negative Judgment the *whole* of an Affirmative Judgment (e.g., "the soul is mortal") is denied, but in an Infinite Judgment we *affirm* that the soul belongs to the class of things which are not-mortal. Since this class is "boundless," the Judgment is Infinite. It must be admitted the distinction (based as it is on the verbal form of the Judgment) is not very clear.[10]

A complete analysis of these tables and of all the logical questions involved would take us out of our way. Full discussion of the categories, in general and in particular, will be found in the commentaries on Kant available in English: Paton, Vleeschauwer, Ewing, etc.

We will limit ourselves to the category of causality, to which Coleridge gives considerable attention. To affirm Causality as a Category in Transcendental Logic is Kant's answer to Hume's Critique. Hume had argued that causality cannot be proven from experience. Kant acknowledged the impossibility of empirical proof of causality, but argued that it is nevertheless valid for us because it is a part of the system of categories which our intellect imposes upon the multiplicity of phenomena. All we know are the appearances of things. "But appearances are only representations of things which are unknown as regards what they are in themselves. As mere representations, they are subject to no law of connection save that which the connecting faculty prescribes" (B 163–64). Causality is one such connection, and therefore it is necessarily valid for us.

More exactly, the category involved in the notion of causality is the second category in the third class (Relation), which Kant elsewhere (B 431) calls Ground and Consequence. The corresponding type of judgment is the Hypothetical: proposition B follows inevitably if proposition A is assumed, so "if A, then B." This is a purely logical principle; it can become a law of nature only if we introduce into it the notion of time, with the succession of one phenomenon upon another. Then the principle becomes that of causality, in which the effect B inevitably *follows* upon the cause A, every cause *preceding* the effect. Kant points this out later, in the section dedicated to the Principles of the Understanding (B 232). He equated "cause" with "ground" in B 249, and "effect" with "consequence" in B 234.[11] This correlation involves the further concept of "schema," which will be discussed after the categories.

Coleridge's adhesion to the doctrine of the categories goes back to 1809, in the first version of *The Friend* (No. V): "the Understanding or regulative faculty is manifestly distinct from Life and Sensation; its *function* being to take up the *passive affections* into distinct Thought of the Sense both according to its own essential forms.* These Forms however as they are first awakened by impressions from the Senses, so they have no Substance or Meaning unless in their application to Objects of the Senses."

A footnote, after referring to Aristotle's categories, goes on: "The best and most orderly arrangement of the original forms of the Understanding (the *Moulds* as it were both of our Notions and judgments concerning the Notices of the Senses) is that of Quantity, Quality, Relation, and Mode, each consisting of three Kinds." [12]

Kant is not mentioned here, but he is quoted in a parallel passage in the *Biographia* upon the twelve "categorical forms." A footnote specifies: "videlicet, quantity, quality, relation, and mode, each consisting of three subdivisions. Vide *Kritik der reinen Vernunft*, pp. 95 and 106. See too the judicious remarks on Locke and Hume" (*BL*, I, 94).

In the final version of *The Friend* (1818) the Understanding is "that faculty, the functions of which contain the rules and constitute the possibility of outward experience" (p. 96, First Landing Place, Ess. 5). He also speaks of "the moulds and mechanisms of the Understanding, . . . which consist in individualization, in outlines and differencings by quantity, quality and relation" (*F*, 340, Sec. II, Ess. 11). So, too, in Z, 227.

And there are references to the doctrine also in later writings. In the *Statesman's Manual*, Appendix E, Coleridge defines "incomprehensible" as "not reducible to the forms of sense, namely, time and space, or those of those of the understanding, namely quantity, quality and relation" (p. 294).

In the dissertation "On the difference in Kind between Reason and the Understanding" which is included in *Aids* (p. 150), the "constituent forms of the Understanding" appear again. Kant is referred to for the definition of Understanding a few pages later (p. 153), and on the following page there is a fuller definition of the categories as "pre-conceptions (*conceptus antecedentes at generalissimi*—conceptions antecedent and very general) of Quantity and Relation" (p. 154).

In the so-called *Essay on Faith* he is even closer to Kant in his reference to the classes of categories: "The faculty of the finite is that which reduces the confused impressions of sense to their essential forms, quantity, quality, relation, and in these action and reaction, cause and effect, and the like; thus [sic] raises the materials furnished by the senses and sensations into objects of reflection, and so makes experience possible. Without it, man's representative powers would be a delirium, a chaos, a scudding cloudage of shapes; and it is therefore most appropriately called the understanding or substantive faculty" (*Aids*, 345–46).

As the reader may have noticed, the classes of the categories in the last references have dwindled, from four, first to three and then to two. This may be simply an incomplete reference, but there may be a deeper reason. In a note of 1815 Coleridge wrote: "A sound Dialectic has taught me to reduce the Forms or Modes of Action of the reflex Faculty to the three Categories of Quantity, Quality, and Relation; while Modality is the synthesis of the Three, considered as possible, as real, or necessary;

and in all the Categories it is noticeable that the first and second are Thesis and Antithesis, and the third, the Synthesis of both." [13]

The terminology of the last sentence is Hegelian, but the idea is Kantian. It was Kant himself who called attention to the fact that categories go by threes. True, the triads in turn fall into four classes, but Kant is more attracted by triads than by quaternions. He said himself that the point was one of the "nice points" of the Table, "which may perhaps have important consequences" (B 109). Few predictions have been so over-whelmingly verified. Kant observed that "the third category in each group always arises from a combination of the second category with the first" (B 110). This is the first appearance of what was going to be that great engine of metaphysics, the dialectic of Hegel. Kant's demonstration of the connection be-tween the members of a triad (which members he calls "Mo-ments," A 76, B 101, another term which will pass into Hegel) reads like a passage in Hegel's *Logic*: "*allness* or *totality* is just plurality considered as unity; *limitation* is simply reality com-bined with negation; *community* is the causality of substances reciprocally determining one another; lastly, *necessity* is just the existence which is given through possibility itself" (B 110). He adds that this combination of opposites into a third moment "requires a special act of understanding" (*ibid.*), i.e., it is not automatically given by the concepts but requires an ulterior process of reflection, or what will later be called dialectical thinking.

In the Introduction to the *Critique of Judgment* Kant re-affirms the triadic principles and justifies it against its critics: all a priori concepts involve three moments, "1) a condition, 2) a conditioned, 3) the concept arising from the union of the conditioned with the condition" (p. 39). This is on one side close to Plato (*Philebus*), on the other side closer to Hegel.[14]

Now this trichotomy, which in its Hegelian form has been the object of much criticism, was entirely approved by Cole-ridge. He says that "trichotomy . . . forms the prominent excellence in Kant's *Critique of Pure Reason*" (Snyder, 129*n*). It is true that he accompanies this judgment with the claim that "the merit . . . belongs to R. Baxter, a century before," i.e., Richard Baxter, a seventeenth-century divine of whom Coleridge thought very highly. But Wellek showed that there is no foundation for Coleridge's claim: "Baxter had not the slightest glimpse of the dialectic, but merely indulged in speculations on the *Vestigia Trinitatis* in the Macrocosmos and the Microcosmos" (*W*, 85). Baxter like Augustine argues that, since "man is made in the image of God" and God is a trinity, there must be trinities in everything human: e.g., the three faculties "Vegetation, Sensation and Intellection," the last being also subdivided into three, "Posse, Scire, Velle," and so on.[15] In none of these triads is the last term the synthesis of two preceding opposites and therefore is not dialectical.

But although the triadic process was called dialectics later by Hegel, its three "moments" being for Hegel affirmation, negation, and finally negation of negation, Kant himself, as we have seen, uses the term Dialectic in a derogatory meaning, for the part of philosophy that refutes the errors of metaphysics. In spite of this, Kant was building the foundations for the positive use of dialectics as it will be found in the metaphysics of his successors. We shall take up later its repercussions in Coleridge's thinking.

The concept of "schema" arises out of Kant's attempt to develop all the basic assumptions of science from the categories, through a gradual progress from the general to the particular. The stages of this development are called *Schemata* and *Principles of the Understanding*. Kant's argument is rather complicated, but all we need here is an idea of its general purport.

Categories, being the most general concepts, must be the foundation of all later knowledge of phenomena. But a category, taken by itself, or in its abstraction, is not yet a principle that can guide us in the particular investigation of nature. To afford such guidance, a category must be connected with the pure form of perception, i.e., with time, and it then becomes a schema. In other words, a schema is the temporalization of a category. We have already seen an example in the manner in which the category of "Ground and Consequence" becomes the concept of causality: that concept, which involves time, is a schema. The same process is applied to all categories (or at least to all the classes of categories) and we obtain a set of *schemata* in correspondence to the table of categories. For instance, Number for the class of Quantity, Degree for the class of Quality, and six other schemata for the six categories of Relation and Modality.

Coleridge does not seem to have taken much notice of schemata, and the words schema and schematism appear to have a different meaning in him.[16]

But schemata are merely general concepts, they are not statements of principles that can be actually applied to specific questions. To become principles, schemata must be developed into propositions: e.g., the concept of Causality, or the schema of Necessary Succession in Time, must be formulated as the proposition "Every event must necessarily be preceded by its cause." In this shape it can be applied to a specific question: e.g., B follows A, can B be the cause of A? Answer, of course No.

So from the schemata Kant develops in this way a set of general principles of scientific investigation of phenomena. Although these principles are thus deduced a priori, there is nothing metaphysical or transcendent about them, and most of them would be probably taken for granted by a modern scientist. They are: 1) all phenomena are measurable, i.e., are extended in space and / or time; 2) all phenomena have a certain degree of intensity, even though this may not be measured;[17] 3) the total quantum in nature is neither increased nor diminished by any change; 4) all changes occur in conformity to the law of causality; 5) all substances are in reciprocal interaction.

Kant classified them under the following headings: 1 under Axioms of Intuition (= *Anschauung*, sometimes translated Sensation), 2 under Anticipations of Perception, 3–5 under Analogies of Experience; then he added another three as Postulates of Empirical Thought.

The second principle of the last group is the Postulate of Existence or of Actuality, which means that "the perception which supplies the content to a concept is the sole mark of actuality" (A 225, B 273), or as it might be put today, the only way to verify it. This could be what the principle of "verification," one of the mainstays of modern logical positivism, reduces itself to. But Kant includes in "perception" the a priori conditions of perception (A 220, B 267), which are over and beyond the confines of positivism.

All Kant's principles of knowledge fit into his "architectural" scheme, as follows:

Classes of Categories	Schemata	Principles of the Pure Understanding
Quantity	Number	Axioms of Intuition
Quality	Degree	Anticipations of Perception
Relation	Permanence	Analogies of Experience
	Causality	
	Coexistence	
Modality	Possibility	Postulates of Empirical Thought
	Existence	
	Necessary existence	

We will not attempt to expound all this table, which also involves a number of debatable points. But we will note that Coleridge accepted the main doctrine of the "principles of the Understanding." In the already quoted passage from the first version of *The Friend* he goes on to say: "the Understanding, with all its Axioms of sense, its Anticipations of Apperception, and its Analogies of Experience, has no appropriate Object, but the material World in Relation to our worldly Interests" (*op. cit.*, p. 80). These three groups of principles will be found in the third column of the table above, with some slight variation in the rendering of terms like *Anschauung* (intuition or sense). Coleridge omitted only the last group, Postulates of Empirical Thought, not necessarily because he rejected it, but possibly because he thought it unnecessary to quote the entire list.

Wellek's remark about the schemata is worth quoting as a criticism of Kant. Kant tried to solve the problem of bringing together "sensibility and understanding," which he had too sharply divided, "by the introduction of schemata, which subsume the manifold of experience under the general a priori. But obviously the solution is unsatisfactory. . . . Experience cannot be arrived at by subsumption but merely [i.e., only] by synthesis" (*W*, 83).[18] This is a pertinent criticism. Coleridge also criticized the way in which Kant subsumed the manifold (*mannigfaltig*) material of experience under the general a priori categories in an important marginalium quoted also by Wellek (*W*, 82–83), which begins: "How can that be called *ein mannigfaltiges* υλη which yet contains in itself the ground why I apply one category to it rather than another?"

This may have been one of those "doubts during a first perusal," as Coleridge headed these marginalia in his copy. In any case, he accepted the peculiarly Kantian doctrine of schemata and principles in *The Friend* of 1809, and confirmed his allegiance to it in later references, as we have seen. According to this doctrine, all the fundamental laws of nature can be derived logically from the a priori concepts of the Understanding in conjunction with the a priori forms of perception, but with an increasing element of empirical knowledge. Kant expanded this doctrine in his *Metaphysical Foundations of the Science of Nature* (1786), about which we shall see something more in Chapter 8. Here we will point out an important aspect of Kant's doctrine of the categories: not only are the categories necessary to us, the knowing subject, in order to turn the chaos of phenomena into the orderly and rational world of natural science (this is the subjective Deduction), but experience itself must be such that it fits into the Categories (this is the objective Deduction).

We have already noticed in Coleridge a tendency to turn back from the extreme consequences of transcendentalism and return to traditional theism. Here is another instance, relative to the present subject: "The fact therefore that the mind of man in its own primary and constituent forms represents the laws of nature, is a mystery which of itself should suffice to make us religious; for it is a problem of which God is the only

solution, God, the one before all, and of all, and through all!"
(*Statesman's Manual*, Appendix B; *C&S*, 273).

The first part of the paragraph is Kantian: the "primary and
constituent forms" of mind are the categories, which according
to Kant "represent the laws of nature." But in the strict context
of the *Critique of Pure Reason* there is no solution in God, nor
a feeling of mystery to make one religious as Coleridge becomes.

In the analyses of the *Critique* the function of the Imagination is repeatedly mentioned, and this has led to a misunderstanding, by critics who believed that this was the aesthetic
imagination. First of all, Kant distinguished the Productive
Imagination from the Reproductive Imagination, but neither of
them has an aesthetic function. They are not concerned with
the Beautiful, and are not productive of art or of poetry. They
are instead functions of the Understanding that operate in the
organization of empirical knowledge.

The Reproductive Imagination is a little more than memory.
It recalls previous representations, connecting them blindly,
according to the laws of association (B 152). These laws, formulated by Locke, are recognized by Kant only in the limited
area of the Reproductive Imagination, as empirical laws.

The Productive Imagination, or "pure a priori imagination"
(A 142, B 181), operates in the construction of schemata (A
140, B 179). We have seen how schemata are a mediation between the categories and the general principles of science, such
as the law of causality. This is enough to show how far the
Productive Imagination of the *Critique* is from the domain of
aesthetics. Who could speak of the schema of causality as
something poetic? Hence it is hard to follow D. G. James in his
extension of Kant's theory of the Imagination.[19]

On the other hand, it may look as if Kant introduced the
concept of the unconscious mind, at least in the workings of the
Reproductive Imagination. He defines it "a blind but indispensable power of the soul, without which we should have no
knowledge whatsoever, but of which we are scarcely ever conscious" (A 78, B 103). Still it should be noted that even here
Kant, like the Captain, speaks of "scarcely ever," and does not

say "never." He says elsewhere that if we were not conscious "the manifold of representation would never, therefore, form a whole, since it would lack that unity which only consciousness can impart to it" (A 103). At the next higher level, the understanding is always conscious, being "the faculty whereby the a priori is always brought to consciousness" (*Co*, 264).

Yet even this slight reference to the unconscious was apparently not without consequences in later philosophy, where the unconscious takes an important place, as we shall see in Schelling.

A shortcoming of Kant's Table of Categories is that the concepts listed therein refer only to the physical world, and none of them refer to human or moral conditions or objects, such as the will, the person, and the character, good or bad, of human actions. If our experience were determined solely by the Table of Categories, we would see around us only material objects and not a living creature. We would see the bodies of human beings as bodies but never as people, since we would be lacking in the category necessary for that perception. This deficiency was remedied, to a considerable degree, in Kant's succeeding *Critiques*. The *Critique of Practical Reason* introduces the concept of Person, and the *Critique of Judgment* the concept of living beings or organisms.

In conclusion we may say that Coleridge adopted from Kant the doctrine of the categories and preserved this attitude for the rest of his life. But his fullest exposition of the doctrine, which is in the MS. "Logic," cannot fairly be said to be "slavish," since it is professedly an exposition of Kant; it might rather be called "faithful." It is in other respects that Coleridge diverges from Kantian thought, e.g., in the extreme consequences of transcendental idealism. These were largely determined by another doctrine of Kant's, to which we turn in the next chapter.

In confirmation of these conclusions, here is an unpublished attempt by Coleridge to set up a kind of Table of Categories and Principles of his own, modeled on Kant's but differing in content:

"The rational being asks (for a reason)

Quantum?	measure
What?	being
How	cause—ground
Why	end

it requires: Universality, Permanence, Harmony, Finality. It rests satisfied having discovered:

The Many in the One
The Real, or the Actuality of the Potential
The Adequateness of the Potential to the Actual
The Necessity of the Actual

The discovery is effected by the opposition of the

One ✶ Many
Essential ✶ Actual
Ground ✶ Manifestation
Will ✶ Reason

It asserts this discovery as a Judgment in the form of a correspondent Mesotheta—

Omneity
Reality
Idem = Alterity
Law.

These may be regarded as regulative ideas, and the intellectual correspondents of the constitutive Ideas of Reason

Omneity = Universality
Reality = Permanence
Idem-Alterity = Harmony
Law = Finality." [20]

(Add. MS. 34, 225, fol. 159)

CHAPTER 4

Kant III—The Transcendental Unity of Apperception

i

THE TRANSCENDENTAL DEDUCTION of the Categories actually introduces a new principle, which is not itself a category but the ultimate foundation of all categories, and indeed of all experience and all mental processes. It is therefore of the greatest importance. Yet Kant introduces it without preliminaries of any kind, not even one of those paragraph headings of which he is sometimes generous. Nor is it mentioned in the Preface among the important points of the book to which the reader's attention is called (e.g., A xvi–xvii, B xxxviii).

This principle, upon which everything else is now shown to depend, is the act of self-consciousness, or as Kant designated it "the *I think*." In his terminology, self-consciousness constitutes the Transcendental Unity of Apperception. It is Transcendental, because it is the a priori condition of all experience: without awareness of self there can be no awareness of anything else. It is a Unity—even a "numerically identical" Unity (A 107)— because there is only one *I*, one center of consciousness. Finally it is a unity of Apperception, because by Apperception Kant means self-consciousness (B 66; cf. Paton, I, 346).

As "the supreme principle of all employment of the understanding" (B 136), it might have rated, one assumes, at least a chapter to itself. Instead, it is buried in the convolutions of the Transcendental Deduction. This may be due to the late emergence of this principle in the long period of composition of the *Critique*. It is said to appear in a rudimentary form for the first time "shortly before 1781" (*Co*, 234). In any case, his successors made up for this abundantly, by making it the central principle of reality.

The meaning of this principle may be briefly stated thus: all representations must be accompanied by the awareness that they belong to one and the same consciousness (A 123–24, B 132). If consciousness does not recognize a sensation as its own, that sensation would not exist for consciousness, and therefore would not exist at all (A 115, B 132), since its existence consists in being a conscious phenomenon. We may of course conceive modifications of bodily condition of which one may not be aware at the time, but these modifications have not yet become sensations. "To become part of experience, sensations and representations must be cognized as belonging to a subject, or known by the *I think*" (A 120, B 132).

This is probably the most complete answer to empiricism formulated by a philosopher. As we have seen, empiricism in all its forms, ancient and modern, maintains that all our knowledge comes from sensations and from no other source, there being no knowledge in our mind that is obtained independently of sensations. Indeed the more radical empiricists, such as Hume, maintain that there is no such thing as the mind, or the I, but only a bundle of sensations and of traces of sensations. Consciousness has been termed an "epiphenomenon" or an end-product, a pale reflex or residue of repeated impressions. As we saw, Hume maintained that he could not find the self in himself:

"For my part, when I enter most intimately into what I call *myself*, I always stumble on some particular perception or other, of heat or cold, light or shade, love or hatred, pain or pleasure. I can never catch *myself* at any time without a perception, and never can observe anything but the perception" (p. 252).

Now Kant agreed that the self is always to be found thinking of something and never without an object (B 276), but he also believed that the knowing self, the "I think," is distinct from every particular object and logically prior to it. It is, in his language, transcendental (A 341, B 399). The reason why Hume could not find the self in himself was that he looked in the wrong direction. He should have looked not for the "me," but for the "I," not for the known but for the knower, not to the object of thought but to the subject. Hume's argument actually implies the personal identity which the argument denies, for if the argument is to be valid, the "I" who "enters most intimately" must be identical with the "I" who "stumbles," and both must be identical with the "I" who "can never catch itself." It is to the "I" that knows, thinks, asks questions, and finds answers, that Hume should have directed his inquiry, as Kant did.

Instead of deriving this "I" from the residua of sensations, Kant considered its self-consciousness as primary and sensations as secondary. Becoming aware of a sensation is the a priori condition for connecting it with other sensations in any kind of association or combination. The laws of association, upon which empiricism relies to bring together sensations and build out of them the world of experience, are indeed valid for Kant, but as we have seen only to a limited degree, and presuppose the previous recognition of the sensations in a single consciousness. If sensation A belonged to the consciousness of Mr. X, while sensation B belongs to the consciousness of Mr. Y, they would never associate in a single experience, but go their separate ways in different consciousnesses. Or as William James put it, more in the way of a parable than of an argument, but with his usual stylistic vigor: "Take a sentence of a dozen words, and take twelve men and tell to each one word. Then stand the men in a row or jam them in a bunch, and let each think of his word as intently as he will; nowhere will there be a consciousness of the whole sentence." [1]

And not only representations, made up from sensations in the three-fold syntheses of apperception (A 99–104), but also general ideas (or "empirical concepts") would be impossible without the unity of consciousness (B 131). A general idea for Kant is derived from a multiplicity of representations, abstracting from each the quality it has in common with other representations. For instance, through experiencing several representations of red objects, we obtain the concept of the color red and of the quality of redness (B 133). Through repeated experiences of hot objects, we abstract the concept of heat. These two representations are often associated, so we may take a further step and formulate empirical generalizations: red things are hot, hot things are red. Like all empirical generalizations, these are not always true. But we could not reach even an empirical generalization if the representations involved were not brought together as the objects of one and the same consciousness. If all the representations of red belonged to one consciousness, and those of heat to another, neither could reach the conclusion that red things are hot. So all consciousness involves self-consciousness, and the identity of consciousness in the various acts of thought presupposes the unity of consciousness with itself. If I were not aware of myself, I could not recognize myself in successive acts of perception and unify them in a generalization. The unity of consciousness with itself is a priori, for, far from being derived from sensations, it is the necessary condition for the possibility of the perception of any sensation.

This may perhaps suggest the reason why Kant took hold of Coleridge's mind "as with a giant's hand." Here was the complete refutation of empiricism that Coleridge had been looking for since he became dissatisfied with Locke and Hartley. The refutation was accompanied by a positive account of the way in which experience is built up by the mind, and a final rejection of the concept of mind as passive or inert.

However, there is a passage in the *Biographia Literaria* (Ch. IX, I, 99), from which it appears that Coleridge had some difficulty with the doctrine of the Unity of Apperception. We shall consider this difficulty in Chapter 7, since it concerns also Fichte. Coleridge says he overcame the difficulty "soon," having found an explanation of it which we will also consider then.

But what is really this Unity of Apperception, this supreme

condition of all knowledge? It is, in one sense, an ultimate, for Kant says that self-consciousness, although it "must be capable of accompanying all other representations," yet "cannot itself be accompanied by any further representation" (B 132). In other words, it conditions all other knowledge but it is itself unconditioned. Now what is unconditioned is absolute: does this mean that Kant has been able to find an absolute principle of knowledge? And if it is absolute knowledge, what is its status in the sphere of reality? Is it a concept, a notion, or a substance, or a quality, or what? Could it possibly be *the* Absolute, from which all reality depends? All these are concepts which have been presented at different times in the history of philosophy, and Kant was well acquainted with them. He could not escape the question of their possible relation to the Unity of Consciousness. What does he say about it?

Here as elsewhere, Kant oscillates between what seems the inevitable trend of his thinking and his habitual mistrust of "dogmatic philosophy" in all its forms. At times, when he is following the predominant trend of his thoughts, he will answer that the Unity of Apperception is not just another notion but "an act," and specifically "an act of spontaneity of the mind" (B 130), i.e., an act which is not determined by anything outside the mind. He will also say: "Being an act of the self-activity of the subject, it cannot be executed except by the subject" (B 130). He will even go so far as to say: "the *I think* expresses the *actus* whereby I determine my own existence" (B 157*n*, as quoted in *Co*, 324). Here he speaks practically like Fichte. Furthermore the use of the Latin term *actus* connects with Aristotelian and scholastic theories of God, whose being is pure act. We are getting into deep water indeed.

At other times, Kant succumbs to his habitual fears of transcendent speculation, and says that the "I think" is only "a representation" and that it merely "accompanies" all other representations. But we have just seen that it does something more than accompany: on Kant's own showing, it *conditions* every other mental operation. Furthermore, in the Transcendental Dialectic Kant elaborately argues that we cannot know anything about the inner nature of the human soul. Like the inner nature of things in general, it is a noumenon and we can only know its phenomena, the fluctuating motion of states of mind which our inner sense perceives. Nor can we call it a substance and then try to define its attributes, because all statements that refer to the soul as a substance are shown by Kant in the Dialectic to be subject to insoluble contradictions. Therefore the Unity of Apperception is definitely not what philosophers call a "substantial ego."

So this view provides no support for belief in the spirituality and the immortality of the soul, conceived as a permanent substance (Paton, I, 407). It does not, and cannot, assert the simplicity and immateriality of the soul. Previous philosophers had based arguments for immortality on its power of reflecting upon itself;[2] but Kant rejects that argument.

However, in the same section Kant also makes the already mentioned distinction between the self as knowing and the self as known (B 155). This distinction runs through the whole *Critique* (see B xxviii; B 147; A 341–42, B 399–400; B 429; A 443, B 471; and A 429, B 520) and will be termed "by Kant's followers," as Coleridge knew (*BL*, I, 184*n*), the distinction between the transcendental self and the empirical self. Kant does not put it in such a clear-cut dichotomy, but the terms are there: e.g., the "transcendental subject" is distinguished from the "empirical" appearance of "our mind as object of consciousness" in A 492, B 520.

Coleridge repeatedly refers to the distinction. In the passage from the *Biographia* he speaks of "the distinction between the conditional finite I (which, as known in distinct consciousness by occasion of experience, is called by Kant's followers the empirical I) and the absolute I AM, and likewise the dependence or rather the inherence of the former in the latter" (*BL*, I, 184*n*). This is repeated in the MS. "Logic," with an additional German quotation: "the distinction . . . which is so far not improperly termed by the followers of Kant the empirical I (*das empirische Ich*) and the absolute 'I am,' " etc. (II, 75 v.). In a marginalium to Kant he noted: "the difference between the original Unity of consciousness and empirical consciousness, is the great point." [3] When we come to the MS. "Logic" we shall see how far Coleridge actually entered into the doctrine of the Unity of Apperception.

The distinction between the empirical and the transcendental self is a distinction fundamental for post-Kantian idealism. The empirical self is the shifting current of moods and thoughts, of sensations and impulses which are connected by the Inner Sense, and categorized by the Transcendental Unity as belonging to my experience. This shifting current is rather like "stream of consciousness" of later psychology. In a word, the empirical self is "the object of Inner Sense" (A 342—B 400). But the Transcendental Self is not the observed but the observer, not the object of knowledge but the knowing subject, "the vehicle of all concepts" (A 341—B 398). In this awareness "I am the *being itself*" (B 429), which in Kant's system means not an appearance but a reality, a noumenon. But what is the ultimate ground of the Transcendental Self and how does this duplicity, this split into the two Selves, empirical and transcendental Self, come about? These are questions which Kant does not answer, indeed he hardly raises them. He seems to do so in B 155, where he merely answers them by repeating the statement that mental states are the objects of the Inner Sense (B 156). But these questions will be raised persistently after him, and will become basic with the post-Kantian idealists.

All that Kant says in the *Critique* about the nature of the *I think* is that it is "one and the same in all consciousness" (B 132), indeed numerically one, as he insists: "the numerical unity of this apperception" he says in A 107, and "numerical identity is inseparable from it"—i.e., "self-consciousness"—"and is a priori certain" (A 113). For Kant it is self-evident "that the 'I' of Apperception, and therefore the 'I' in every act of thought, is one (*ein Singular*), or cannot be resolved into a plurality of subjects" (B 407), and is a "logically simple subject." Post-Kantian idealists interpret this as meaning that there is only one mind, one Transcendental Unity, in the whole world, operating through empirical selves, and "one and the same in all consciousness." This is rejected by philosophers who believe in the multiplicity of Egos and who argue that in Kant "the whole context shows, not that it is one in all thinkers, but only that . . . it is one and the same in all consciousness, while it is different in different thinkers." [4] But whatever Kant's ultimate intent and meaning were in the *Critique*, he never speaks in it of the "I think" as "different in different thinkers." Indeed such a concept would contradict all his doctrine of the unity of apperception. For if the "I think" is merely a thought which may be different in different thinkers, how do we know that it has the same meaning for each of them? and particularly that it operates in all of them in the manner described by the *Critique*? How can we affirm that it unifies sensations, that it possesses two transcendental forms of intuition—only two, and *those* two (space and time)—that works with categories and the categories are those twelve, and only those twelve? At each of these steps in the process of knowledge, variation is possible if the selves are different, and with each further step variations not only accumulate but multiply. Surely it is clear that just as for Kant "there is only one space and one time" (A 110), so there is only one Unity which uses them as its forms of intuition. If every self enjoyed his own private space, how could these selves ever meet? If each of these selves had their own private time, how could they ever synchronize? How could they live with each other, communicate with each other, work with each other?

A post-Kantian historian of philosophy, who was also an absolute idealist, J. E. Erdmann, gives another argument for the unity of the transcendental self.[5] It is required to guarantee the objectivity of our experience. The objects of consciousness for the empirical self are merely subjective, for their union consists only in time-succession, since the empirical ego is nothing else than sensations of the inner sense bound together in a time-series. For instance: "for me, sadness follows sunshine." But the judgment of experience has universal validity: e.g., "warmth is due to sunshine." This happens in virtue of the facts that validity for *a* consciousness only now ceases, and in its place we have the universal *I*, "which is also the condition of the empirical *I* and may be called Transcendental." "The act of combination now falls within the I underlying every empirical *I*. I no longer speak for *me* but for all or in general." This is genuine objectivity, and something not external to consciousness but inside it.

In the Transcendental Dialectic Kant refutes the errors of reason when it tries to go beyond experience and to build up metaphysical doctrines. One of these doctrines is the substantiality and immortality of the soul, and it might be thought that Kant's doctrine of the *I think* could be used to support it. But Kant puts up a strenuous resistance to any attempt in this direction, in keeping with the whole trend of the Transcendental Dialectic, which might be called in this respect sceptical. However in the course of this dialectical resistance Kant comes up with concepts and with distinctions which further extend the principle of the Unity of Apperception, and which were to have important consequences in later speculation.

First of all Kant asks the question: "Can this Transcendental Unity be said to exist?" or "can we attribute existence to it?" This may appear to be a quibble, since Kant in the Transcendental Analytic not only asserted that the Unity was there, but assigned to it the overall functions that we have seen. How could it exercise these functions of unification and organization of experience if it did not exist? We shall see in Chapter 8 how Schelling and Coleridge answered that question. But the concept of existence has turned out in the Transcendental Analytic to be one of Kant's pure concepts of the Understanding, or Categories, and therefore according to his philosophy it is only applicable to the manifold of sense data. Now the Unity by definition is no manifold, and is also a priori and a condition of all experience, hence not sensuous at all, hence "existence" is not applicable to it.

It is true that for Kant there is a self which is like the sensuous manifold in that it is known through one of the forms of perception, the Inner Sense. It is the experienced self, the self that consists of feelings, pleasures, pains, moods and other psychological phenomena. But this self, the object of the Inner Sense and thus perceived *in* Time, not out of it, is as we have seen not identical with the knowing subject, the *I think*, of the Unity of Apperception. If the latter is the actual subject of knowledge, the former is only an *object* of knowledge and never the subject.

Now if the category of Existence (which is really what Kant calls a schema, corresponding to the Assertoric category) can apply to the objects of perception, then it can apply to the empirical self, but not to the Self which actually applies the categories to unify experience within itself. This is explicitly asserted by Kant (cf. B 429).

Yet obviously this Self must possess some sort of being, if not of existence. Kant after laboriously struggling with the dilemma reaches the very reluctant conclusion that the *I think* may be said to *exist*, but not in the same sense of the category of Existence: it is neither a phenomenon nor a noumenon, but it is "something real that is given," "something which actually exists" (B 423*n*). But after having denied that the *I think* is a noumenon (otherwise we would have knowledge of at least one noumenon, or thing-in-itself), he says that "in the consciousness of myself in mere thought I am the *being itself*," which appears to be a direct contradiction of his usual viewpoint. However, he hastens to add "although nothing in myself is thereby given for thought" (B 429). By this he may mean that no other information about the self or its inner nature ("nothing *in* myself") is thus provided. In his caution not to overstep the narrow boundaries which he assigns to the notion of the *I think*, he even speaks of it as "this I or he or it (the thing) which thinks" (A 346, B 404)!

Yet, being the profound thinker that he is, all the time he is well aware that there is a big problem here in the relation of the knowing self to the known self, between the subject to the object, when the object known is the subject itself. He says so in one of his most tortuous utterances (B 155).[6]

In his effort to limit the range of this extremely powerful principle which he had himself discovered, Kant affirms that the proposition "I think" must be considered a purely analytical judgment (B 135). This means that nothing new is known through it, that it is a mere tautology, an empty identity, or A =

A. If Kant admitted that it was a synthetic proposition, then we would have acknowledged that there is a synthetic a priori judgment possible about the essence of the mind; but such a judgment it is his object to disprove in the Dialectic. Nevertheless it may be shown, without going beyond Kant's own statements, that the *I think* is not a purely analytical judgment. For the *I* that is known in self-consciousness, and which being an object we may call the *me*, is, of course, the same as the *I* that knows (analytical judgment); yet at the same time, being the object known and not the subject knowing, it is *not* the same: and this difference constitutes a synthetic judgment. In other words, if the *me* were not the same as the *I*, there would be no self-consciousness; and if it were not different, there would be no consciousness at all, but only a self-contained existence without awareness. So the logical conclusion from Kant's own presentation of self-consciousness is that the *I think* is a very special kind of judgment, both analytical and synthetical at the same time. To go beyond that is to go beyond Kant, but that much may be affirmed within the Kantian limits. Of course such a judgment, both analytical and synthetic, is unique; but so is self-consciousness, and it should not be surprising that the attempt to analyze it should lead to other unique positions.

Kant's conception of the "I" underwent a change when he passed from the *Critique of Pure Reason* to the *Critique of Practical Reason*, from the study of the cognitive process to a study of the conative or practical process. He then discovered that the *I think* was not a mere representation but actually a noumenon (*Co*, 328).[7] This makes it all the more necessary to revise the definition of the *I think* as a purely analytical judgment (B 135). The "I" is not only a thinking subject but an acting will. Both these activities are transcendental but they are not the same, they are spheres which can only be described as "distinct" from each other. In our own century this was Croce's term for them, and no better term has yet been found, though Croce has been criticized for not "deducing" action from thought, or vice versa, or both from some higher principle.

Unquestionably, Croce started from a purely empirical statement of their distinction: they are distinct because they are commonly so found to be. Later he gave a more abstract logical formula, that of the unity in distinction and distinction in unity. A more Kantian formulation would be the definition of the *I think* as a *synthesis* of distinct activities. This would include the aesthetic activity, since Kant finally recognized still another function for the I, which we might call the "I taste," or the appreciation of beauty. Of Action and Thought, we can say what Kant says of Virtue and Happiness: "they form a *synthetic* unity, that is to say, the one is not implicit in the concept of the other" (Cassirer, 84). This problem does not seem to have been discussed by Coleridge, much as he stressed the Will as a metaphysical principle in his later speculation.

But for the post-Kantian idealists the "I" becomes the center of the universe, and the creator of the universe itself. It was this dark divinity which we glimpsed in the depths of the abyss within our consciousness of which we became aware when studying the ideality of space and time. It is this absolute which after Kant becomes the theme of philosophical speculation and the problem around which the systems arise.

ii

IN SPITE OF Coleridge's difficulties, there is evidence that he had grasped early and firmly Kant's doctrine of the I. Early, because in 1804 he wrote in his notebook: "Memo. To write to the Recluse (Wordsworth) that he may insert something concerning *Ego* / its metaphysical Sublimity—and intimate Synthesis with the principle of Co-adunation—without it every where all things were a waste—nothing, &c." (*NB*, II, 2057). Firmly, for twelve years later he repeated: "Without this latent presence of the 'I am,' all modes of existence in the external world would flit before us as coloured shadows, with no greater depth, root or fixture, than the image of a rock hath in a gliding stream or the rainbow on a fast-sailing rain-storm" (*C&S*, p. 273; Appendix B to the *Statesmans Manual*).

But the metaphysical Ego must not be confused with the Ego as the idea that a mere individual has of himself, and consequently with the Ego of "egotism" or selfishness, as in *NB*, I, 904, 1801, before Coleridge's deep study of philosophy; nor with Coleridge's early aesthetic use of "egotism" to mean lyricism in poetry (*NB*, I, 62; cf. the Prefaces to the *Poems* of 1796 and 1797).

An undated marginalium in Coleridge's copy of the *Critique* may relate to what he himself called "doubts during a first perusal" which later were overcome (*W*, 84):

"I have for a moment been inclined to understand it (Kant's meaning) as something similar to Averroes,[8] that all men participate in *one* Understanding, each the whole, as—to use a very imperfect illustration—a 1000 persons may all and each hear one discourse of one voice. At least, the difference between the original Unity of consciousness and empirical consciousness, is the great point—the germ." [9]

The reference to Averroism is explained by an early notebook entry. In 1798–99 he read in a German book (I translate): "the opinion of the Averroists that the intellectual soul is one in all men" (*NB*, I, 374 Fol. 3–4).

The subject will come up again, in connection with Fichte.

CHAPTER 5

Kant IV—The Transcendental Dialectic

i

WE NOW COME to the most negative part of the *Critique*, the Transcendental Dialectic. So far we have seen Kant in the Analytic carefully reconstructing the world of experience and the world of science (including the mathematical sciences), although giving them a purely subjective validity. We have followed him in his exploration of the depths of the Transcendental Self and seen what positive, if disconcerting, discoveries he made there. These discoveries will be the springboard for the great philosophical enterprises that immediately follow Kant, the idealistic systems of Fichte and Schelling. All this is "critical" philosophy, in Kant's positive sense of the word. But there is also in Kant a critic in the negative sense of the word, and the "critique of Pure reason" is also a refutation of pure reason. It is here that Coleridge parts company with him.

We have seen the three cognitive functions of the human mind according to Kant: sensibility, understanding, and reason. The first is the faculty of sense and is purely receptive; the other two are "spontaneous" or a priori. But the forms of perception, space and time, are also a priori. The Understanding is the faculty of concepts, including the pure concepts of categories, which apply to the representations from the sensibility. Pure Reason is the faculty of Ideas, i.e., of concepts applied to objects which are beyond experience and therefore transcendent (not transcendental). Since this is, according to Kant, not a legitimate extension of the use of concepts, the branch of the *Critique* that deals with them is not the Analytic but the Dialectic of Pure

Reason. Dialectic for Kant is the refutation of illusion (A 62, B 86). In it Kant roundly declares that Reason is a "deceptive extension" of the understanding that pushes its concepts beyond the limits of all possible experience (A 295, B 352). The Ideas of Reason are "pseudo-rational" (A 644, B 672) and "produce illusion" (A 642, B 670). The pure concepts of the understanding, or categories, are valid only when referred to appearances or phenomena; they do not apply to things in themselves, or noumena, which are beyond experience. The "empirical employment" of the categories is their only legitimate use (A 296, B 352). Any attempt to extend the concepts of unity, substantiality, causality, or any of the other categories, to objects that transcend experience (such as the soul of man or the spirit of God) is erroneous (*ibid.*). For an Idea "no corresponding object can be given in sense experience" (A 327, B 383) and Ideas have therefore no objective validity, whereas the pure concepts of the understanding, while "thought a priori antecedently to experience" (A 310, B 366), possess an "objective reality . . . founded solely on the fact that. . . . it must always be possible to show their application in experience" (A 310, B 366).

But Ideas have also a positive function, and for them Kant coins another pair of terms: they are "regulative" and not "constitutive" (A 180, B 222). These two terms are adopted by Coleridge, even where he contradicts Kant on this part of his doctrine (e.g., *C&S*, 302). What they mean is that Ideas do not give us knowledge of any reality; in this respect, they are illusory. Yet according to Kant they have "an excellent and indeed indispensably necessary regulative employment, namely that of directing the understanding" toward ideal goals, such as those of totality or absolute completeness in any branch of knowledge. These ideas will stimulate further and further investigations and results in more and more discoveries, even if they will never reach their objects, i.e., totality. This lies outside experience and will remain "a purely imaginary point, a mere idea" (A 644, B 672), but we must proceed in our research *as if* the Ideas were absolutely valid (A 672, B 701) and not merely regulative. This is the famous *as if* that gave rise to Vaihinger's philosophy.

H. W. Cassirer's commentary on this aspect of Kant's doctrine will be found illuminating: "Kant's whole doctrine of Ideas, and the distinction between constitutive and regulative principles on which it rests. . . . is part of a philosophy which regards human knowledge as limited to empirical objects, but which at the same time believes that the world of experience cannot be the only world and that the existence of another world must be assumed. This is the doctrine peculiar to transcendental philosophy. Every other philosophical system would believe either that the Ideas gave us knowledge of real objects or that they were devoid of all meaning. Empiricism would hold the latter view, dogmatism the former. It is only if we assume the transcendental principles that we can deny both views, and can hold that the Ideas of Reason do not give us knowledge of things in themselves and yet enable us to make our enquiries into natural objects subject to the Ideas of objects belonging to a supernatural world." [1]

Kant proves his position by means of a systematic critical analysis of the Ideas which occupies most of the second half of the *Critique* and is the most detailed discussion in the whole work. Kant here takes the basic doctrines of traditional metaphysics on the existence of God, the immortality of the soul and the structure of the universe, and refutes them one by one. His immediate target is the school of Wolff in which Kant had been brought up until Hume "broke his dogmatic slumbers." He therefore comes to agree with the negative attitude of empiricists toward metaphysics, but his method is different. Kant shows that speculation on these metaphysical problems gives rise inevitably to pairs of contradictory propositions on each point, both of which can be logically defended but which contradict each other completely. He lists the arguments on each side in parallel columns, usually known as Antinomies, though Kant used the term for only one group of them. The first group he calls "the Paralogisms of Pure Reason" and they are the arguments in favor of the unity, simplicity, and immortality of the soul. They are shown to be "mere Ideas," unsubstantial hypotheses which cannot be proved or refuted. He is particularly emphatic in arguing that no support for them can be drawn from his theory of the Transcendental Self (A 345, B 403 ff.).

In the next section, "Antinomies of Pure Reason," Kant shows that when Reason attempts to go beyond experience and define the nature of the universe, it again lands into opposite and irreconcilable conclusions. For instance, it can be equally proved that the universe is, and is not, limited in space and in time. Finally in a third section he attacks the three traditional arguments for the existence of God: the ontological, the cosmological, and the teleological or argument from design. It is in connection with the first of these that Kant brings forward his famous argument that "existence is not a predicate" (A 598, B 626), which Coleridge was to adopt in his paper "On the Philosophic Import of the Words, Object and Subject" (*Notes and Lectures*, 1849, II, 287), and in his MS. "Logic" (II, 66). See also *Aids*, 120–21 (Shedd, I, 220–21).[2]

The Dialectic, with its systematic refutation of all previous "dogmatic" systems of metaphysics, is what earned Kant in his own day the epithet of *alles-zermalmender*. Coleridge calls it "the striking but untranslatable epithet, which the celebrated Mendelssohn applied to the great founder of the Critical Philosophy 'Der alleszermalmende KANT,' i.e., the all-becrushing, or rather, the *all-to-nothing crushing* KANT" (*BL*, II, 69*n*). In popular opinion Kant has remained the liquidator of metaphysics and of theology. The Italian nineteenth-century poet Carducci equated Kant with Robespierre: "one guillotined the King, the other God," nor was he alone in this opinion. But such was not Kant's ultimate intention. Even in the *Critique* his final aim was constructive. In the preface to the second edition, he goes so far as to say that his object was to "make room for faith" (B xxx). This aim becomes apparent in the second Critique, the *Critique of Practical Reason* (1788), in which Kant brings forward his own way of demonstrating the Ideas of God, Freedom, and Immortality, as postulates of the practical reason. And even in the Dialectic there are positive doctrines of great importance.

Just as in the Analytic Kant introduced without warning the

Transcendental Unity of Apperception, so in the Dialectic, over and beyond his negative conclusions, he introduces without warning some highly-charged philosophical concepts of far-reaching importance. They are nothing less than the Unconditioned (A 307, B 364) and the Absolute (A 324, B 380). If we add the Idea (A 311, B 368), the three concepts converge in one: the Idea is the unconditioned and the absolute, and we run again into metaphysics.

True, Kant surrounds these concepts with the customary qualifications and reservations, precautionary rules and safety devices. To begin with, these concepts are only "regulative," i.e., hypothetical, and not "constitutive," i.e., true knowledge. They are in fact a source of possible delusion, which criticism must dispel. But still they are useful for euristic purposes, as a sort of ideal pattern of completeness to stimulate investigators.

Kemp Smith accounted for this apparent ambivalence by distinguishing two conflicting trends in this part of the *Critique*. One is the Kantian "critical" view, according to which all statements that transcend experience are delusive: man cannot possibly acquire knowledge of an unconditioned whole of which only a conditioned part is accessible to him. But the other trend leans strongly toward philosophic Idealism: ideas of the whole provide knowledge of the unconditional (*Co*, 429–31). As Kant put it in one of his loose notes (*Reflexionen*), "Idea is the representation of the whole in so far as it necessarily precedes the determination of its parts" (*Co*, 433). In his *Logic* Kant says that "an Idea cannot be obtained by composition, for in it the whole is before the part." [3]

This results in the legitimation of what Kant calls "the apodeictic use of reason" (A 646, B 674), i.e., conceiving the Idea "as a whole which is prior to determinate knowledge of the parts and which contains the conditions that determine the a priori for every part its position and relation to the other parts" (A 645, B 673). This actually seems to provide us with a priori knowledge of the particular. "If reason is the faculty of deducing the particular from the universal, and if the universal is already *certain* in itself and given, only the *faculty of judgment* is required to execute the process of subsumption, and the particular is thereby determined in a necessary manner" (A 646, B 674).

One sees Kant's Idea turning into something very like Hegel's Idea, which is a priori and from which all the particulars of experience may be deduced. For instance, if the concept of Tragedy were an Idea (which I doubt, even for Kant), it would be possible to deduce from its definition a priori the actual structure, plot, and characters of all existing tragedies, just as from the general definition of Art, Hegel deduces the phases of the historical development of all arts and even all individual works. But Kant ends this long discussion of the Idea with the usual caution: that it is only regulative and not constitutive (A 680, B 708).

Whence did Kant obtain those three metaphysical concepts, the Absolute, the Unconditioned, and the Idea? There is only one on which he answers that question explicitly, and that is the Idea. It comes of course from Plato, as Kant points out in a remarkable chapter in which he makes full acknowledgment to his great predecessor (A 312, B 368, foll.). Here he says that "Plato made use of the expression 'idea' in such a way as quite evidently to have meant something which not only cannot be borrowed from the senses but far surpasses even the concepts of the understanding (with which Aristotle occupied himself)" (A 313, B 370). Note the limitation of Aristotle to "the concepts of the understanding." If the traditional dichotomy of Platonism versus Aristotelianism, of which Coleridge was very fond, were reliable, which it is not, then Kant should be considered on the side of Plato, of whom he says: "He knew that our reason naturally exalts itself to forms of knowledge which so far transcend the bounds of experience that no given material object can ever coincide with them, but which must none the less be recognised as having their own reality, and which are by no means mere fictions of the brain" (A 314, B 371).

This shows that Coleridge was wrong when he classed Kant as mainly an Aristotelian. Rather is Kant to be considered as the thinker who brought Plato's ideas from heaven down to earth and made them functions of the human understanding. The absolute and the unconditioned he probably got from his immediate predecessors in German philosophy, the Wolffian metaphysicians; the unconditioned may arise from logical theory.

The absolute is a term which Kant introduces with some apology. He intends it to mean "valid without restriction" (A 326, B 382), distinguishing it from what is "restricted by conditions," so the absolute *is* the unconditioned. And since the idea is both absolute and unconditioned, the three terms, as we were saying, merge into one. This is the source in Kant of the metaphysical Absolute which plays so important a role in Hegelianism. The *source* of the idealist theory, but not the idealist theory itself. For in Kant these terms are still considered regulative and not constitutive, at least in the *Critique of Pure Reason.*

So the result of the discussion of the Transcendental Ideas in the Dialectic is an ideal of knowledge as a system in which every part is conditioned by every other part, and cannot therefore be grasped except as an unconditioned whole, or the Absolute. Such knowledge is for Kant merely an ideal toward which the human mind strives necessarily but vainly, while organizing according to its dictates the particular truths that are gathered from ever-widening research.

But the post-Kantians, like Schelling, will point out that this ideal, being a concept, is itself knowledge. We actually know *now*, in the present, that truth is an organic system, and this knowledge is already ours, not something just beyond the horizon. Hence the post-Kantians will open up the road for inquiries into the Absolute which Kant refrained from, and systems of absolute idealism will be constructed out of the ideas that Kant formulated but did not wholly trust himself to.

ii

THIS IS ALSO the point where Coleridge, who accepted Kant's division of the three cognitive faculties (e.g., *The Friend*, First Landing Place, Ess. 5, p. 97; Shedd, 146), parts company with

Kant. He could not be satisfied with the purely regulative status of Ideas; for him, they are constitutive. Here is a considered statement, made in a letter of January 14, 1820, to J. Gooden: "there neither are, have been, or ever will be but two essentially different Schools of Philosophy: the Platonic and the Aristotelian. To the latter, but with a somewhat nearer approach to the Platonic, Emanuel Kant belonged; to the former Bacon and Leibniz and in his riper and better years Berkeley—and to this I profess myself an adherent. . . . He for whom Ideas are constitutive, will in effect be a Platonist—and in those for whom they are regulative only, Platonism must be a hollow affection" (*UL*, II, 264–66).

Compare also: "Whether Ideas are regulative only, according to Aristotle and Kant; or likewise constitutive, and one with the power and life of nature, according to Plato, and Plotinus . . . is the highest problem of philosophy" (*C&S*, 302). This seems to imply that the regulative-constitutive dichotomy was present in ancient thought, which is one of Coleridge's unhistorical projections of Kant in the past.[4]

Coleridge in this respect always proclaimed himself a Platonist; but it would have been more accurate to call his view in Kantian terms Dogmatism, that being the term employed by Kant for a metaphysic made out of pure concepts (B 35), and Coleridge accepted that usage ("Logic," II, 66–67 and 329ᵛ).

Coleridge does not seem to have grasped firmly and continuously the fact that the categories of the understanding, in Kant's system, are a priori and not derived from experience. At times, he seems to believe that the categories are a posteriori formations, "conceptions formed by the Understanding from materials furnished by sense" (*PhL*, 426). At other times he is closer to Kant's view, as we have seen in Chapter 2; but he also tends toward the view that the Understanding merely abstracts from sensations, operating entirely a posteriori. No particular authority is given for this view, but in the *Aids* he claims to find "word for word, the very definition which the Founder of the Critical Philosophy gives of the Understanding" (*Aids*, 143) in a phrase of Archbishop Leighton's: "natural Reason judging according to Sense" (*Aids*, 137). Actually this definition, "word for word," is neither Kant's nor Leighton's: for Leighton speaks of Reason and not of the Understanding, and Kant does not call the latter the faculty of judging according to sense, but the function that judges according to a priori concepts.

While acknowledging that Coleridge derived some secondary points from Kant's Dialectic—such as the list and definitions of technical terms in *C&S*, 301, from A 320, B 376–77—Winkelmann affirmed that Coleridge did not discuss the Dialectic and went his own way without thinking it through (Winkelmann, 175 and 246–47). Certainly Coleridge did not choose to grapple with the specific problems of the Antinomies, although he took note of the critique of the ontological argument, as we saw above. Also, when Coleridge expounded the *Critique* in his MS. "Logic," he stopped short of the Dialectic. But he had certainly read it and taken good note of it. In the "Logic" itself there is a terse summing up of the basic idea of the Antinomies in one paragraph, but with an important variation: the Antinomies are referred to the Understanding and not to Reason, thus altering Kant's analysis of the two faculties: "When from two premises, both of which are affirmed with equal right by the Understanding, the Understanding itself can arrive at two contradictory conclusions, the only possible solution of the difficulty is found in assuming that the Understanding has been applying its own forms and functions or those which it had borrowed from the sense to objects that do not fall under its cognizance, as for instance, the Understanding applies the forms of time and space, of quantity, quality, and relation to the Idea of the Supreme Being, or to the things themselves contradistinguished from phenomena" (II, 190 v.).

The last error is exactly the one that Kant attributes to the pure Reason.

Since he attributed the Antinomies to the Understanding and not to Reason, Coleridge was consistent when in a note to Tennemann's *History of Philosophy* written apparently in 1818–19 (*PhL*, 18) he spoke of "the Kantean supposed Antinomies of Reason" (*PhL*, 425).

Coleridge went even further. Probably under the stimulus of post-Kantian dialectics, he maintained that the truths of Reason appear to the Understanding in the shape of contradictory pairs of propositions (*Aids*, 154*n*; Shedd, I, 272*n*).

Working along these lines, Coleridge developed a Dialectic of his own, which does not seem to have been noted by previous students. The purpose of this Dialectic was the refutation of such heretical and impious doctrines as Atheism, Pantheism, Unitarianism and so forth. All these errors arise because the limited concepts of the Understanding are applied to the universal Ideas of Reason. In *The Friend* he boldly announced: "I have no hesitation in undertaking to prove, that every heresy which has disquieted the Christian Church, from Tritheism to Socinianism, has originated in and supported itself by, arguments rendered plausible only by the confusion of these faculties, and thus demanding for the objects of one, a sort of evidence appropriate to those of another faculty" (*F*, 110*n*, Sec. I, Ess. 3).

In the *Aids* he gave an instance (*Aids*, 109–11; Shedd, I, 210–12) which I interpret as follows. Unity being a category of the Understanding, it is "one of the necessary *Forms* of thinking, taken abstractedly." "By the aid of the Imagination" or of the "Fancy"—the two are not differentiated here—this category is turned into a real thing, a "substantiated notion," i.e. that of the "ONE as the ground and cause of the Universe, in which in all succession and through all changes is the subject neither of Time nor Change. The ONE must be contemplated as Eternal and Immutable."

"But if from the Eternity of the Supreme Being a Reasoner should deduce the Impossibility of a Creation; or conclude with Aristotle, that the Creation was co-eternal; or, like the later Platonists, should turn Creation into *Emanation,* and make the Universe proceed from the Deity," then "it would no longer be the God in whom we *believe,* but a Stoical FATE, or the superessential ONE of Plotinus," or "the indivisible one and only substance of Spinoza."

What is the answer to this "Reasoner"? "We have only to demand of him, by what right and under what authority he converts a Thought into a Substance, or asserts the existence of a real somewhat corresponding to a Notion not derived from experience of his senses." The last words are Kantian: existence can only be proved from experience. But then Coleridge proceeds to define his own concept of Reason. The proper way to build up the Idea of God is to refer to Religion and to the requirements of Conscience and of Morality: then "this Idea presents itself to our mind with additional attributes, and these too not formed by mere Abstraction and Negation [by the Understanding]— with the attributes of Holiness, Providence, Love, Justice, and Mercy," and of God "as our Creator, Lord and Judge." In other words, the personal God is reaffirmed.

He concludes: "Where the evidence of the Senses fails us, and beyond the precincts of sensible experience, there is no reality attributable to any Notion, but what is given to it by Revelation, or the Law of Conscience, or the necessary interests of Morality."

Thus the proper use of Reason serves to correct the errors of the Understanding, and it is possible to affirm through the Reason what the Understanding rejects as contradictory or absurd (cf. *Aids*, 159, Shedd, I, 256–57 and *NB*, I, Notes, 455).

This dichotomy of Reason and Understanding is one of Coleridge's fundamental ideas, upon which he was to rely at all times. We find it stated as early as 13 October 1806, in a letter to Thomas Clarkson, who had asked him a series of deep philosophical questions. In his answer Coleridge begins by giving first the Greek equivalents of the two terms and then the German equivalents: "the difference between the Reason, and the Understanding (νοῦς καὶ ἐπιστήμη: *Vernunft, und Verstand*)" (*CL*, II, 1193). The presence of the German points to Kant, and the Greek terms show that Coleridge had made the connection with the original Platonic dichotomy.[5] In the body of the letter, when he gives his definition, he shows himself aware of the Greek sources of the Kantian *phenomena* and *noumena*, and although he does not mention Kant, his definition is based on the *Critique*: the Understanding deals with *phenomena*, Reason with "all such notices, as are characterized by

UNIVERSALITY and NECESSITY . . . and which are evidently not the effect of any Experience, but the condition of all Experience, & that indeed without which Experience would be inconceivable, we may call Reason" (II, 1198). For Kant this is true only of the categories of the understanding. Then Coleridge returns to traditional metaphysics: "Reason is therefore most eminently the Revelation of an immortal soul, and it's best Synonime—it is the *forma formans*,[6] which contains within itself the law of its own conceptions" (*ibid.*).

In this letter Coleridge rightly traced the distinction back to Greek thought. In the *Biographia* he not only restates the distinction, but claims to trace it to his favorite seventeenth-century English theologians: "Lastly, I have cautiously discriminated the terms, THE REASON, and THE UNDERSTANDING, encouraged and confirmed by the authority of our genuine divines and philosophers, before the revolution." And he quotes Milton (*PL*, V, 485–90), where the two terms appear, but not in juxtaposition (*BL*, I, 109, Ch. X).

He then goes on: "I had previous[7] and higher motives in my own conviction of the importance, nay, of the necessity of the distinction, as both an indispensable condition and a vital part of sound speculation in metaphysics, ethical or theological. To establish this distinction was one main object of THE FRIEND" (II, 110).

In the *Statesman's Manual* (1816), Appendix B, Coleridge returned to the distinction and gave it further formulation. Still fuller is the discussion he gave to it in *Aids to Reflection* (1825), where there is a whole dissertation dedicated to it in the body of the book, and also an Appendix with "A synoptical summary of the scheme of the argument to prove the diversity in Kind, of the Reason and the Understanding."

We will not attempt to trace further the development of this dichotomy in Coleridge's writings. This is part of the complete history of Coleridge's mind, left to other students. But we may pause for a moment to consider the philosophical value of the dichotomy, when it is removed from its Kantian base and its terms altered.

It was of course open to Coleridge as a philosopher to set up his own definition of Reason and Understanding, and reject Kant's if he did not find it satisfactory. But can one accept, as Coleridge did, the basic theses of Kant's Analytic, and yet withhold assent from the Dialectic, which is based upon it and logically derived from it (cf. *W*, 80–81)? This is the problem that Coleridge should have met when he set up his own dichotomy. But, at least in his published works, he did not. Instead, he went on repeating, with all the power of his eloquence, that there *is* such a distinction and that all the great problems of philosophy are solved by it. In the end it seems that we are left with little more than the expression of a wish to reconcile philosophy with religion, if not with Carlyle's "sublime secret of believing by the reason what the understanding had been obliged to fling out as incredible" (*Life of Sterling*).

As for the "anticipations" of the distinction which Coleridge claimed to find in seventeenth-century theologians, it may well be asked: in which English thinkers of the seventeenth century is the distinction between the Reason and the Understanding clearly and definitely expressed? The most recent student of the background of Coleridge's religious thought states that such a distinction was made only "in a hazy, general, way," "not always clear" and "not defined sharply" (Boulger, 69 and 72), and that it was from Kant that Coleridge derived his sharper view (*ibid.*, 72).

Shawcross had already observed: "The distinction of Reason and Understanding may have been long familiar to Coleridge, but it was no doubt in Kant that he first learned its value as a weapon against the empiricists and necessitarians" (*BL*, I, 250, *n.* 110).

iii

AT THIS POINT note should be taken of the latest critical discussion of the Reason-Understanding dichotomy, due to the eminent philosopher A. O. Lovejoy. In what was to be his last book, Lovejoy made a study of this subject, referring repeatedly to Coleridge.[8] He gave a critical and historical account of the dichotomy as it was developed in German thought "between 1795 and 1839" (p. 1), but made no reference to its roots in earlier thought. With this qualification, the historical account is brilliant and erudite, as usual in Lovejoy, while the critical account, as is also usual, is oriented in favor of his own brand of realistic philosophy. This means that it is adverse to the dichotomy, a hostility which ends by affecting even the accuracy of his historical narrative. Lovejoy evidently endeavors to discredit the dichotomy by connecting it closely to another doctrine, that of "intellectual intuition," which in this age means immediate knowledge of transcendent realities, such as God or the immortal soul (pp. 35 ff.). Now there is no logical connection between the Reason-Understanding dichotomy and the doctrine of intellectual intuition, which was indeed usually urged against it. Nor is there a close historical connection between them. Leading thinkers of this period like Kant and Hegel maintained the dichotomy but rejected intellectual intuition. The one thinker of this time who maintained them both was Jacobi, and Lovejoy consequently makes much of him. But no critic attacked Jacobi on this ground with more persistency than did Hegel (*Enc.*, # 61–78, 467–68 and *passim*).

Lovejoy's hostility against idealism sometimes made him unable to see an obvious point. For instance, he asks: "why do the new epistemologists insist that self-knowledge is the only true knowledge of reality?" (p. 46). The answer, as Schelling pointed out, is simple: because of self-knowledge is the most complete realization (indeed, the only realization) of the traditional definition of truth as "*adaequatio rei et intellectus*," coincidence of the object with the knowing mind (*SW*, I, 366; cf. Ch. VIII), as Schelling noted (see Ch. 8, Sec. 1 of this volume).

Lovejoy is one of the few scholars to take notice of the "wall" passage in the *Notebooks* discussed in Chapter 7. There we shall see that it contains an echo of Fichte, missed by Lovejoy.

Finally, Lovejoy neglected an important practical consequence of the dichotomy, however unsound it may be on strictly philosophical grounds (and I am not defending it on those grounds). The practical consequence is that acceptance of the dichotomy makes for a tolerant attitude toward doctrines which logically one cannot accept. A doctrine refuted by showing that it belongs to the understanding rather than to reason is not rejected as being mere error or crafty sophistry or sheer nonsense, but shown to be partially true. Its truth is limited to the sphere to which it properly belongs, but within that sphere it is a valid statement. Such an attitude is not possible for philosophers who rigidly admit of only one faculty of truth, such as empiricism or abstract rationalism.

iv

THE READER who has followed our exposition of the *Critique* in the preceding chapters, incomplete and simplified as it was, will by this time have become aware of the important differences between Kant and Cudworth. To sum them all up in one sentence, Cudworth's point of view is still dogmatic (in the Kantian sense, B xxxv), while Kant's is critical. Cudworth's is a traditional system of metaphysics of the Neoplatonic type, and Kant formulated a radical objection to all metaphysics. Their relations to science also compare unfavorably: Cudworth only draws some illustrations from science and from mathematics, while Kant set up full-fledged theories about the nature and function of the sciences, of mathematics as well as of physics.

In this last respect allowance must of course be made for the differences in the historical situation of the two thinkers. Cudworth had in front of him only the empiricism of Hobbes; even Locke was still to come and modern science was then beginning. Kant had before him a much more radical empiricist, Hume, and the full development of Newtonian science, with its apparently complete system of the universe. Hence Cudworth is inevitably less advanced than Kant in the history of thought, and Kant is much more modern. This is usually ignored by the propounders of the anticipation theory.

In his epistemology Cudworth certainly stressed the a priori character of knowledge, but this was common ground in the rationalist school, as we saw in Chapter 2. His ingenious analysis of sensuous perception quoted in Chapter 1 is still too abstract; Cudworth does not perceive a white object, but the whiteness of objectivity. His description of the sense datum as a "phantasm" is too generical and still unanalyzed: Kant distinguished form and content in sense data, and formulated the theory of the a priori forms of perception, space and time. Furthermore Kant set up a full table of a priori concepts, aiming at completeness; Cudworth was apparently against this attempt on principle, but still gave lists of categories, which are only partial and, in the words of a sympathetic critic, "present a somewhat uncritical medley." [9]

One of Cudworth's lasting merits is the firm assertion of the "self-active" character of thought, which Kant called its "spontaneity." In the field of ethics, this means freedom of the will, in which both thinkers believed. Kant however, as we shall see, provided a philosophical proof of it. Another lasting merit of Cudworth's in his affirmation that concepts are not dead things, already quoted. For Kant, concepts are a synthesis, and synthesis is an act (B 153); and he provided a much deeper analysis of the act in the Transcendental Deduction.

But it is time to make the quotation from James Martineau, promised in Chapter 1. In his book, Martineau refers to Dugald Stewart's claim (1815) that Kant may be indebted to Cudworth for some of his "leading ideas," such as the a priori element in sensible experience:

"The comparison only shows how very superficially even a practised philosophical critic may read and judge the most exact and severe productions in the history of human thought. The supposed resemblance disappears on the mere mention of two marked differences. 1) With Cudworth, the endowment of Sense supplies no a priori elements; with Kant, it gives us Space and Time, its own forms. 2) With Cudworth, the Understanding's 'intelligible ideas' (*noémata*) are themselves its *objects of knowledge*, and constitute the essences of things, and therefore introduce us to the nature of things in themselves: with Kant, they are merely subjective, inherent only in the make of our faculty, so that we cannot help thinking under these categories, but have no right to treat them as valid for reality irrespective of us. Thus, the ideality of human cognition, which the two writers hold in common, was used by Cudworth to prove, by Kant to disprove, the absolute validity of our knowledge: with the one, it was the means of reaching, with the other, the excuse for surrendering, eternal and immutable truth: with the former, it carries us into Infinite Nature, with the latter, it shuts us up in our own." [10]

Let us now consider the other thesis, that Coleridge received Kantian conclusions by anticipation from the Cambridge Platonists.[11] The first witness to the contrary is Coleridge himself. Not only did Coleridge fail to recognize the Kantian anticipation in the Cambridge Platonists, but he repeatedly and vigorously criticized them for not having instituted Kant's critical method. One of the principal causes of their "imperfections and errors" (he says, *à propos* of Henry More) was the "want of that logical *propaideia dokimastiké*, that critique of the human intellect, which, previously to the weighing and measuring this or that, begins by assaying the weights, measures and scales themselves; that fulfilment of the heaven-descended *nosce te ipsum*,[12] in respect to the intellective part of man, which was commenced . . . by Lord Bacon . . . and brought to a systematic completion by Immanuel Kant in his *Kritik der reinen Vernunft, der Urtheilskraft* and *Metaphysischen Anfangsgründe der Naturwissenschaft*" (LR, III, 157).

In another note, on John Smith, he says of the whole group that although they called themselves Platonists, they were "more truly Plotinists. Thus Cudworth, Dr. Jackson . . . , Henry More, this John Smith, and some others. . . . What they all wanted was a pre-inquisition into the mind as part organ, part constituent, of all knowledge, an examination of the weights, scales, and measures themselves abstracted from the objects to be weighed or measured by them; in short, a transcendental aesthetic, logic and noetic" (*LR*, III, 415–16)—in one word, Kant.

Still more deficiencies of the group are enumerated in the notes on Henry More (*LR*, III, pp. 157–58). There is here no grateful recollection of intellectual help received at a critical moment, no such enthusiastic recognition as is afforded Kant in Chapter IX of the *Biographia,* not even such gratitude as is expressed for Boehme and for Berkeley.

As a matter of curiosity it may be noted that Coleridge was aware of the existence of unpublished works in MS by Cudworth and regretted they were still unknown. In the *Table Talk* he said: "there are valuable works of Cudworth prepared by himself for the press, yet still unpublished by the University which possesses them, and which ought to glory in the name of their great author!" (II, 365).

Coleridge assumed that these MSS were in Cambridge; but they are in the British Museum, and there they were recently studied by J. A. Passmore, as we have already seen.[13]

There is in the marginalium on the Unity of Apperception quoted at the end of the last chapter a philosophical simile which Coleridge may have derived from Cudworth. In the passage on "ectypal participation" quoted in Chapter 1, Cudworth makes a simile to illustrate the participation of men's minds in the mind of God: one and the same idea is in a thousand different minds "as one and the same voice may be in a thousand ears listening to it."[14]

Coleridge described the Unity of Apperception in the many empirical Egos "as—to use a very imperfect illustration—a thousand persons may all and each hear one discourse of one voice." The simile is the same as Cudworth's, down to the number one thousand. On the other hand, one thousand for a large number is common, and Coleridge himself declares it "a very imperfect illustration." So, if it is an echo from Cudworth, it did not help Coleridge very much with Kant.

In conclusion, it seems clear that Coleridge made determined efforts to reach a purely rational conception of man's capacity to attain the truth, and he must accordingly be evaluated as a philosopher. It is true that in his complex personality there were tendencies toward other approaches, that might be called mystical or emotional or, as is now the fashion, "existential" (Boulger, 76–93). But the view that Coleridge relied mainly upon the latter for his philosophy was indignantly rebutted by Muirhead [15] when Coleridge was apparently presented under this light as a follower of Jacobi.

In this chapter we have seen that Coleridge took good note of Kant's Transcendental Dialectic, deriving from it the dichotomy of Reason and Understanding, but with an important change: the Antinomies that Kant found in pure Reason, Coleridge assigned to the Understanding, and Reason had for him valid knowledge of constituent Ideas. From this he developed a dialectic of his own, directed against heretical doctrines. The dichotomy has a long history behind it, and Coleridge's variation from it is more like Kant's predecessors. Cudworth provided only a generic statement of the self-active character of the mind.

As a conclusion to these chapters on the first *Critique*, let us say that Coleridge subscribed to the Aesthetic and the Analytic, but modified the Dialectic. Whether this modification can stand is questionable.

CHAPTER 6

Kant V—Ethics and Aesthetics

i

IN HIS WRITINGS on the theory of ethics, especially the *Critique of Practical Reason* (1788) and the shorter *Fundamental Principles of the Metaphysics of Morals* (1785), which preceded it as a popular introduction, Kant set himself to do for ethics what he had done in the first *Critique* for knowledge, i.e., investigate the a priori element in it. In ethics this a priori element constitutes the Practical Reason, and a critique of it is "a critique of reason as it judges in practical matters." [1] In ethics the a priori element is to be found in the moral obligation, or concept of Duty; the empirical or a posteriori element being the natural inclination of man. The concept of obligation belongs to pure reason and involves absolute necessity and unconditional requirement. The many natural impulses and appetites of man belong to his physical or empirical nature, and they are the material upon which the ethical will operates, as the sensational manifold is the material upon which the pure forms of mental activity operate in knowledge.

It is notable that in the domain of ethics the concept of pure Reason is entirely positive: its dictates are real and not apparent, or, to use the terms of the first *Critique*, constitutive and not regulative. In ethics the "pure practical reason" yields knowledge that is valid and absolute, not only phenomenal but noumenal. In the practical reason supersensuous objects, says Kant, "become immanent and constitutive, being the source of the possibility of realising the necessary object of pure practical

reason (the *summmum bonum*); whereas apart from this they
are transcendent, and merely regulative principles of speculative
reason, which do not require it to assume a new object beyond
experience, but only to bring its use in experience nearer to
completeness" (*Critique of Practical Reason*, I, ii, 2, # 7;
Abbott, 233).

If Kant had followed in his ethics the same phenomenalist
tendency that he follows in his epistemology, he would have
had to argue that we cannot know what the Good is in itself,
or what Duty is in itself, but only what they appear to us to be,
while their inner nature remained inaccessible to us. But, as
Ewing notes, "it would be futile for ethics to tell us only what
seems to be our duty, not what our duty really is." [2] So in
ethics Kant acknowledges that we know the thing in itself,
the noumenon. We also come to know man as he is in himself:
the human subject is "conscious of himself as a thing in himself,"
and as a self-determined source of causality he is no less than a
"noumenon" (*Critique of Practical Reason*, I, i, 3; Abbott, 191).

Operating in the noumenal sphere, pure practical reason
proceeds wholly a priori. While in its cognitive function reason
always needs sense data and the concept without the intuition
is empty, in its moral function reason draws directly from itself
its guiding principle. This principle, being the quintessence of
rationality, is simply "the universal conformity of . . . action
to law in general" (Abbott, p. 18), i.e., the action should be
such that it can become a universal law. This is the origin of
Kant's famous ethical principle, the categorical imperative (or
unconditional command): act in such a way that your action
can become a universal rule (Abbott, 18).

Since "rational nature exists as an end in itself," the imperative may be formulated also: "So act as to treat humanity . . .
in every case as an end, never as means only" (Abbott, 47).

The will of man is good when it follows these dictates of
reason, and there is nothing else in the world—or out of it,
adds Kant—that is good except the good will. Indeed, this is
the very first statement at the beginning of the *Fundamental
Principles of the Metaphysics of Morals*: "Nothing can possibly

be conceived in the world, or even out of it, which can be called good, without qualification, except a good will" (Abbott, 9). All other things that are called good are so only in relation to the good will.

But in following the categorical imperative, practical reason is following its own law, and to follow one's own law is to be free. So freedom of the will is a logical presupposition of all moral action. Thus the idea of freedom of the will, which in the *Critique of Pure Reason* was said to be only regulative, is shown to be constitutive in the realm of ethics.

Acceptance of the idea of freedom opens the way to a justification of the other two Ideas that Kant could not demonstrate in the theoretical sphere: God and immortality. The existence of God and the immortality of the soul are defended in the *Critique of Practical Reason* (I, ii, 2, # iv and v) as "postulates of the practical reason" (Abbott, 218–21).

Immortality is defended on the ground that moral progress requires unending effort, "a progress *in infinitum*," which is not possible in the short life of man; hence the soul, to satisfy this requirement (which is purely ethical and not metaphysical) must be immortal (Abbott, 218–19). The existence of God is defended on the ground that justice (another ethical imperative) calls for a happiness proportionate to that morality in infinite progress, hence a cause capable of producing it, which can only be God: so moral law postulates the existence of God (Abbott, 220–21).

In this way Kant has demonstrated the validity of the three Ideas of reason which he had invalidated in the first *Critique*, but only as postulates of ethical action: our theoretical knowledge of the supersensuous is not thereby extended in any way, and we cannot make any use of these postulates to expand our metaphysical knowledge of reality (Abbott, 232). Thus Kant is again balancing himself on the razor's edge.

Perhaps the best known aspect of Kant's doctrine of duty is its rigorism: natural inclinations must be always resisted. Since practical reason is wholly a priori, it must have no admixture of the sensuous element. The only way to be sure one is not acting under a sensuous impulse is to act *against* it. Morality requires not only devotion to duty but the repression of our natural inclinations.

Also, being categorical, the imperative does not admit of exception. To show how far Kant will carry this, take for example the command: "Tell the truth." This being categorical, we must tell the truth unreservedly under all circumstances to all people, *even to a murderer who asks us where his intended victim is to be found:* man never has the right to be untruthful (Abbott, 360 ff.).

The above account of Kant's practical philosophy does not go into the same detail as the account of his theoretical philosophy, not only because Kant himself dedicated comparatively less space to it, but also, and principally, because Coleridge dedicated correspondingly less attention to it. For the same reason the exposition of the ethical theories has been drawn indifferently from both the *Fundamental Principles* and the *Critique*, without distinguishing the contents of each. To show Kant's loyalty to his "architectonic," we will add only that the *Critique of Practical Reason* is also divided into an Analytic and a Dialectic, and that it contains a Table of Ethical Categories, or "Categories of Freedom relating to the Notions of Good and Evil," grouped by threes under the four headings of Quantity, Quality, Modality, and Relation (Abbott, 158). For our purposes this brief account of Kant's ethics may suffice.

ii

COLERIDGE BEGAN rather early to make a study of Kant's ethical theories. In December 1803 he was reading the *Fundamental Principles of the Metaphysics of Ethics* and taking notes in his *Notebooks* (I, # 1704–5, 1710–11, 1717, and 1723; other entries may also arise out of this reading). There is an important marginal note which he made at the time in his copy of the book (note to # 1705).

In reading these early notes one should remember Coleridge's own definition of his notes on Kant as "Doubts during a first perusal, i.e., struggles felt, not arguments objected," quoted in our first chapter. In the notes of 1803 we can see Coleridge in this area of philosophy still enmeshed in empiricism, struggling to understand Kant's transcendentalism, and failing to do so at his first attempt, but succeeding later. Coleridge was apparently still looking for a psychological theory of ethics, i.e., an account of what goes on in the mind in terms of feelings, emotions, faculties, and their interplay, while Kant was seeking for the rational ground of moral obligation, the universal and necessary reasons for right conduct, not what happens, but what *should* happen, rationally: in his own terms, the fundamental principles of the metaphysics of ethics.

Not finding psychological analysis in Kant's book, Coleridge condemns him at first as "a wretched Psychologist" (# 1717, cf. 1710). In the marginalium he gives his reason more fully: "Kant and all his school are . . . bad analysts of all but notions" (1705*n*). But that was precisely Kant's object: to analyse the "notion," the universal and necessary principle of morality, not to describe emotions and distinguish the fine shades of feelings, a task for which a poet like Coleridge was better qualified.[3]

We have already seen in Chapter 2 this distinction between Kant's method and the psychological approach, and how the second is not relevant to the first. Coleridge came to see it himself, and in later statements accepted Kant's principles of ethics without the psychological reservations which he made on his first contact with them. Even this marginalium ends with a postscript highly praising Kant for two paragraphs which are copied out in the *Notebooks* (# 1723), and in which duty is opposed to inclination not on psychological a posteriori grounds, but on a priori philosophical grounds: where "principles dictated by reason" are required to be "wholly *a priori*," unalloyed by "empirical motives" and by "every empirical element": nothing from inclination," everything from pure reason (*W*, 88–89).[4]

When he comes across the Categorical Imperative, Coleridge here demurs at it: he seems to call it "mere empty generalization" and gives a revised version of it, more empirical, referring it to "the Race" rather than to Reason; but by the end of the paragraph Coleridge hesitates and then goes back to the absolute formulation of Duty as Duty, pure and absolute, "categorical" as Kant would say: "it is each individual's Duty to perform" his duty "—because it is his Duty" (# 1711). In later statements that we shall see, Coleridge repeated Kant's Categorical Imperative without any reservations.

A similar oscillation is to be found in # 1717. Coleridge begins by criticising Kant's statement (quoted in German) that "the will is nothing else but practical reason." "This I doubt," Coleridge observes. "My will & I seem perfect Synonimes—whatever does not apply to the first, I refuse to the latter," and so comes to the conclusion, already quoted, that Kant "is a wretched Psychologist."

But then follows a pause, represented by a blank in the MS., and after-thoughts follow: "Yet it is, doubtless, a most abstruse Subject. In all inevitable Truths . . . I feel my will active: I seem to *will* the Truth, as well as to perceive it. Think of this!"

And he thought of it, and later came to accept at least the term "practical reason": in the *Aids* he speaks of "the *practical* reason of man, comprehending the Will, the Conscience, the Moral Being." and "the *practical* reason, that is, the power of proposing an *ultimate* end, the determinability of the Will by IDEAS" (*Aids*, 115 and 164; Shedd, I, 215 and 261).

In these notes there is also a quotation from Schiller's "On naive and sentimental poetry" (# 1705 [i] n.). But Coleridge does not bring in Schiller's concept of the "Beautiful Soul," which is a clever solution of Kant's opposition between inclination and duty.

This opposition was accepted by Coleridge two years after. In a note of April 1805 he says: "we are to contemplate and obey *Duty* for its own sake, and . . . we must see it . . . in direct opposition to the *Wish*, the *Inclination*." This "is the *Ideal*, which . . . every human being ought to try to draw near unto." [5] Only an angel "finds his Duty in Enjoyment" (# 2556).

Later still, between 1807 and 1810, he accepts the Categorical Imperative as far as it goes, i.e., "in the Intellect," and supplements it with the golden rule "in the heart". " 'Be able to *Will*, that thy maxims (rules of individual conduct) should be the law of all Intelligent Being.' In the heart, or practical Reason, Do unto others, as thou would'st be done by" (# 3231, fol. 13v).

In the same entry he adopts Kant's argument for immortality based upon ethical reasons: "*From* what reasons do I believe a *continuous* and ever continuable *Consciousness?* From *Conscience!*" (*ibid.*, fol. 14). The rest of the entry makes it clear that he is speaking of "immortality." He then firmly rejects miracles as proof of it (fol. 14v).

But the fullest and most unqualified statements of Kantian ethics are to be found in *The Friend.* Here is the Categorical Imperative, although it is not attributed to Kant: "So act that thou mayest be able, without involving any contradiction, to will that the maxim of thy conduct should be the law of all intelligent beings—is the one universal and sufficient guide to morality. And why? Because the object of morality is not the outward act, but the internal maxim of our actions" (Sec. I, Ess. 4; *F*, 122).

Kant's principle that human beings must always be treated as ends, and never as means, is formulated in a more concrete form:

"All morality is grounded in reason. Every man is born with the faculty of reason; and whatever is without it, be the shape what it may, is not a man or a person, but a thing. Hence the sacred principle, recognised by all laws, human and divine, the principle indeed which is the groundwork of all law and justice, that a person can never become a thing, nor be treated as one without wrong" (*F*, 118; Sec. I, Ess. 4).

Kant's doctrine of the autonomy of the will is here presented as follows: "as the faculty of reason implies free agency, morality (i.e., the dictate of reason) gives to every rational being the right of acting as a free agent and of finally [through finality?] determining his conduct by his own will, according to his own conscience: and this right is inalienable except by guilt, which is an act of self-forfeiture" (*ibid.*).

In *Aids to Reflection* Coleridge adopts Kant's distinction

between the practical reason and the theoretical reason, while maintaining his own interpretation of the latter: "the Practical Reason alone *is* Reason in the full and substantive sense. It is Reason in its own sphere of perfect freedom; as the source of IDEAS, which *Ideas*, in their conversion to the responsible Will, become Ultimate Ends. On the other hand, Theoretic Reason, as the ground of the Universal and Absolute in all Logical *Conclusion* is rather the *Light* of Reason in the *Understanding*, and known to be such by its contrast with the contingency and particularity which characterises all the proper and indigenous growths of the Understanding" (Note to the "Synoptical Summary of the Scheme of the Argument" on the Reason and the Understanding, in Appendix A, p. 277).

It was not to be expected that Coleridge would be permanently satisfied with Kant's conception of the three Ideas as mere logical postulates. In a letter of May 23, 1818, to H. J. Rose, he wrote of Kant's "system" of "scientific theology": "No! for his proofs are *moral*—and he himself expressly entitles the result, *Vernunft-Glauben,* i.e., a belief consistent with reason—expressly declares that even a praktische *Vernunft,* or reason proceeding on a praeterrational Ground, demands only that we should act *as if* the proof were scientific" (*CL,* IV, 863).

Among the still unpublished MSS. of Coleridge there is a work preserved almost complete in two volumes in the Coleridge collection at Victoria College, University of Toronto. They were formerly known as Say MSS. II and III; Muirhead called them MS. B. The work has at present no title, but it might be called a Philosophy of Religion. It consists of a philosophical demonstration of the truths of Christianity, based on the sole assumption of the existence of a moral will in man. Once the existence of a "responsible Will" has been admitted, the next step is the deduction of the "difference between Good and Evil" (III, 13). Then follow deductions of the Conscience, the "transcendence of God," the personality of God, and the doctrine of the Trinity. Since Coleridge had covered in the *Aids to Reflection* the doctrines of Original Sin, of Redemption, and of Baptism, it would appear that he had actually accomplished a large part of his plan for a philosophical defence of Christianity, which for many years after his death was thought to be a mere pipe dream.

Most of Chapter 8 of this work, "On Faith and Conscience," is an expansion of the so-called "Essay on Faith," which was published in Coleridge's *Literary Remains* and since often reprinted (e.g., Shedd, V, 557–65). It is therefore already known to students of Coleridge, at least in substance. But it became a part of a larger work which is still awaiting publication.

Muirhead, who saw this MS., noted that Coleridge quotes in it Kant's striking statement of the good Will, which we have mentioned above, "probably for the first time in English ethical literature" (Muirhead, 156–57, n.).[6] Here are Coleridge's words, quoted more fully from the MS.: "There is, observes the great restorer* of the Stoic Moral Philosophy, nothing in the world, yea! nothing out of the world within the powers of human conception, that can without qualification or limit be regarded as good, save the good will alone" (III, 64).

The note* gives the following information on Kant: " *Immanuel Kant, *Grundlegung zur Metaphysik der Sitten*, with which[7] I accord only as far as it is opposed to the modern Epicurean, whether under its grossest form in the philosophy of Helvetius and his scholars or in its more plausible religious dress, as it presents itself in the writings of Paley, Priestley and the other masters of the school which began or rather attained the predominance from the ascension of Charles 1st to the death of his son and successor. The points, on which I disagree with the illustrious sage of Königsberg, those namely in which he differs from the Christian code, and the philosophical grounds of my disagreement will appear in its place in another part of this work" (III, 63).

We may have to wait for an edition of this work to know if Coleridge maintained this promise. Meanwhile, in the "Essay on Faith" there is reference to the categorical imperative (III, 109; Shedd, V, 557). There are also two references in this MS. to Kant's *Only possible proof of the existence of God* at II,

53–54 and 168 v.: the first is also quoted in *BL*, I, 133–34 (cf. *W*, 91–92 and 305–9), as we have seen in Chapter 1.

Another remarkable point about this work has been noted by Chinol: Coleridge reverses Kant's argument on the freedom of the will in connection with the moral law. For Kant, we have first the moral law as an absolute certainty, and from that we deduce, as its presupposition, the freedom of the will: "we ought, therefore we can." But Coleridge here starts from the "good will" as the primary certainty, and from that he deduces the law of morality (Chinol, 52–53). Obviously, Coleridge's argument is suggested by Kant's and very close to it, but Coleridge shows independence in his reversal. A full study of this MS. work will no doubt add to our appreciation of Coleridge's thought.

Apart from the presumed un-Christian element in Kant referred to by Coleridge in the last quotation, the Kantian doctrine that Coleridge (like almost everybody) finds objectionable in Kant's ethics is its rigorism. That is the implication, I believe, of the title "restorer of the Stoic moral philosophy," bestowed by Coleridge upon Kant in the above quotation, and elsewhere (cf. *PhL*, 62). Even more emphatically in a letter to J. H. Green, of Decemeber 13, 1817: "I reject Kant's *stoic* principle, as false, unnatural, and even immoral, where in his Critik der practischen Vernunft he treats the affections as indifferent (ἀδιάφορα) in ethics, and would persuade us that a man who disliking, and without any feeling of Love for, Virtue yet *acted* virtuously, because and only because it was his *Duty*, is more worthy of our esteem, than the man whose *affections* were aidant to, and congruous with, his Conscience. For it would imply little less than that things not the Objects of our moral Will or under it's controul were yet indispensable to its due practical direction. In other words, it would subvert his own System" (*CL*, IV, 791–92).

Finally it is interesting to note that Coleridge, in this vein, quoted the most eloquent protest ever made against Pharisaic puritanism, and used it as a motto in *The Friend* (Sec. I, Ess. 15, p. 204); Jacobi's "letter to Fichte," which Coleridge translated as follows: "Yes, I am that Atheist, that godless person, who . . . would lie as the dying Desdemona lied; lie and deceive as Pylades when he impersonated Orestes; would commit sacrilege with David; yea, and pluck ears of corn on the Sabbath, for no other reason than that I was fainting from lack of food, and that the law was made for man and not man made for the law."

The above does not claim to exhaust the references to Kant's ethics to be found in Coleridge; but it is not possible here to go further. Also, it is not possible here to go into the philosophy of religion in Kant (for which see *W*, 88–95) and in Coleridge beyond the references already given. A detailed discussion of both these topics will be found in Winkelmann (pp. 187–223).

iii

IN 1790 KANT PUBLISHED his third and last Critique, the *Critique of Judgment*. This work has always been the object of admiration, especially on the part of idealistic philosophers, for its attempt to breach the gap left between the world of necessity and the world of freedom in his first two Critiques. In the third Critique the gap is bridged by the faculty of Judgment, as he then proceeded to define it. Judgment is now "reflective judgment," or the faculty that sees system and order in nature according to law. Art and poetry are also subject to this faculty, but in their case law must be defined rather differently. This analogy between art and nature accounts for the fact that the Critique consists of two parts, one dedicated to the aesthetic judgment, and the other to the supreme example of system and order in nature, viz. the natural organism.

It is therefore significant that Coleridge joined in the admiration for the third critique. In November 1810 he told Crabb Robinson that he "thought the *Kritik der Urteilskraft* the most astonishing of all his [Kant's] works." [8]

As in the other Critiques, Kant's task is to seek and define the a priori element, this time in the aesthetic judgment, or in Kant's terms "the judgment of taste," where Kant runs into an even stronger current of scepticism than in epistemology and ethics. Although the "absoluteness of taste" was maintained by some aestheticians, the opposite belief prevails in popular opinion: nothing is so relative as taste, and there is no arguing about tastes.

The first part of the third *Critique* is dedicated to aesthetics, or "the judgment of taste," i.e., the aesthetic judgment, or the evaluation of something as beautiful. Like the other Critiques, it is divided into an Analytic and a Dialectic. In the former, the Beautiful is defined under four headings, which correspond to the four classes of judgments in the first *Critique*: quantity, quality, modality, and relation. The Beautiful is then distinguished from the Sublime, according to eighteenth-century aesthetics, and the latter receives its definition: the sublime is "the absolutely great" (# 25). In the Dialectic Kant discusses the Antinomy of Taste: "there is no arguing on taste" *versus* "one can argue about taste" (# 56). The arguments pro and con are balanced, as in the Antinomies of theoretical reason, but here Kant offers a solution of the dilemma (# 57), as he shortly before had offered a solution to the dilemma of Genius versus the Rules (# 46).

For our purposes, the most important point in the second part of the *Critique*, which deals with design in nature, is the definition of the organism as a system in which "every part is reciprocally end and means" (# 66). For Kant then makes the observation that there is an analogy between the natural organism and the work of art, thus establishing a classical demonstration of what is know as organic (or "organismic") aesthetics. Less known is the other important fact, that he also defines the differences between a natural organism and a work of art (# 65), thus avoiding the trap into which critics hostile to organic aesthetics believe it falls.

The four headings under which the definition of Beauty is given in the first part of the *Critique* are the following:

1) Quality: Beautiful is that which gives pleasure without interest (i.e., without an interest in the real existence of the

object which has beauty). Disinterestedness is thus the *quality* of beauty (# 2).

2) Quantity: Beautiful is that which gives *universal* pleasure apart from concepts (# 6).

3) Relation: Beautiful is what exhibits *purposiveness* without a real purpose (# 11).

4) Modality: Beautiful is that which gives pleasure *necessarily* to all (# 22).

These famous definitions of disinterested pleasure without contingency, purposiveness without purpose, and universality and necessity without concepts, lay the foundations for a definition of art and beauty which is strictly autonomous. Beauty is thus sharply distinguished from logical values (the universal and necessary concept), from utilitarian values (interest), and even from mere hedonism, for the pleasure afforded by art is in Kant's definition a purely intellectual satisfaction, *das reine intellektuelle Wohlgefallen* (Introd., IX). Disinterestedness even excludes the Good (# 4). The judgment that an object through its structure causes such a satisfaction must according to Kant be clearly distinguished from the judgment that an object through its sensuous qualities gives us sensuous pleasure: this judgment is called by Kant an aesthetic judgment *of sense* (# 14) using "aesthetic" in the meaning which it has in the first *Critique* (A 21, B 36) as equal to sensuous. The judgment on beauty is for Kant an "aesthetic judgment of reflection" (Introd., # viii) since it sees system and order in the object. *Vergnügen* or sensuous pleasure is sharply distinguished from *Wohlgefallen*, sometimes translated as "satisfaction" and sometimes "approval": it is a sensation of pleasure arising out of the perception of congruence or harmony in the parts of a beautiful object.

A work of art for Kant consists of a system of parts related to each other so as to form a whole. Although Kant does not say in so many words that a work of art possesses organic unity, so that all the parts agree with each other and with the whole (in keeping with Plato's definition, *Phaedrus*, 264), this definition may be said implicit in the third *Critique*, especially in # 65, where he traces the "analogy" between a work of art and natural organism, and also defines the differences between them. These are, first, that in an organism "parts produce one another; it is self-organising" (*F*, II, 10); secondly, that an organism that goes out of order "repairs itself"; and thirdly, that a natural organism "propagates" or reproduces itself. Kant warns that there is no real analogy between nature and art, because the art product necessarily involves an "artificer" and nature does not. His final definition of the natural organism is in terms of teleology: "An organized product of nature is one in which every part is reciprocally purpose and means" (# 66), a basic definition for later philosophical speculation and particularly for Coleridge. On the other hand, the work of art is devoid of purposefulness, as we have seen, but has merely the appearance of purpose: the parts are connected together artfully "as if" there was a purpose, and produce the intense but absolutely disinterested pleasure of the Beautiful.

Thus the organic concept is formulated in the abstract by Kant as the relation of the parts to the whole. An important development of this concept is its extension to the relationship between the form and matter, or the form and the content, of a literary composition. Since form and matter are the parts of a work, the applicability of the organic concept is obvious. Hence the idea of Organic Form and its opposite, Mechanical Form, which were to play such an important part in later criticism. Did Kant formulate the idea of Organic Form in aesthetics?

If he did not (and he does not seem to have done so explicitly), he certainly laid the foundation for it. In the Introduction the term "form" suddenly emerges as the condition for the sensation of aesthetic pleasure: "pleasure is bound up with the mere apprehension of the form of an object of intuition" (Sec. VII). What is specifically meant by form is not defined, but Kant later says that "what is formal in the representation of a thing" is "the congruence of its manifold with a unity" (# 15).

The concept of Organic Form in aesthetics was further developed by Schelling, as we shall see in Chapter 9, with notable consequences for literary criticism.

We cannot assert the purposiveness of natural products because according to Kant purposiveness is an Idea and Ideas transcend experience: they are, as we saw in the Dialectic, regulative and not constitutive. On the other hand, the judgment we pronounce on the pleasure we receive from a beautiful object is, says Kant, "constitutive" (Introd., Sec. IX). This is an extraordinary admission. It means that we find in aesthetics another noumenon which is within reach of our knowledge. It means that the aesthetic judgment is given a solidity and a universality which place it above the flux of relativism. It ranks Beauty as a noumenon along with the ethical Will and the personality of man, if not directly, at least through the intermediary of the disinterested pleasure it provides.

We take a further step into the noumenon when we analyze the antinomy of taste: "It is possible to discuss about tastes— it is not possible to argue about tastes" (# 56). The solution lies in a reference to the "supersensuous foundation of all human beings," which makes them all see the same thing as right and the same objects as beautiful. Kant concludes: "the antinomies force us against our will to look beyond the sensible and to seek in the supersensible the point of union for all our *a priori* faculties, because no other expedient is left to make our reason harmonious with itself" (# 57).

Furthermore in the production of the work of art two other factors are involved: Genius and the Imagination. Kant now comes to recognize the aesthetic imagination, which was excluded from the first *Critique*. In his epistemology, as we have seen, Kant noted the faculty of imagination operating as purely reproductive, or as productive of scientific concepts such as the schema of causality and the schema of number. Now Kant discovers that there is also a faculty of imagination which is active in the production of beautiful things. This faculty, as he says, underlies our judgment of taste and "is both productive (not merely reproductive) and free, for it is independent of any determinate laws of the understanding" (# 49). Thus Kant frees Art from all subjection to the intellect.

Then there is Genius. For Kant, writing in that period of German literature which has been called the age of genius

(*Genieperiode*) because of the stress laid upon that power, Genius is the faculty that produces the beautiful. Throughout the preceding age of classicism, critics might have admitted that, but added immediately:—Yes, but Genius must follow the rules of art, and not let itself run loose. It must be curbed and guided by Judgment.—But in the Storm and Stress period, which is another name for the *Genieperiode*, Rules had been declared null and void, Genius had claimed complete freedom, and showed it by going against the Rules and breaking them at every opportunity.

Kant tackled this situation magnificently. First of all, he gave no attention to Judgment in the peculiar and restrictive sense which the classicists used: it was, as he had already shown, Imagination and not Judgment that produced the Beautiful. As for rules, art was not lawless and did not pursue irregularity for its own sake; but it prescribed its own rules to itself. "Genius," Kant defined, "is the talent that gives rules to art" (# 46). In this definition both Genius and rules are preserved; but the rules are the laws that the aesthetic faculty sets up for itself in the process of its creation, and not the pre-established precepts of Rhetoric or of Poetics, the traditional patterns of genres or types, the conventions of external regularity and traditional models.

Kant's formula is a genuine synthesis of opposites, and as such it may not be superseded by the mere repetition of one of the opposites which it already includes within itself. That would be falling back upon the unresolved antithesis to which the formula provided a solution.

The doctrine of the Imagination as the supreme aesthetic faculty Kant owed to English aestheticians of the eighteenth century, who had slowly developed it empirically, without giving it a philosophical foundation.[9] Such a foundation was given to it by Kant's predecessor N. Tetens.[10] But its roots appear to be in Italian criticism of the sixteenth and seventeenth centuries,[11] culminating in Vico, who is the author of the most complete identification, upon a philosophical basis, of the Imagination (*Fantasia*) with the cognition of the particular. Even in Kant, sixty years after Vico, the Imagination differs from

the cognition of the particular, or *Anschauung*. The *Einbildungskraft*, discussed in Kant's *Anthropologie* (# 25), is merely
the faculty that brings back an image of an object in the absence of that object, hence little more than the memory. The
image, *Bild*, is presumably the object of *Anschauung*, but Kant
does not say it. It was Vico who made the all-important connection, and assigned poetry to the sphere of the particular.

In English Neoclassicism, and in the philosophical school
which is usually its foundation, Empiricism, the imagination is
at most a connective faculty, not an organizing one. Defined as
the faculty that perceives resemblances, and designated at times
as Wit, it has in literary composition a purely ornamental function, providing similes or metaphors to prettify this or that passage, but it has nothing to do with the total organization of the
work. The structure of a composition is reserved by Neoclassicism to Reason and Judgment, operating by means of general
concepts: a character is the embodiment of a concept, e.g.,
Achilles is the embodiment of anger in a young man: the right
emotion for the right type of person, according to Aristotle:
so literary beauty consists in the logical congruence between
the genus and the species, or the logical subsumption of the
particular under the general.

Besides the concept of the Beautiful, Kant also accepted
from contemporary aesthetics the concept of the Sublime, as
distinct from the Beautiful and not a variety of it. This dichotomy of the Sublime and the Beautiful has a long history
behind it, which has been expounded in a well-known book
by S. H. Monk.[12] Kant received it from English criticism, where
it had obtained a classic formulation in Edmund Burke's essay
On the Sublime and Beautiful (1786).

Kant, as usual, gives the traditional dichotomy a new turn,
which makes him the ancestor of the German concept of
romanticism: "The Beautiful in nature is concerned with that
form of the object the essence of which is limitation. The sublime, on the other hand, is to be found also in a formless object
in so far as it either immediately involves or else provokes the
idea of boundlessness" (# 23).

Here are two of the concepts which will be used by Friederich Schlegel in his first definition of the Classic and the Modern: the former is both formed and limited, the latter is limitless and formless. This dichotomy will shortly afterwards turn
into the Classic and Romantic dichotomy, as shown by Lovejoy.[13]

In the course of the *Critique* Kant discusses also the theory
of Ideal Beauty which had developed in Germany in recent
years, e.g., by Winckelmann, who in his celebrated writings on
the history of ancient art had advocated a revival of the Platonic
theory of Ideas concerning the Beautiful, and the adoption of
a norm of perfect human beauty. Kant objects that such a norm
would not be beautiful because it cannot contain anything individual: "a perfectly regular countenance ordinarily tells us
nothing because it contains nothing characteristic"; it would
be "merely correct" and not beautiful (# 17). Through the
characteristic we approach the concept of the individual, which
is the object of art according to the doctrine we have traced to
Vico.

Toward the end of the book Kant brings up a theory of
so-called "Aesthetic Ideas," which appear to be nothing more
than what we would call the great themes or commonplaces of
literature and of the arts, such as love and death, fame and immortality, the universe, etc. (# 49). Finally, in the last paragraph of the treatise, he boldly outlines a theory which would
make all art symbolic of morality (# 59).

So far Kant had steered clear of traditional intellectualism
in aesthetics. He rejected over and again the concept as the
content of art; the Beautiful for him does not embody any concept and there are no rules (or concepts) that account for it;
and so forth. But Ideas for Kant are different. They are notions
of the supersensuous, and while purely subjective, still universal
and necessary (regulatively). A symbol is defined by Kant as
an intuition, or sensuous representation, which stands for an
Idea in a relation which is beyond the reach of concepts. But
no sensible intuition can be adequate to an Idea, so presumably
an unlimited series of representations are required to convey a

single Idea. And the Idea which is symbolized in art in general is for Kant the Idea of Morality, i.e., the unity of the theoretical faculty with the practical, whose ground is supersensuous. Thus Kant again avoids, though narrowly, falling into intellectualism, and takes his stand in the supersensuous which he had discovered in the *Critique of Practical Reason.*

These ideas that we have found in the third *Critique*—the autonomy of art, genius and the imagination as the aesthetic faculty, organic form versus mechanical, the infinite and the supersensuous as the foundations of art, and the symbol and the characteristic—might be easily identified with a well-known literary movement: Romanticism. Is Kant the standard bearer of Romantic aesthetics? In a sense he is, and in another sense he is not. He is, since most of the ideas mentioned above were adopted and developed by critics who raised the Romantic banner in literature, such as the Schlegels; but not only by them. Some of those ideas are to be found also in critics like Goethe and Schiller, who in Germany are labelled classics: "die deutschen Klassiker." [14] Also, if Romantic is opposed to Classic, and the latter is given the meaning of Greek and Latin writers, it has already been shown, and could be shown more fully, that some of these ideas, if not all, have their roots in ancient thought, so that they may be called classical as well. Romantic should not be opposed to "classic," for even great Romantic writers can become classics, but to "classicist" or "neoclassical," as has been done above.

This whole set of Romantic ideas has recently been called by Wellek "the central idealist tradition in aesthetics" [15] which it may well be called, since these ideas constitute a luminous tradition of European thought which continues to shed its light even in the twentieth century and in other continents.

iv

WHILE THE INDIRECT influence (i.e., through intermediaries) of the ideas in Kant's third *Critique* on Coleridge was considerable and, as has been said of the German influence in general, "qualitatively incalculable," the direct influence from the *Critique* itself was materially not very extensive. As well known, it is to be found mainly in the four "Aesthetic Essays" which Shawcross appended to his edition of the *Biographia* (*BL*, II, 219–63). We will take them in chronological order:

1) The fragment of "An Essay on Taste" (1810) which Wellek judges "little more than the beginning of a statement of the central problem of the *Critique of Judgment*" (*W*, 110). Taste is here defined as "a sense of immediate pleasure in ourselves with the perception of external arrangement" (II, 248). Immediate here means "disinterested" (*W*, 110–11). The problem of the relativity of taste is raised, and the solution is hinted "to be found in those parts of our nature, in which each intellect is representative of all" (II, 249), corresponding to Kant's "supersensuous substratum" of humanity (II, 247–49).

2) "On the Principles of Genial Criticism concerning the Fine Arts" (1814; II, 219–46) is perhaps Coleridge's most serious attempt to set up an aesthetic, but it does not go very far (*W*, 111–14). I interpret "Genial" in the title to mean "sympathetically evaluating Genius," as has been shown by previous students[16] and is confirmed by a marginalium: "the genial judgment is to distinguish accurately the character and characteristics of each poem, praising them according to their force and vivacity in their own kind—and to reserve reprehension to those who have no character."[17] First a distinction is made between different kinds of pleasure: "complacency" here corresponds to Kant's *Gefallen*, while *Vergnügen* is represented by "delight" (II, 224) and by the "agreeable" (231–32), and Beauty is defined as "multeity in unity" (230 and 232). The beauty of Raphael's Galatea (which Coleridge knew only in a black and white print)[18] is shown to be "in the balance . . . effected between these two conflicting principles of FREE LIFE, and of confining FORM" (235), which is reminiscent of Schelling's *Discourse* (see Chapter 9). After the quotation from Plotinus which we have discussed in Chapter 1, Coleridge gives this final definition of Beauty, which unites the Kantian concept of dis-

interest with that of organic unity: "*The sense of beauty sub-sists in simultaneous intuition of the relation of parts, each to each, and of all to a whole; exciting an immediate and absolute complacency, without interference, therefore, of any interest, sensual or intellectual.* The BEAUTIFUL is thus at once dis-tinguished both from the AGREEABLE, which is beneath it, and from the GOOD, which is above it: for both these have interest necessarily attached to them" (II, 239).

And so on, in an entirely Kantian vein. This essay contains also an anecdote derived from the *Critique*, illustrating the dif-ference between the agreeable and the beautiful: the story of the red Indian in Paris, who was indifferent to the architecture, but thought the cook's shops beautiful (II, 241–42; cf. *Critique*, # 2).

3) The "Fragment on Beauty" (1818; II, 250–52) reaffirms the difference between the Beautiful and the Agreeable (251) and the "disinterestedness of all taste" (252), and also refers to "the living balance of excited faculties" (251), which may be an echo of Kant's Introduction to the *Critique of Judgment*, VII.

4) Finally, "On Poesy or Art" is Lecture XIII of the course of 1818 (II, 253–63) and contains some important ideas from Schelling, as we shall see in Chapter 9. The term "Poesy" is extended to cover all the arts (II, 255), somewhat as the Ger-man *Dichtung* includes not only poetry but all creative writing. The concept of expression appears (II, 254–55), and the Neo-classic formula, "art is the imitation of nature," is subjected to criticism (II, 255–56) by means of the distinction between imitation and copy, a favorite one of Coleridge's,[19] though not one of his most profound, since both imitation and copy are a denial of creativity. They have in common the reference to an external object on one side, and on the other the lack of reference to the creative power of the artist.—Then, "unity in multeity" is reaffirmed as the "principle of Beauty" (II, 262).

There is here a hint of the concept of organic form in juxta-position to mechanical form: "Remember that there is a dif-ference between form as proceeding, and shape as superinduced" (II, 262). Coleridge had already made a parallel distinction in 1805, but with no reference to aesthetics. It was in a discussion of the problem of human generation: "The difference between Fabrication and Generation becomes clearly indicable / the Form of the latter is *ab intra, evolved*, the other *ab extra, impressed*." This he describes as "the inducement of Form on pre-existing material" (*NB*, II, 2444), but this Form is not literary form.

The formula quoted above from *Genial Criticism* as a definition of Beauty, "unity in multeity," was a favorite of Coleridge and often repeated by him,[20] sometimes in Italian: "il più nell'uno" (*TT*, 268, 1 January 1834). This Italian phrase is sometimes attributed to St. Francis de Sales (*PW*, I, 481*n.*, and *IS*, 106), but de Sales wrote in French; and sometimes to the "Roman school of painting" (?) (*TT*, 146, 27 December 1831). It is even projected by Coleridge into a quotation from Dante (*NB*, II, # 3201, 1807–8). Could it be a phrase which he heard from some Roman *cicerone?*

The problem of the One and the Many and their relation is of course one of the oldest in the history of philosophy. It was raised by the pre-Socratics, who wondered how unity could be reconciled with multiplicity and viceversa, or, as Coleridge once put it, "how the *one can be many*" (*NB*, I, # 1561, 1803; and still earlier, # 556, of 1799). Plato showed the solution in the *Philebus:* "the one is many and the many are one," or "an identical unity is found simultaneously in unity and in plurality" (14 E, 15 B).[21] Furthermore Plato showed in the *Phaedrus* (264) how the work of literary art organised many parts in the unity of the whole, and Aristotle recognised that in beauty "the scattered elements are merged into unity" (*Polit.*, III, 11, 1281 B). Then Plotinus conceived Beauty as unity in multiplicity (I, 6, 2) and as unity in variety (I, 6, 3), in that passage which we have already seen in Chapter 1 may have been known to Coleridge early in life. These two formulas for Beauty, unity in multiplicity and unity in variety, occur in many later writers of all countries, including literary critics known to Coleridge.

As a definition of Beauty, unity in multiplicity suffers from a limitation which also affects its more elaborate version "organic unity": it defines other things besides Beauty. In effect, it belongs to almost every complex unity, natural or ideal, philosophical or scientific. Coleridge himself uses it to define life in general: "life . . . as the principle of unity in *multeity*" (Shedd, 1, 387). Coleridge also defined "Nature herself" as "under the two primary Ideas of Identity and Multeity, i.e. alternately as one and many," in the Notebook of 1825 quoted by Muirhead (p. 124). Kant's frequent references to the "synthesis of a manifold" (unification of a multiplicity) would strengthen the formula in Coleridge's mind: in Kant it is referred to cognition in general, and sense cognition in particular.

Coleridge in addition took good note of Kant's definition of the natural organism in the *Critique of Judgment* (# 66). It appears unexpectedly, but appropriately, in Coleridge's famous statement on the distinction between Organic Form and Mechanical Form, which is mainly a translation from Schlegel.[22] Here he inserts parenthetically this definition: "and what is organization but the connection of parts to the whole, so that each part is at once end and means?"[23] Since neither Kant nor the *Critique* are referred to, it escaped the students of Coleridgean criticism until M. H. Abrams pointed it out in 1953.[24]

All in all, it may be said that the basic concepts of Kant's aesthetics were adopted and absorbed by Coleridge,[25] even to the extent of occasionally improving upon them. But the contribution of Schelling was even more important, as we shall see in Chapter 9.

CHAPTER 7

Fichte

i

WITH THE END of our discussion of Kant we hope to have achieved the first aim that we set out with, viz. to see what there was in Kant that Coleridge saw in Kant. But it is not possible to stop here without giving some account (even if not a complete account) of the philosophical developments that followed immediately in Germany, as a direct consequence of Kant's teaching. For one thing, we have already been throwing out anticipatory hints of these developments, and the reader may expect to learn something more about them: were all anticipations realized, did all consequences take place? For another, one of these developments, viz. the philosophy of Schelling, was considerably influential upon Coleridge: indeed, as Wellek notes, it was through Schelling's doctrines that Coleridge criticized Kant himself. But Schelling, to be intelligible, must be taken in conjunction with Fichte, just as Fichte, to be intelligible, must be taken in conjunction with Kant. In any case there are enough references to Fichte in Coleridge to make some account of him justified.

As Kant's *Critique of Pure Reason* became better known and began to find followers, the need was felt for a positive and constructive formulation of his philosophy: i.e., a formulation which would bring together all the philosophical truths contained in the *Critiques* and systematize them under one general principle, according to the method that Kant himself advocated at the end of his work (A 832, B 860). This was attempted by a disciple of Kant, Karl L. Reinhold, who found the required general principle in the representation, thus: "in consciousness the Representation is distinguished by the Subject from the Object, and referred to both." [1]

The Kantian world of experience was thus reduced to two factors, the Subject and the Object, together with the relation between them. We are getting close to Fichte's I and not-I. Indeed, Fichte began by discussing this doctrine in a book review of 1792, printed in 1794 (*GW*, I, 1 ff.). Fichte found the formula deficient because it related only to theoretical philosophy and not also to practical philosophy, and was not therefore broad enough for a universal principle.

Criticism of a more radical kind was beginning, and the first part of Kant's system to fall was the doctrine of the noumenon, or thing in itself. Kant had assumed its existence as the cause of our sensations but argued that we could know nothing else about it, since our cognitive concepts, i.e. the categories of the understanding, were applicable only to phenomena.

There lurks here an inconsistency, which was pointed out not by one critic only but by several acting independently.[2] Most of these critics were disciples of Kant's and aimed merely at making a system out of the *Critiques*: only one was a philosopher of the sceptical school, E. Schulze in his *Aenesidemus* (1792). They all noted that since causality was one of the categories applied by mind to phenomena, its employment could not be extended to things in themselves without falling into one of those paralogisms that Kant criticized in his Dialectic. But the only thing that Kant knew about things in themselves is that they were the causes of our sensations. Clearly, we cannot assert even that, since causality is a category. Then the only remaining prop for the support of the existence of things in themselves, or noumena, falls to the ground.

What are we then left with? Only the *I think*, the transcendental unity of consciousness, weaving its complex web of forms of intuition, categories, and schemata to build up an image of the world in space and time out of our sensations, which are subjective phenomena to which no objective cause can now be assigned. The next step is to conclude that, consequently, sensations are also somehow produced by the transcendental self, and the result is a system of philosophical idealism. Kant had always tried to ward off idealism, on the ground of the existence of things in themselves. But these were now exploded, and so we have the idealistic philosophy of Fichte.

Fichte began his career as a devoted disciple of Kant. Under his master's inspiration Fichte wrote a fourth *Critique*, directed against dogmatic religion, which Kant helped him to publish anonymously: the *Critique of all Revelation* (1792). In completely Kantian terms, Fichte defined religion as essentially morality, and then proceeded to inquire how it came about that a system of pure ethics was transformed into a body of supernatural beliefs. This transformation took place through a process that Fichte called "alienation," thus using apparently for the first time in philosophy a term which was to figure so largely in later and "existentialist" thinking. Through this process, which according to Fichte is something necessary to humanity's spiritual welfare, the purely inward law of ethics became an external Lawgiver, and loyalty to one's duty was turned into supernaturalism.

But in the early nineties the trend among students of Kant was toward the elimination of things in themselves, and Fichte participated in this trend. He turned his attention to the one principle of transcendental philosophy which still remained standing, namely Kant's *I think*, and made it the foundation of his own system, the *Ich* or Ego, from which everything else is to be derived, or rather "deduced." His own system he called *Wissenschaftslehre* or Doctrine of Science, which is again Kantian, for that is what Kant had in effect produced in the first *Critique*: a theory of knowledge, a doctrine of science. Kant had more cautiously called his own work a *Critique* of knowledge, because it showed the limitations of human thought; Fichte more boldly spoke of a Doctrine and built it upon Kant's *Critique*.

In one of his early writings, the *Second Introduction to the Doctrine of Science* (1797), Fichte addressed the orthodox followers of Kant who declared that he was going beyond his master, saying: "As long as Kant does not expressly declare in so many words that he derives sensations from the impact (*Eindruck*) of a thing in itself, or, to use his own terminology, that sensation is to be explained by the presence of a transcendental object independently existing outside ourselves, I will not consent to believe what these expositors tell us concerning Kant" (*GW*, I, 486). He did not have to wait very long for an answer. On August 28, 1799, the old philosopher (Kant was then 75) published a statement in which he expressly repudiated Fichte's interpretation of his doctrine, and referred the reader who wanted more information straight back to the text of the *Critique of Pure Reason*, literally interpreted.[3]

This repudiation marks the break of strict Kantianism with the later idealistic speculations, a break which might have been fatal to idealism if Kant had only explained how to reconcile noumena with causality, how to define the manner of existence of the *I think*, which was not according to the category of existence, and the other problems of his philosophy. All he was able to do at this advanced age was to refer back to the text of the *Critique*, and as we have seen it was out of that text that these problems arose. Even so, Fichte could always quote Kant's own words on endeavoring to understand a great philosopher (like Plato) better than he understood himself (A 314, B 370).

Fichte therefore stuck to his view, which makes the *Ich*, or the thinking subject in general, his fundamental philosophical principle. Fichte argued that since this is a fundamental principle, it does not depend on anything else; for if it depended on something else, that something else would be the fundamental principle. So Fichte thus formulated his philosophy in 1794: "The I posits absolutely and originally its own being" (*GW*, I, 98). At the same time the I posits also its object, the Not-I, as well as the relation between them. This accounts for everything in the world: the universal mind, the world it creates, and the process of creation.

There have of course been idealistic systems of philosophy before Fichte, such as Berkeley's, but this was an entirely new kind: it was transcendental idealism, based on Kant's analysis of knowledge. As has been well said, "Berkeley, as well as Descartes, had resolved bodies into representations, in part or in whole: but these representations were for them functions of thinking substances. For Fichte, self-consciousness is an act which, instead of presupposing a thinking substance, produces it itself." [4]

We have seen this view gradually emerging from Kant's complicated and guarded statements. So modern objections to Fichte that his idealism involves a "thinking substance," or even worse "a ghost in a machine," are based on a misunderstanding. Fichte's I is not a substance, for the concept of substance had been subjected to criticism in different ways both by Locke and by Kant, and Fichte builds upon Kant while rejecting things in themselves. Fichte calls his *Ich* an act, a *Thathandlung* (e.g., *GW*, I, 8) and it is an act which posits itself,[5] an absolutely free act, and an act which every thinking person must perform by himself and for himself, in order to acquire dignity as a man.

For Fichte did not present his philosophy as a purely theoretical conception, a solution to a metaphysical problem. He gave it a strong ethical cast and turned it into a call to action, to effort, to energetic living, and finally into a political drive.

By conceiving that the I makes itself, and making itself makes the world, Fichte rejected the static conception of Being which had dominated philosophy since the ancients, and replaced it by absolute becoming. There is for Fichte no such thing as simply *being*, being oneself or being something, a static, unchanging condition which persists under the appearance of change, "being in itself, being limitless" (*F*, 340, Sec. II, Ess. 11). The practical consequence of this is that a man can never affirm that he *is* wise or that he *is* good, but only that he is *becoming* wise or good, and that only if he is continually striving toward that goal. Even the I is an I only in so far as he is not I but strives to be I. The world has not been made once and for all, as a solid system of being which we must accept and to which we must conform. It has to be made anew every day, and it is up to man to make it, since it is *his* world. This is the ethical bearing of Fichte's idealistic metaphysic.

ii

BUT COLERIDGE[6] not only fully grasped Fichte's metaphysical principle; he praised it highly. In the often quoted Chapter IX of the *Biographia* he extols Fichte, then follows up with some sharp criticism: "Fichte's Wissenschaftslehre, or Lore of Ultimate Science, was to add the key-stone of the arch; and by commencing with an *act*, instead of a *thing* or *substance*, Fichte assuredly gave the first mortal blow to Spinozism, as taught by Spinoza himself: and supplied the idea of a system truly metaphysical, and of a *metaphysique* truly systematic (i.e. having its spring and principle within itself). But this fundamental idea he overbuilt with a mass of mere *notions*, and psychological acts of arbitrary reflection. Thus his theory degenerated into a crude egoismus, a boastful and hyperstoic hostility to NATURE, as lifeless, godless and altogether unholy" (I, 101–2).

In a contemporary letter in which he criticizes Fichte's ethics, Coleridge repeated his acknowledgement that "he has the merit of having prepared the ground for and laid the first stone of, the Dynamic philosophy by the substitution of Act for Thing" (*CL*, IV, 792).

In the *Biographia* Coleridge expounds what he means by "crude egoismus" in a metrical squib, of which some lines will give a sufficient idea:

> Here on the market-cross aloud I cry
> I, I, I! I itself I! . . .
> The inside and outside, the earth and the sky,
> I, you and he, and he, you and I,
> All souls and all bodies, are I itself I!
> All I itself I!

Coleridge of course knew, or should have known, that Fichte's "I" being a universal principle was not to be identified with a particular self: Kant's distinction between the transcendental self and the empirical self applies here too. Merely as a stylistic parody of the repetition of the word "Ich" in Fichte's early writings Coleridge's squib has some point, but not much. Asserting the "I" was not the fundamental philosophical concern of Fichte: for that he relied on Kant. Fichte's problem was, once granted the universal I or transcendental self, to derive from it the objective world, or the not-I. It is to this end that the various versions of his system written in Fichte's early years tend, trying one formula after another to effect the deduction of the not-I. The most successful of these deductions, according to a friendly critic of Fichte, was that of 1801,[7] but it remained unpublished until 1834, and Coleridge could not have seen it, so we will not go into it. Curiously enough, its central concept is that of "reflection," but it does not fit into Coleridge's formula quoted above, that of "psychological acts of arbitrary reflection," at least if one accepts, as Coleridge did, the idea of that kind of metaphysical speculation.

In view of the criticism with which Coleridge ends his praise of Fichte in the *Biographia*, it is necessary to recall that earlier he had absorbed Fichte's way of thinking and returned to it in his own thoughts. There are several references in letters and notebooks during the years 1801–05 (indicated in the notes). There is also a remarkable entry in the notebooks of 1801, which deserves minute analysis, and which we will now proceed to examine.

iii

THIS ENTRY is dated "February–March 1801" and numbered 921 by Professor Coburn:

—and the deep power of Joy
We see into the *Life* of Things—

i.e.—By deep feeling we make our *Ideas dim*—& this is what we mean by our Life—ourselves. I think of the Wall—it is before me, a distinct Image—here. I necessarily think of the *Idea* and the Thinking I as two distinct & opposite Things. Now <let me> think of *myself* —of the thinking Being—the Idea becomes dim whatever it be—so dim that I know not what it is—but the Feeling is deep & steady— and this I call *I*—identifying the Percipient & the Perceived—.

This is a note that calls for explanation, and Miss Coburn has given it considerable attention. First of all, she notes that the verse quotation with which it begins is from Wordsworth's *Lines written a few miles above Tintern Abbey*, ll. 49–50. The poem is familiar, but a reference to the exact context of the lines quoted by Coleridge may help. Wordsworth is speaking of "that blessed mood . . . In which the heavy and the weary weight / Of all this unintelligible world / Is lighten'd" and we "become a living soul." Then "with an eye made quiet by . . . the deep power of joy / We see into the life of things."

Coleridge however appears here to contradict this. He affirms instead that "by deep feeling we make our *Ideas dim*," so presumably we cannot then see into the Life of Things. On the other hand, we can and do see into ourselves, for "this is what we mean by our Life—ourselves." Then, for some strange reason he goes on to "think of the Wall." He may mean that when the mind turns upon itself, its ideas of all external objects, such as a wall, "become dim," "so dim that I do not know what the object is—but the Feeling of Self is deep and steady —and this I call *I*."

Having thus reached a state of self-awareness, Coleridge notes that in it "the Percipient and the Perceived," "distinct and opposite" in ordinary thinking, have become identical. This point is appropriately referred by Miss Coburn to the Schellingian "Theses" in the *Biographia Literaria*, Chapter XII, and particularly to the passage in Thesis VI, where Spirit is defined as "identity of object and subject": "in this (i.e. the Self), and in this alone, object and subject, being and knowledge, are identical, each involving and supporting the other" (*BL*, I, 183).

The alternation of emotion and reflection in this entry leads Miss Coburn to think that it refers to the process of poetic composition. It seems to me concerned rather with epistemology, not at the very beginning perhaps, but afterwards increasingly so. It is certainly not a crystal-clear entry, and the transitions are somewhat abrupt. In particular, why that sudden turn of thought, "I think of the Wall"? Why a wall? where does the wall come from? and how does it lead to a statement on the identity of subject and object in self-consciousness?

When I first saw this entry, I was reminded of something I had read in the preface to a translation of Fichte's popular works which does bring in an unexpected Wall. It is a vivid description of Fichte's manner as a lecturer: "The following graphic sketch of Fichte's personal appearance and manner of delivery is taken from the Autobiography of Henry Stephens." [8]

And here is the sketch, shorn of unessential details: "Well acquainted with the metaphysical incapacity of his hearers, he took the greatest possible pains to demonstrate his propositions . . . 'Gentlemen,' said he, 'collect yourselves—go into yourselves—for we have here nothing to do with things without, but simply with the inner self.' Thus summoned, the auditors appeared really to go into themselves . . . 'Gentlemen,' continued Fichte, 'think the wall,'—(*Denken Sie die Wand*). This was a task to which the hearers were evidently all equal; they thought the wall. 'Have you thought the wall?' asked Fichte. 'Well then, gentlemen, think him who thought the wall.' It was curious to see the evident confusion and embarrassment that now arose. Many of his audience seemed to be utterly unable to find him who had thought the wall."

This remarkable illustration of Fichte's skill as a teacher obviously reminds us of the puzzling sentences in the Coleridge note: reflection upon a wall is the starting point of a train of thought which ends in self-consciousness, an act in which the object is the same as the subject. The wall and self-consciousness are thus brought together. But by what means could Coleridge have got hold of that anecdote of Fichte, if he did get it from that source?

The translator of Fichte who wrote the note quoted above

cites as his authority "the Autobiography of Henry Stephens." But who was Henry Stephens, auditor of Fichte and describer of his lecture manner? In the *Dictionary of National Biography* (reissue, XVIII, 1061) I found that the most prominent Henry Stephens in the last century was an authority on agriculture who lived during the years 1795–1874 and was the author of *The Book of the Farm* (1844), the standard textbook on farming in the Victorian age, often reprinted both in England and America. Not much that is Coleridgean here; but the *DNB* states also that Stephens had toured the Continent in his youth (1818–19). Fichte died in 1814, but four years afterwards Stephens could still have met with students of his in Germany and heard of this enthusiastic idealist and his striking manner of teaching, and this might be mentioned in his autobiography. But where was his autobiography, cited by the translator of Fichte? The *DNB* refers to an autobiographical preface to the second edition of his book (1849–51). I looked in vain for this edition in libraries accessible to me in the States, and finally found it in the library of the British Museum. Unfortunately the autobiographical preface contains very few details of his visit to the Continent, and absolutely no mention of any German philosopher asking his pupils to "think of the wall."

Having reached a dead end I turned back to my source, Smith's translation of Fichte, and considering it from all angles I now noted that it was the fourth edition of the work. So I looked up the first edition (1848), which of course is in the library of the British Museum, and there found the key to the puzzle: an unforeseeable translation of a German surname into an English one. The man who had described Fichte so vividly was not Henry Stephens, but "Henry Steffens"! [9] Light at last dawned upon me. (In a case like this, it is hard to avoid lapsing into the manner of J. L. Lowes.) Steffens, the German *Natur-philosoph*, whom in later years Coleridge was to praise so warmly: "the clear-headed, perspicuous Steffens, whom I love and honor with heart and head" (*BL*, 2, 399; cf. *CL*, IV, 792) and from whom he was to derive ideas for his *Theory of Life*;[10] Steffens was of course a contemporary of Fichte and must have known him. Sure enough, I found at the Museum Steffens' diffuse *Autobiography* (*Was ich erlebte*, 1840–44) in no less than ten volumes, a work so much admired in its day that there is a contemporary English abridgement of it (1863). And there, in the complete text, is a passage quoted in Smith, describing Fichte telling his students to "think of the wall" at Jena, in the year 1799 (IV, 78–80).[11]

But the date of the *Autobiography* is 1840 *et seq.* and the passage in question is in the volume of 1841. So Coleridge in 1801 could not have seen it. However, Coleridge studied in Germany for a semester in 1799, the year in which Fichte was lecturing at Jena; at Göttingen Coleridge associated with German students, nor did he ever conceal from them his deep interest in philosophy: he spoke of nothing else, according to Carlyon who was there with him. Is it not possible that he heard of Fichte's manner of lecturing from some fellow-student who had attended Fichte's lectures at Jena? Fichte's lectures were very popular, he was followed eagerly by many students, and the injunction "think of the wall—think of yourself" is striking enough to be remembered by any one who had heard it. As we saw, one auditor, Steffens, was impressed so deeply by it that he remembered it vividly in all its details thirty years later. A student who heard it less than a year before could have reported it to Coleridge.

All this of course is likely, but still hypothetical. However, we do not have to rely only on a possible oral source for Coleridge's acquaintance with this dictum of Fichte's. There are printed sources available, well anterior to Steffens' *Autobiography*: Fichte's own publications. The injunction to think of the wall, and then of oneself, is to be found in his *Attempt at a new exposition of the Doctrine of Science* (*Versuch einer neuen Darstellung der Wissenschaftslehre*) published in 1797.[12] In it Fichte repeatedly invites the reader to think of some common object, such as a wall, and then to think of himself. The passage that perhaps comes nearest to Coleridge is: "When you thought of your table or your wall (*deine Wand*), you, my intelligent reader, *you* who are conscious to yourself of the activity of your thought, you were yourself *the thinker* in your thinking; but *the thing-thought-of* (*das Gedachte*) was for you not yourself, but something different from yourself. In short . . . the thinker and the thing-thought-of must be two. But when you think *yourself*, you are not only the thinker, but also at the same time the thought-of (*das Gedachte*); thinker and thought-of must therefore be one" (*GW*, I, 522).

But was Coleridge acquainted with Fichte as early as February 1801, date of the entry in the Notebook? Miss Coburn's note tells us that there is no evidence that Coleridge read Schelling as early as 1801 (this is early for Coleridge, for it was in 1801 that he began to grapple with German philosophy). But Schelling now turns out *not* to be the source, and Fichte becomes the probable original. Now it was precisely in the month of February 1801 that Coleridge was reading Fichte—to be precise, his *Ueber den Begriff der Wissenschaftslehre* (*On the concept of the Doctrine of Science*) of 1794—and quoting a long passage of it to Dorothy in a letter of February 9, 1801. Here is part of it, in Coleridge's translation (with additions by him), quoted here because it illustrates another aspect of self-consciousness: "The Proposition, A = A, holds good originally only of the I: it is abstracted from the Proposition in the Science of *absolute* Knowledge, I am I—the substance therefore *or sum total of every Thing*, to which it may be legitimately applied, must lie in the I, and be comprehended under it" (*CL*, II, 674; italics mark Coleridge's additions).

It is clear from this that Coleridge was acquainted with Fichte in 1801, but the book that he quotes is not the one that has the Wall passage, and the one that does have the passage is not quoted by Coleridge at this time. However, the uniqueness of the combination of ideas, and the difficulty of finding any other explanation, make the connection with Fichte morally certain.[13]

iv

LET US NOW COME to another question, which also is connected with Fichte.

In a remarkable entry of December 1804 (*NB*, II, # 2382)

Coleridge discusses the classification of mental faculties made by previous philosophers, beginning with the most common division of three faculties: feeling, perception, and thought. (Imagination is here identified with perception, in keeping with Kant's first *Critique*; the creative imagination is not considered.) Now some philosophers make the first faculty, the most fundamental, and reduce to it all other mental acts. Others reduce the first and the third faculties to the second, and make all mental acts derive from perception. Others again, and these include Fichte, reduce all the other faculties to thought—pure abstract thought, it may be added. At this point Coleridge affirms emphatically: "My *Faith* is with Fichte!"—a full conversion to idealism if it had been maintained. "But," he immediately adds, "never let me lose my reverence for the *three distinctions*, which are human & of our essence, as those of the 5 senses."

The discussion continues, and Coleridge adds two other faculties to the list, Will and Action.[14] He does not return here to Fichte; but this note shows how seriously he considered Fichte's philosophy, even if he did not pin his faith on him. It is also a correct interpretation of Fichte to say that according to him all so-called faculties are reduced to thought: as we have seen in Kant, all mental acts must be accompanied by the *I think*, which is the basic act of consciousness. This is also true of later formulations of absolute idealism such as Gentile's, against which Croce also maintained his "reverence" for the distinction of mental acts, not in a psychological but in a transcendental sense.

In the intellectual autobiography that Coleridge sketched out in Chapter IX of his *Biographia Literaria*, he fully acknowledged the deep effect that Kant's philosophy had upon him. Kant's thoughts, as we saw, "took possession of me as with a giant's hand" (*BL*, I, 99). Yet he also acknowledged that there were passages in Kant which he did not fully understand, at least for a time: "The few passages that remained obscure to me, after due efforts of thought (as the chapter on *original apperception*), and the apparent contradictions which occur, I soon found were hints and insinuations referring to ideas, which Kant either did not think it prudent to avow, or which he considered as consistently left *behind* in a pure analysis, not of human nature *in toto*, but of the speculative intellect alone" (*ibid.*).

The Chapter of the *Critique of Pure Reason* here referred to, is either the whole of the Transcendental Deduction of the Categories, designated by Coleridge through its most important doctrine, the Transcendental Unity of Apperception, or (according to Sara Coleridge) the specific # 16 of the Deduction as given in the second edition of the *Critique*, viz. the paragraph entitled "# 16, The Original Synthetic Unity of Apperception" (*BL2*, I, 264*n*). From the point of view of the doctrine it does not matter very much whether the whole section or the specific paragraph is intended; both present definitely the doctrine of self-consciousness as "the highest principle in the whole sphere of human knowledge" (# 16, B 135).

Whatever the version, first or second edition, in which Coleridge originally read the "Unity of Apperception," he declares that he had some difficulty with it; but he goes on to say that he "soon" found an explanation for it. It was either a doctrine "which Kant . . . did not think it prudent to avow," or which was necessitated by the limitations of the purely theoretical approach of the *Critique of Pure Reason*. Let us take these two explanations in turn.

1) What could there be in the doctrine of the original, or transcendental, apperception, that Kant found it prudent to suppress? Some clue is given by Coleridge in the passage immediately following: "He (Kant) had been in imminent danger of persecution. . . . The expulsion of the first among Kant's disciples, who attempted to complete his system from the University of Jena," proved that Kant's "caution was not groundless" (I, 100). Also, when Kant was asked to settle disputes among his interpreters "by declaring what he meant," he politely declined "the honors of martyrdom" (I, 101).

The disciple of Kant referred to is obviously Fichte. As Shawcross reminds us, he "in 1798 was driven from Jena on a charge of Atheism" because of his defining God as merely "the moral order of the Universe" (I, 246). Kant had himself had a brush with the Prussian government on account of his ideas on religion. But what is there in the doctrine of original apperception that can concern religion to the point of risking a charge of Atheism? Only the inference, which Fichte was to draw later, that the I is the fundamental principle of the universe, thus eliminating the objective Deity of traditional religion. If this is what Coleridge had in mind, then he interpreted the doctrine of apperception in the same way as Fichte did, i.e., in the way of absolute idealism, and so it must have been no longer obscure to him, but simply alien, for Coleridge in spite of vacillations and temptations from different sources, never seems to have abandoned theism completely. This would be confirmed by Coleridge's last statement, quoted above, the reference to Kant's reply to the disputes of his commentators, which is a clear reference to Kant's famous statement of 1799 in the *Allgemeine Literatuzeitung* in answer to Fichte's interpretation of transcendentalism as absolute idealism, rejecting it.

2) On the other hand, we have the alternative hypothesis of a doctrine which was necessarily one-sided because of the limits of the purely theoretical inquiry of the *Critique.* Coleridge developed this point as follows: "Here therefore he was constrained to commence at the point of *reflection,* or natural consciousness: while in his moral system he was permitted to assume a higher ground (the autonomy of the will) as a POSTULATE deducible from the unconditional command, or (in the technical language of his school) the categorical imperative, of conscience" (I, 99).

Since Kant's "moral system," as expounded in the *Critique of Practical Reason* and other writings on ethics, ends by grounding the truths of religion on the Postulate so deduced, Coleridge may still be thinking that the original apperception was unmitigated idealism, grounded on a restricted "analysis . . . of the speculative intellect alone" (I, 99), and therefore to him unpalatable.

But Coleridge's last word throws everything into doubt again. He concludes the discussion thus: "In spite therefore of his own declarations, I could never believe, that it was possible for him to have meant no more by his *Noumenon*, or THING IN ITSELF, than his mere words express: or that in his own conception he confined the whole *plastic* power to the forms of the intellect, leaving for the external cause, for the *materiale* of our sensations, a matter without form, which is doubtless inconceivable. I entertained doubts likewise, whether in his own mind he even laid *all* the stress, which he appears to do, on the moral postulates" (I, 100).

The questioning of the Thing in Itself may be an echo of Fichte's criticism of it, possibly in the version it appears in Schelling, as Sara Coleridge noted.[15] "Plastic" means productive or creative,[16] and the extension of mental creativity to the production of the very material of our sensations is another doctrine of absolute idealism. Finally, the depreciation of Kant's moral postulates ("doubts . . . whether he laid all the stress . . . on the moral postulates") tends to weaken the argument in favor of the existence of God.

All this paragraph therefore would seem to go in the direction of a Fichtean, or Schellingian, idealism. This is confirmed by the presentation, which immediately follows, of Fichte's doctrine as "the key-stone of the arch" of Kant's system: "By commencing with an *act*, instead of a *thing* or a *substance*, Fichte supplied the idea of a system truly metaphysical, and of a *metaphysique* truly systematic" (I, 101). Fichte's Act was of course the act of self-consciousness, the I being aware of itself.

But then Coleridge goes on to say that "his theory degenerated into a crude egoismus" (I, 101), and makes other criticisms of Fichte, in keeping with his generally theistic trend. So we can only conclude that the doctrine of original apperception gave a lot of trouble to Coleridge until he clearly perceived that it led to absolute idealism. This may have attracted him for awhile, as evidenced by some of the statements in the *Biographia* that we have seen above (*W*, 82–85). But finally his theism prevailed and he rejected the idealistic thesis, though on grounds the logic of which is not apparent.

Like Kant, Fichte relies upon the faculty of the imagination to round out the process of cognition. As in Kant's first *Critique*, this is not the poetic imagination but a purely cognitive and empirical faculty. In Kant, the imagination was almost unconscious, but not entirely. In Fichte an unconscious imagination is introduced to explain the fact that, while philosophy teaches us that it is our mind that creates the world of experience, we ourselves are not conscious of creating it. It is done by the imagination working unconsciously.

This unconscious factor has been taken by some contemporary critics as akin, if not an anticipation, of the Freudian concept of the unconscious. But it is of a different character. The modern unconscious mind is the domain of the irrational, of the instinctive and of all bestiality, and its philosophical ancestor is the arch-pessimist Schopenhauer. But the unconscious or subconscious of the transcendentalists is instead the gateway to the spiritual and even to the divine. Coleridge said it in so many words: "But yet tho' one should unite Poetry, Draftmanship and Music—the greater and perhaps nobler, certainly all the subtler parts of man's nature, must be solitary—Man exists herein to himself and to God alone. Yes, in how much only to God— how much lies *below* his own Consciousness" (*NB*, # 1554, dated 1803; spelling modernized). Hence modern enthusiasm over depth psychology in Coleridge is misplaced.[17]

An important consequence of the elimination of the things in themselves is the disappearance of the distinction between reality and appearance in Kant. Since for the idealists there is nothing beyond what appears to the self in consciousness, appearance is all there is to know in the objective world. There is no such thing therefore as the "representation" of an object; we know the object itself, or what there is of it. So the speech of absolute idealists will sound at times like that of commonsense realists, as Fichte when he says: "of the thing that exists, and that can exist, thou art immediately conscious." But he goes on to say that the thing that exists, and that can exist, is only thought projected by the mind out of itself: "Thou thyself art the thing; thou thyself . . . art thus . . . projected out of thyself; and all that thou perceivest out of thyself is still—

thyself only" (this is in the fervid eloquence of the *Vocation of Man*, Part II).[18] Schelling as we shall see made much of this line of argument.

Intellectual intuition, declared impossible by Kant, is acknowledged by Fichte as an act of the mind, *Handlung* (I, 472), and will gain in importance with Schelling. The result of the rejection of these Kantian distinctions is a totally monistic view, overcoming Kant's basic dualism: it is here that the influence of Spinoza is noted by modern historians of philosophy.

There is a very interesting but neglected writing of Coleridge's in which he seems to be attempting the same task that Fichte attempted in his Doctrine of Science, viz., deduce the objective from the subjective. This writing is entitled "On the import of the words Object and Subject" and was published in 1821 in *Blackwood's Magazine*.[19]

In it Coleridge derives the idea of external reality step by step from simple consciousness of self. Nothing more than the elementary data of self-consciousness is required to obtain the notions of "real" and of "external." "In the superinduction of the sense of *outness* on the feeling of the *actual* arises our notion of *real* and *reality*" (p. 291) and "*outness* is but the feeling of otherness (alterity) rendered intuitive, or alterity visually represented" (p. 295). This is not Kant, but it is very much like Fichte. It must be considered an original attempt by Coleridge to construct his own epistemology on lines parallel to those of Fichte but with different steps. Unfortunately after a lively beginning it peters out in a discussion of the problems of terminology and the possibility of ghosts.

We have already seen in the *Critique of Pure Reason* the doctrine of the synthesis of opposites into a third concept which includes both of them, leading to the dialectical movement that proceeds by three stages of trichotomy. We find it again in Fichte, but in a somewhat different manner. Fichte's fundamental principles, the I and the not-I, and the reciprocal interaction of the two, present the reconciliation of opposites that Fichte explicitly marks out as an essential part of his philosophy, beginning with the *Fundamental Principles of all the Doctrine of Science* of 1794, sect. III (*GW*, I, 107). Hegel's dialectic was gradually emerging.

It should be added that Fichte in this work not only deduced the not-I from the I, but he also brought back the most basic of Kant's categories, though in no particular order: i.e., the categories of reality, quantity, substance, causality and reciprocity. Although he rejects Kant's systematic arrangement, Fichte still feels the need to "deduce the categories." We shall see that his successor, Schelling, will also undertake the same task.

Coleridge reproached Fichte for his hostility to "NATURE." That Fichte's philosophy was deficient in this respect was the reason that made Schelling turn to the philosophy of Nature, so Coleridge here agrees with Schelling. In the passage quoted above, Coleridge goes on to say: "while his religion consisted of a mere ORDO ORDINANS, which we were permitted *exoterice* to call GOD; and his *ethics* in an ascetic, and almost monkish, mortification of the natural passions and desires."

The reference to Fichte's religious views makes sense if we, following Shawcross, refer it to an early paper "On the grounds of our belief in a divine government of the universe" (1798), in which God is defined as simply "the moral order of the universe" (*BL*, I, 246). But in his later philosophy Fichte became much more religious and supported Christianity, or at least gave a philosophical interpretation of it. Coleridge does not seem to have given proper attention to these later developments, though they should have chimed in with his own religious concerns. For instance, Part III of Fichte's *Vocation of Man* (1800) is definitely a religious philosophy,[20] but Coleridge apparently noted only the earlier parts, which expound the Doctrine of Science, for he criticised the "equivoque of the word I" (*BL*, I, 247*n*). Religion pervades the whole of the *Anweisung zum seeligen Leben* (1806) and piety inspires its title, translated *The Way to the Blessed Life*; but this is Coleridge's marginalium: "O woful love whose first act and offspring is self! 'I,' and this is not a present 'I am,' but a poor reflection thereof. In his better (days?), *I* taught a better dogma—viz., the generalization of the thou in all finite minds." [21]

Finally, the "monkish mortification of the natural desires" may fit some of the more extreme ethical doctrines of Kant, but it does not do justice to the strong ethical inspiration of Fichte's metaphysics, which we have seen above.

Besides these high ethical conceptions, Fichte had also un-monkish theories on politics and even on economics, with which Coleridge was in part acquainted, but which he apparently did not grasp in their essence, to judge from his critical marginalia in Fichte's *Closed commerical State* of 1800.[22] This is just as well, since they are strongly nationalistic and bear an unfortunate affinity with later German nationalism.[23]

On the whole, it may be said that Coleridge clearly grasped Fichte's central concept of the Act and the dynamic character of his metaphysics, but remained by and large hostile to the more detailed developments of his theory, indifferent to his politics and ignorant of his religious philosophy.

CHAPTER 8

Schelling I—Metaphysics

i

SCHELLING BEGAN as a disciple of Fichte. His earliest philosophical writings (1795–97) are brilliant and lively expositions of the *Doctrine of Science*, much more readable than Fichte's own laborious and scholastic dissertations.[1] Gradually Schelling developed a system of his own. During the years 1797–99, when he taught at Jena and there associated with the German Romantic School, the Schlegels and their friends, he began to bring out his own contribution to idealism in the form of a philosophy of Nature, or *Naturphilosophie*.

Among the writings of Schelling's Fichtean period there is a group entitled *Essays in Explanation of the Idealism of the Doctrine of Science* (*Abhandlungen zur Erläuterung des Idealismus der Wissenschaftslehre*, 1796–97) which made a deep impression upon Coleridge (*W*, 99–100). It is, as its author claimed, a lucid defence of Fichte's system in its difference from Kant, to be recommended even today to anyone who wants a clear account of that position. Coleridge not only made use of it in the *Biographia*, incorporating several of its arguments in his own text, but even made a direct quotation from it, naming both the author and the work—once (*BL*, I, 171, Ch. XII).

In these, as well as in other early writings, Schelling presents a critique of the common doctrine of epistemological realism. This doctrine holds that we perceive objects because they exist outside ourselves, independently of our perception. Schelling asks:—How does perception occur?—Realism, briefly stated, argues that if we see an object it is because the light from that object strikes our eye, producing an image on the retina. This image is transmitted by the optic nerves to our brain, and in our brain somehow perception occurs and we become aware of an image produced by the object. A classic statement of this theory is to be found in Newton's *Optics*.[2] After the image is produced, we go through a process of reasoning, arguing that the image must be caused by an object existing outside ourselves, and we conclude that what we see is a real object.

Schelling observes that if this is true, we never have direct knowledge of the object. What we have is the consciousness of the image transmitted from the retina to the brain, and as we know the inverted image in the retina is not the same as the straight image in our brain. Intermediate stages are then assumed, and at the end of the stages we also assume a process of reasoning by cause and effect. This is anything but direct cognition. At each intermediate step the possibilities of alteration multiply. As to the final process of reasoning by inference from effect to cause, in ordinary experience we are not aware of it, so that doubt may be cast on its actual occurrence.

So realism, instead of guaranteeing the validity of our perceptive process, multiplies the risks of distortion and error, and provides at best an indirect and inferential knowledge of objects. Schelling's idealism instead claims that we have direct and absolutely valid cognition of objects: what we perceive *is* the real object, all there is of it, and not a copy of a reflected image of it.

Schelling calls the doctrine that he is criticizing sometimes Realism, sometimes Dualism, sometimes even by the name of Improper Idealism (*SW*, III, 427). According to him, it results in the belief that, living in a world of transmitted images, we live in a world of illusion: "improper idealism" is "a system that turns all knowledge to illusion" (*loc. cit.*). According to Kant, such was the idealism of Berkeley, since it transformed all experience into a mere illusion (B 71).

In the *Biographia Literaria*, Coleridge accepted wholeheartedly this critique of realism made by Schelling. If this fact is still unacknowledged universally, it may be partly because

Coleridge himself dispersed the arguments in two chapters, 8 and 12, separated by an interval, partly because of the little knowledge of philosophy among the literary students of Coleridge. But all the points that Schelling makes against Realism are repeated by Coleridge in these chapters, with embellishments that do not detract anything from the power of the argument.

The first of Schelling's *Essays* (*SW*, I, 345–63) starts from the Fichtean rejection of the things in themselves. If there are no things in themselves, what are we left with? Only with the representations in our minds, and our mind's activity in organizing them. But, as we have seen in Fichte, these representations are the only real objects, these are the things-in-themselves. The view that they represent something existing outside ourselves is subjected to the above quoted rebuttal of Realism. Schelling insists that the man who believes that his perceptions are mere images of a reality which exists beyond him and which he can never directly attain, lives alone in a world of his own, "surrounded on all sides by ghosts" (I, 362). In Chapter VIII of the *Biographia* Coleridge attacks dualism with the same argument: "it places us in a dreamworld of phantoms and spectres, the inexplicable swarm and equivocal generation of motions in our own brains" (I, 92).[3]

Such a dualism is attributed by Schelling to the orthodox Kantians, degenerate disciples of a great master, just as Leibniz had degenerate disciples: referring to which fact, Schelling makes a Latin quotation which Coleridge liked and repeated: "*Doctrinam per tot manus traditam tandem in vappam desiit*" (I, 358; cf. *BL*, I, 180), thus translated by G. Watson: "A doctrine passed down through so many hands ends as flat wine." Watson also notes: "quotation untraced," [4] but makes no reference to its previous appearance in Schelling, though Sara did (*BL2*, 354*n*).

In *Essay II* (I, 363–74) Schelling starts from the traditional definition of truth as the conformity of mind with its object (I, 365; already in Kant, A 58, B 83), and shows that the perfect, indeed "the only example of absolute conformity of thought and object" is "the I, or self-consciousness," where the object known, "me," is the same as the subject knowing, "I." So that mind (*Geist*) may be defined as "the only thing which is its own object (*Objekt*)" (I, 367), this definition of mind was repeated by Coleridge at least twice (*BL*, I, 184, and *PhL*, 371). And yet Muirhead (p. 94) followed by Whalley[5] considers it original.

Then Schelling makes the following observations, which reappear in later idealistic systems: "however mind is not *originally* object, but absolute *subject*, for whom *everything* (including himself) is an *object*. So must it be. What is an object is something *dead*, inert, that being incapable of originating any action is only an *objective* (*Gegenstand*) of action. Mind can only be conceived in action (those who cannot do that are rightly said to be philosophers without mind, *ohne Geist*); it exists only in its *becoming*, or rather it is itself nothing else but eternal *becoming* (*Werden*). . . . Mind therefore *is* not, but *becomes*, its own object" (I, 367 Italics Schelling's).

The principle that the subject of knowledge cannot become an (ordinary empirical) object is already in Kant (A 402). In the sentences that follow, Schelling goes along with Fichte in rejecting the static concept of Being of traditional metaphysics, and replacing it with the concept of reality as process, as becoming, as *Werden*. The negative conception of the object as essentially "dead, inert" is repeated by Coleridge in a significant passage of the *Biographia*: "all objects (as objects) are essentially fixed and dead" (*BL*, I, 202, ll. 16–17, Ch. VIII).

Thus *Werden* becomes one of the key terms of German idealistic thought. Schelling's development of this concept may be seen in the following quotations from the *System of Transcendental Idealism*, which also inspired much later philosophy: "The I is pure act, pure doing" (*SW*, III, 368), it is "eternal becoming" (p. 376) and "infinite activity" (p. 380), and "philosophy considers intelligence in its becoming" (p. 427). We shall see the echo of these ideas in Coleridge when we examine the influence of the *System* in our following section.

In *Essay III* (I, 375–403) Schelling, still expounding Fichte, brings together theoretical and practical philosophy, criticizing the Kantian distinction between them. Coleridge affirmed the unity of the theoretical and the practical in his MS. "Logic" (II, 91–92). In this *Essay*, some characteristic doctrines of Schelling also emerge, such as his deduction of matter and his concept of "self-organization": the latter will be found in *The Friend*, II, x (pp. 329–30).

Essay IV (pp. 403–443) deals with the problems of Kant's practical philosophy when seen from this unified point of view. From it Coleridge derived another spirited defence of philosophic idealism, and its pp. 403–4, slightly altered, became part of Chapter XII of the *Biographia* (*BL*, I, 178–79). Coleridge interpolated a concrete example of his own: "It is the table itself, which the man of commonsense believes himself to see, not the phantom of a table, from which he may argumentatively deduce the reality of a table, which he does not see. If to destroy the reality of all that we actually behold, be idealism, what can be more egregiously so, than the system of modern metaphysics, which banishes us to a land of shadows, surrounds us with apparitions, and distinguishes truth from illusion only by the majority of those who dream the same dream?"

Coleridge inserts here a reference to an English character,[6] then goes back to the *Essay*. There Schelling says: "To this *original* realism we refer you. This believes and intends nothing else, than that the object, which you represent, is also and at the same time the real object" (III, 403). Coleridge translates, even more emphatically: "It is to the true and original realism, that I would direct your attention. This believes and requires neither more nor less, than the object which it beholds or presents to itself, is the real and very object" (*BL*, I, 179).

Such plain statements of Schellingian idealism should be perfectly unmistakable. Yet they have been mistaken, and their Schellingian derivation ignored. On a previous page Coleridge —here too translating Schelling—had rejected the thesis of realism "That there exist things without us" as a "presumption" and a "prejudice" (*BL*, I, 177): again a plain statement of idealism. But the realistic thesis "That there exist things without us" has been taken by another literary student of Coleridge as a statement of Coleridge's own point of view ("Hence Coleridge asserts . . ."). The sentence on "true and original realism" is then quoted in entire ignorance of its idealistic bearing.[7]

Finally, in the *Essay IV*, Schelling advances an *argumentum ad hominem* to convince the reader to accept idealism: "you should feel that you are worth a better philosophy" than this crude realism. This appeal to the reader aroused the preacher always dormant in Coleridge, and he translated: "Oh ye that reverence yourselves, and walk humbly with the divinity in your hearts, ye are worthy of a better philosophy!" (*BL*, I, 179). What follows immediately—"Let the dead bury their dead"— may sound like a continuation of the same Coleridgian homily, but it is genuine Schelling, as is the appeal to "preserve your human nature" (*ibid.*).

Having thus come to somewhat deep waters, Coleridge turns for help to his projected *Logosophia*, the complete system of philosophy and theology (or theodicy) which he repeatedly announced. This work, he says here, will be a new version of "the system of Pythagoras and of Plato, purified from impure mixtures." Then follows the Latin quotation which we have seen Coleridge (I, 180) deriving from Schelling (*SW*, I, 358), although in a different context.

It is from the last page of *Essay IV* that Coleridge takes the quotation from Schelling: "To remain unintelligible to such a mind, exclaims Schelling on a like occasion, is honour and good name before God and man" (I, 169).

But the occasion is more than "like," it is identical: the whole of the preceding page, as noted by Sara (*BL2*, pp. 341–42, *n.*), is translated from Schelling. Coleridge then goes on to give another paragraph from Schelling, with due acknowledgment: "the same writer observes" (I, 169).

These pages of Schelling stress the difficulty of communicating his system to "a man who is not *filled* with the consciousness of freedom" (*SW*, I, 443; *BL*, I, 168), i.e., to a man who has not become aware of the "original intuition" which is the basis of all certainty. This gives rise to the quoted remark upon the honor which this lack of intelligence confers upon the philosopher of freedom.

Finally we come to Coleridge's one complete quotation

from the *Essays* by author and title: it is made for the definition of a postulate (I, 171–72; noted by Sara, p. 344*n*). This derives from the appendix to the *Essays*, entitled "Postulates in philosophy." Three pages of it (*SW*, I, 444–46) are translated by Coleridge with some slight modifications and an explanatory interpolation (*BL*, I, 171–73). They define the difference between "construction" in geometry and in philosophy: an important question of philosophical method which had been raised by Kant. However the goal of the idealists is much broader than Kant's: they aim at "deducing" or "constructing" the world from the Idea. "Construction" means a priori reasoning from established general principles, in the manner of Euclid's geometry, proving each new proposition by means of the preceding ones. The ultimate principle in this passage of Schelling's is shown again to be self-consciousness. At the end of these pages, Coleridge goes off on his own tack: he quotes Plotinus on Nature creating the world by contemplation,[8] and brings in his favorite line from Juvenal about "knowing thyself" (*BL*, I, 268). Then he turns to the later Schellingian version of this argument in the *System of Transcendental Idealism* (*BL*, I, 174 ff.), to which we shall come in the next section of this chapter.

To conclude upon these borrowings from the *Essays*: direct quotations from Schelling are few and made mainly on secondary points, while the meat of the argument is incorporated without acknowledgment.

Let us now come to the real "meat of the argument," viz., the formulation of idealism which Schelling first presented in his *System of Transcendental Idealism* (1800).

ii

SCHELLING'S ORIGINAL CONTRIBUTION to philosophical idealism was the inclusion of nature in the system of absolute mind and this is what powerfully attracted Coleridge. He felt that Fichte's philosophy did not do justice to the problem of nature.

It was right of Fichte to extricate the principle of the "I" out of the Kantian system, removing it from all inconsistent attributes and associations, and to make it consequently the centre of philosophy. But Kant's aim had been to account for the sciences of nature and to provide them with a solid philosophical foundation. In the idealistic dispensation, what became of the sciences? Nature for Fichte is only the not-I "no more than an obstacle posited by the ego in order that it may have something to overcome." [9] But what we call nature is not something purely negative, it has positive reality, and the sciences of nature display realms upon realms of entities, of forces and of structures to be accounted for. This requirement is Schelling's great merit, his permanent contribution to philosophy, the "positive result" which according to Croce he passed on to Hegel, although the use made of it by Hegel seemed to Croce unhappy.[10] The problem remained for later speculation to solve, although the solution may come not from ontology but from epistemology: not by trying to incorporate the entity "nature" into a system of entities, but by analysing the kind of thinking that produces the empirical concepts of the physical sciences. To say therefore of Schelling that he, "for all his magnificent display of dialectic, is no better than a Kant run wild," as was done by a literary scholar who made valuable factual contributions to this historical question,[11] is to ignore the whole philosophical problem and to misunderstand Kant himself.

For Kant in a work which we have not yet examined, *The Metaphysical Foundations of the Science of Nature* (*Metaphysische Anfangsgrunde der Naturwissenschaft*, 1786), had already provided important concepts towards a new philosophy of nature, rejecting the purely mechanical view based upon Newton's physics which had dominated the eighteenth century. In this work Kant resolved matter into force, eliminating the static concept of a solid, impenetrable, inert substance, and replaced it with the interaction of two opposite forces, attraction and repulsion. The so-called impenetrability of matter is only repulsion, and indeed "all reality of the objects of external sense . . . is to be conceived as moving force" (IV, 523). Kant proclaimed the advent of a "dynamic philosophy of Nature" opposed to the "mechanical philosophy of Nature," rejecting the old atomic theory and "accounting for the specific differences of matter by its own motive power of attraction and repulsion" (IV, 532).[12]

Coleridge acclaimed this view. His marginalium to this passage says: "a great idea and worthy of Kant is contained in the construction of matter by two powers."[13] From this work of Kant's Coleridge also derived the distinction between the two meanings of "nature": 1) essential quality of something, and 2) the totality of phenomena, made in a note to *The Friend* (Sec. II, Ess. 6, *F*, 310).[14]

Here we find the origin of the term "dynamic" which Coleridge gave to his own system of philosophy: "the dynamic philosophy" (*BL*, I, 180), "the Constructive or Dynamic Philosophy in opposition to the merely mechanic" (1815, *CL*, IV, 579), "I call *dynamic* or constructive as opposed to the material and mechanical system still predominant" (1815, *CL*, IV, 589) —a system which he believed to be "no other than the system of Pythagoras and Plato" (*BL*, I, 180). *That* "system" can hardly be said to have historical existence.

Schelling extended the dynamic view, in the sense explained above, to everything, from natural phenomena to the operations of the mind, showing everywhere the action and reaction of two opposing forces.[15] In particular, he applied this principle to the speculative interpretation of nature in a series of writings of the years 1797–99. He even founded journals dedicated to such subjects as "speculative physics" and "scientific (i.e., philosophical) medicine." Coleridge was acquainted with a number of these writings, such as the *Ideas for a Philosophy of Nature* (*Ideen zur einer Philosophie der Natur*, 1797, which the poet owned in an edition of 1803), and *Introduction to the Sketch of a Philosophy of Nature* (*Einleitung zu der Entwurf eines Systems der Naturphilosophie*, 1799: see *CL*, IV, 873).[16] He even owned the journals that Schelling edited on "speculative physics" and idealistic medicine (*BL2*, 398 f.): one can only hope that he did not use them to prescribe for himself.

Finally in 1800 Schelling published his comprehensive *System of Transcendental Idealism* (*System der transcendentalen Idealismus*), which brings together the results of all his previous speculations and unites the two preceding trends, Fichteanism and the Philosophy of Nature. Both are declared necessary, as opposites reconciled in a higher synthesis. The book ends with a novelty: a bold speculation on Art and its function in the universe.

Schelling begins by reaffirming self-consciousness as the fundamental principle of all philosophy and refuting the doctrine of realism. He proceeds to deduce Nature from the absolute self-consciousness by means of what he calls "the productive imagination" (*produktive Anschauung*)—a Kantian term trans-valued—first deducing "sensation" (III, 411) as the self-limita-tion of the absolute subject, followed by a series of other successive limitations called "epochs in the history of self-con-sciousness" and which correspond to the "potences" of nature. The main "epochs" include the deduction of matter (III, 440) and end in the deduction of the living organism (III, 491).

Now the act of self-limitation which produces sensation does not lie within consciousness, i.e., it is an unconscious act (III, 450), an important Schellingian qualification which opens the way for the Unconscious in later speculation. Kant, it may be remembered, had already introduced an unconscious mental activity in the workings of the perceptual imagination (B 103), and Fichte had retained it, in the manner we have seen in the previous chapters.

Schelling then proceeds to deduce time and space, the two Kantian forms of intuition (III, 462), and even the categories, though not in the strict Kantian order. Substance and Accident appear first, as a combination of time and space (III, 469); from Substance are derived Causality (III, 471 ff.) and our old Kant-ian acquaintance, Reciprocity or Interaction (III, 475 ff.). Even Schematism reappears later (III, 508 ff.). Finally, with the emergence of the living organism, a concept derived from the *Critique of Judgment*, we reach the human world, and the second part of the system begins with the philosophy of Mind, which includes a philosophy of Law, a philosophy of History and a philosophy of Art.

Just as there is absolute identity of subject and object in self-consciousness, so there is absolute identity of Mind and Nature in the universe. Nature is only unawakened Mind, and Mind is Nature that has achieved consciousness of herself. Identity is one of Schelling's key terms, and his philosophy, at this stage, is known as the philosophy of identity. Later, as in the book on *Freedom* (1809), the term Indifference (*Indifferenz*) becomes prominent. It means "absence of all difference," so that the Identity of Mind and Nature becomes the Indifference of Mind and Nature. This term Indifference appears also in Coleridge's later writings on the philosophy of Nature.[17]

For the apprehension of this absolute Identity Schelling postulated a special faculty which he called "intellectual intuition" (III, 369). He borrowed the term from Kant, who however denied that there was any such metaphysical faculty (B 307). It is remarkable that Coleridge goes out of his way to side with Schelling against Kant on this point: "I take this occasion to observe, that here and elsewhere Kant uses the term intuition . . . exclusively for that which can be represented in space and time. He therefore consistently and rightly denies the possibility of intellectual intuitions. But I see no adequate reason for this exclusive use of the term, I have reverted to its wider signification, authorized by our elder theologians and metaphysicians, according to whom the term comprehends all truths known to us without a medium" (*BL*, I, 190).

The reference to the "elder metaphysicians" should not mislead: "Intellectual intuition" is a key term in Schelling. This passage was rightly interpreted by Wellek (*W*, 87), who was the first to note that Coleridge criticizes Kant from the point of view of Schelling (*W*, 80 and 95–101).

The *System* concludes with a philosophy of Art which asserts that the *aesthetic* imagination (to be distinguished from the *productive* imagination which is active in the construction of the physical world) is the highest organ of cognition in man, being even higher than philosophy, for it is only through art that we attain to the identity of Nature and Mind, of the conscious and the unconscious, which is the essence of reality.

But what Coleridge took from this work when he was composing Chapter XII of the *Biographia* and laying the philosophical foundations for his theory of the imagination, is mainly from Schelling's earlier chapters in which he is still close to Fichte. From them Coleridge drew heavily, without acknowledging that he was quoting from another man's book. This gave rise to the charges of plagiarism hotly debated in the nineteenth century and not entirely extinct today. We shall therefore make a detailed analysis of the text of these passages and also discuss the ideas presented in them, in order to assess the extent of Coleridge's indebtedness and to evaluate the consequences for his philosophy.

The positive approach used by Schelling to maintain his idealistic doctrine was already in Fichte and in Berkeley, but Schelling developed it in a remarkable way. Instead of concentrating on the refutation of the doctrine of an external reality, Schelling stressed the positive argument that the world we know in perception *is* the real world, and common sense is right in believing it so. Thus he neatly turns the tables on the realists, who usually claim that their doctrine is the doctrine of common sense and that idealism runs counter to all the assumptions of everyday life. Schelling becomes eloquent in his plea that idealism is the same as common sense and that it is realism that claims that we live in a world of illusion.

So far this is Kantian (cf. A 372). But Schelling goes on to argue that beyond appearances there is nothing—no things in themselves, no objective reality to fall back upon. The notion of a reality beyond appearances is declared a doctrine of the schools and a construction of the theoretical intellect, not the faith of common sense, and not a direct perception (it cannot be so by definition).

Coleridge follows Schelling faithfully in rejecting external reality and asserting absolute idealism as the faith of common sense, "the true and original realism." He had already presented in Chapter VIII the Schellingian critique of realism, i.e., the theory that "a thought" is explained by "the image on the retina, and that from the geometry of light, if this very light did not present the same difficulty" (*BL*, I, 92). What the "same difficulty" is, will perhaps be made clearer by another passage from Schelling, who, discussing the realistic theory of perception, says: "We only see because the light touches our eyes, etc.—But what then is light itself? Again an object!" (*SW*, I, 389; *Abh*. III), i.e., something external that also has to be turned into something internal, by a process that realism cannot explain. For: "In the first place, by its action on the percipient, or *ens representans*, not the object itself, but only its action or effect, will pass into the same. Not the iron tongue, but its vibrations pass into the metal of the bell. Now, in our immediate perception it is not the mere power or act of the object, but the object itself, which is immediately present" (*BL*, I, 90).

The first and third sentence are literally translated from the *System* (*SW*, III, 428; cf. I, 377), but the second, with its striking simile of the bell, is Coleridge's own contribution to *Erläuterung des Idealismus*.

Coleridge repeated Schelling's arguments against materialism, "a system which could not but be patronized by the philosopher, if only it actually performed what it promises" (*BL*, I, 90 = *SW*, III, 407). On Matter itself, a striking statement of Coleridge's —"Matter has no *Inward*"—with what follows (*BL*, I, 90), is also translated from Schelling: "Daher die Materie kein *Inneres* zukommt," with what follows (*SW*, I, 379, *Abh*. III). According to Schelling's idealism, "inwardness" belongs only to the mind, because only the mind can turn back on itself and reflect upon itself, thus acquiring "an inner world" (*loc. cit.*).

In translating Schelling, Coleridge naturally adopts his terminology, and talks of his own philosophy as "transcendental" and of himself as a "transcendental philosopher" (e.g., *BL*, I, 177 and 186), so that he had little reason to complain in 1825 that "I must be content to remain a high German Transcendentalist." [18]

From the first section of Schelling's "Introduction" Coleridge translates a preliminary discussion on the dilemma which faces the transcendental philosopher at the beginning of his speculations: shall he make his start from Nature or from Mind? This alternative may be said to go back to Kant, when he stated at the outset of the *Critique of Pure Reason*, second edition, that we can either start from the assumption that "our knowledge must conform to objects" or, alternatively, from the assumption "that objects must conform to our knowledge": the former is traditional, the latter is the Copernican revolution that Kant was introducing in epistemology (B xvi). In Schelling however the alternatives are metaphysical: do we deduce Mind from Nature or Nature from Mind? The two possibilities are then formally stated and discussed.

The first alternative (starting from Nature) will lead, according to Schelling, to a philosophy which is "the perfect spiritualization of all the laws of Nature into laws of intuition and of intellect" (*SW*, III, 340 = *BL*, I, 175). This process is already observable in modern science: "the phenomena themselves become more spiritual. . . . The optical phenomena are but a geometry, the lines of which are drawn by light, and the materiality of light itself has become a matter of doubt. In the appearances of magnetism all trace of matter is lost; and of the phenomena of gravitation. . . . there remains nothing but its law" (*SW*, III, 341 = *BL*, I, 176). The conclusion is: "The theory of natural philosophy would then be completed, when all nature was demonstrated to be identical in essence with that, which in its highest known power exists in man as intelligence and self-consciousness" (*BL*, I, 176, expanded from *SW*, III, 341). "This," as Wellek notes (*W*, 284), "is Schelling in substance, now follows Coleridge: 'when the heavens and earth shall declare not only the power of their Maker, but the glory and presence of their God'": a characteristic lapse of Coleridge into Biblical language and traditional theodicy.

To return to Schelling's argument. The first alternative of the dilemma posed at the beginning turns out to be essentially identical with the second: Nature turns out to be Mind. Possibly to balance this, Schelling directs the discussion of the second alternative into a critique of realism, or the belief in the existence of external reality. Coleridge translates this passage faithfully, and adds to it: he criticizes "the assumption of impresses or configurations in the brain, correspondent to miniature pictures on the retina painted by rays of light from supposed originals, which are not the immediate and real objects of vision, but deductions from it for the purposes of explanation" (*BL*, I, 177, Ch. XII). From this vantage point in Schelling's idealism, Coleridge could look down upon his early empiricist masters, such as Hartley with his *vibratiunculae*.

Coleridge also adds a reference to Descartes to support the argument. Then realism is refuted by Schelling on the grounds that the belief that "there exist things without us" itself implies self-consciousness, or awareness of that self, outside which we assert that things exist; he concludes by reverting to self-consciousness as the fundamental principle of philosophy.

At this point Coleridge evidently felt that some further discussion of realism was called for, so he turned back to the *Essays*, where the question is treated more fully. From them he brings in Schelling's argument that idealism agrees with common sense. As we have seen above, he translates Schelling with some omissions and some explanatory interpolations.

Then Coleridge returns to the *System*; but now he follows it less closely. In one of the marginalia to Schelling's Introduction, Coleridge noted: "True or false, this position is too early. Nothing precedent has been explained, much less proved true" (*BL*, I, 269). He may have felt that Schelling asserted too many things after the preliminary discussion of the two alternatives, and did not feel he could follow him step by step. In any case, in the *Biographia*, Chapter XII, he proceeds to condense a dozen pages or so of the *System* into a series of Theses, numbered I to XII. These theses are an abstract of Schelling with some explanatory interpolations, and a larger number of personal additions and corrections than we have met with so far, reaffirming theistic positions. I will summarize the derivations and the disagreements in the following conspectus.

I. This thesis recalls the definition of truth as the concidence of an object with the subject, from which we started in the preliminary discussion (as well as in the *Essays*, *SW*, I, 365). Coleridge adds: "to know is in its essence a verb active," anticipating Thesis VII.

II. Coleridge takes over Schelling's distinction between conditioned and unconditioned knowledge (III, 362), terming it however "mediate or immediate truth": "the former is of dependent or conditional certainty" (*BL*, I, 180). The Scholium, with the simile of the chain without a staple, and the imaginatively presented argument of the cycle of equal truths, is to all appearance Coleridge's own.

III. The concept of absolute truth is here defined as a truth "which is its own predicate" (I, 181). The relation of the predicate to the subject in an absolutely true proposition is discussed by Schelling in Section VI of page 364, but the bold formula of Thesis III is apparently Coleridge's own.

IV. "That there can be but one such principle, may be proved *a priori*" (I, 181). Schelling affirms this on page 354. At the beginning of the following chapter Schelling argues that this principle cannot be derived from any other principle above it (p. 361), which may have suggested Coleridge's more detailed demonstration of the thesis. The Scholium is Coleridge's own and contains a dig at James Beattie, who thought he could refute Hume by means of mere common sense (I, 182). Beattie, incidentally, turned out to be the source of Kant's knowledge of Hume's *Treatise*, as we saw in Chapter 2.

V. "Such a principle cannot be any THING or OBJECT" (I, 182). This point is made in III, 368, but we saw it more fully argued in the *Essays* (I, 367), in the passage quoted earlier in this chapter. The conclusion of the Thesis is the Schellingian "identity" of subject and object (III, 356).

VI. This thesis is one of the most important, since Coleridge here begins by making a perfect statement of the idealistic doctrine of the absolute self-consciousness, and then brings forward his theistic qualifications to it. First, the affirmation of self-consciousness: "In this, and in this alone, object and subject, being and knowing are identical, each involving and supposing the other. In other words, it is a subject which becomes a subject by the act of constructing itself objectively to itself; but which never is an object except for itself, and only so far as by the very same act it becomes a subject" (I, 183).

Coleridge makes here a classic formulation of the doctrine expounded both in the *Essays* and in the *System* (e.g., III, 364–65). But in the Scholium he makes the qualification that this argument refers only to knowledge and not to existence. Actually the argument provides for that when it says that "the subject *becomes* a subject by constructing itself objectively," since to become is to acquire existence. Coleridge goes on to admit that existence and knowledge can be identified, but this occurs only in "the absolute self, the great eternal I AM," and the footnote makes it clear that the latter is the same Spirit in whom St. Paul said that "we live, and move, and have our being" (I, 184, n.), a text quoted also by Schelling, *On human freedom* (*SW*, VII, 349). The reference which follows to "the conditioned finite I . . . called by Kant's followers the empirical I" (*ibid.*) may well be again to Schelling, who repeatedly expounds the distinction between the absolute I and the empirical I (III, 374–75; also I, 442).

VII. In this thesis Coleridge continues to affirm the doctrine of the absolute self, which being the subject cannot be an object. "It must therefore be an ACT; for every object is, as an *object*, dead, fixed, incapable in itself of any action, and necessarily finite" (I, 184–85). Coleridge has gone back to the *Essays* for reinforcements (I, 367). An act, he goes on to say, implies "a will" (I, 185). A very important new concept is here introduced, that of the Will, which Schelling also introduces later in the *System* (*Wollen*, III, 533 ff.), and had already introduced in the *Essays* (I, 393 and 401). It will assume increasing importance in both Schelling's and Coleridge's later speculations. Not much of it, however, is made here, although it returns in Thesis IX.

VIII. An object is always finite: Coleridge is again going back to the *Essays* (I, 367).

IX. The distinction between the *principium essendi* and the *principium cognoscendi* made here is also made, with the same Latin terms, in the *System* (III, 368), and there also the two are identified. Then Coleridge refers back to the preliminary discussion of the objective and the subjective (I, 185, cf. 174–78). But he ends with a reaffirmation of theism: "We proceed from the SELF, in order to lose and find all self in GOD" (I, 186).[19]

X. This thesis is translated with minor alterations and explanatory interpolations from the *System* (III, 355–56). The translation ends at line 30 of page 187. Coleridge then proceeds to refer to the philosophy of Malebranche, "that we see all things in God" (I, 187, ll. 31–32) and from there he passes on to quote a devotional passage from Synesius' *Hymns* (I, 188). He then reverts to transcendentalism, and envisages a philosophical system which will account for the universe by the interaction of "two opposite and counteracting forces." He concludes: "it will be hereafter my business to construct by a series of intuitions the progressive schemes, that must follow from such a power with such forces, till I arrive at the fullness of human intelligence" (I, 188). This programme was exactly the one that Schelling carried out in his *System* (giving to "intuition" its technical meaning), and Coleridge will return to it in Chapter XIII of the *Biographia*.

iii

THESE HOWEVER ARE not the only translations that Coleridge made from the earlier parts of the *System*. Among his MSS. in the British Museum there is an unpublished sheet which the catalogue entitles "the 'I'" (Egerton 2801, fol. 103). This turns out to be the translation of another early section of the *System* (III, 374–76) made according to Coleridge's usual method, with slight alterations and several explanatory interpolations. The watermark is 1812, so it may have been made in the years when Coleridge was working toward, or at, the

Biographia, and may belong to the same impulse that produced the translations and adaptations in the book. The text ties up very closely with the argument that Coleridge took over from Schelling and after quoting it we will take up the question why, if this is so, Coleridge did not incorporate it in that or any other writing of his. His additions are printed in bold type; notes mark his alterations.

THE "I"

"The conception, *I,* involves a far higher [*sic*] than the mere expression of Individuality—it is the act of Self-consciousness, **genetically, absolutely,** coinstantaneous with which the consciousness of Individuality will doubtless introduce itself, **as its Shadow or Derivative,** but which doth itself contain nothing Individual. For we are now speaking of the **Absolute I**—and this is no other than the **eternal** Act of Self-consciousness in its universality—and from this, **as from its creative source,** all Individuality must be derived.

"Still less under the I, as Principle, must be understood [20] the empirical (*experienced*) I, the I which presents itself to an empirical **or natural** consciousness. The *pure* consciousness variously determined, **conditioned,** and limited, gives the empirical—the latter is differentiated from the former by its limits only[21]—remove the limits, **or outline** of the empirical I, and there remains the I absolute, **Illustrated by concentric circles:—**

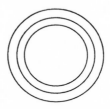

But the pure self-consciousness is an Act, which lies *out of* all Time, **yea,** it is that which constitutes Time; **while** the empirical Consciousness is that which is self-generated *in* Time and in the succession of representations—*Fit et facit, creat et creatur.* **They differ as Time and Eternity, as Man and God.**

"The question whether the I is a Thing (**a reality,** το οντως ων) or a Phaenomenon = **Appearance,** is senseless. It is in no sense any thing, neither Thing in itself, nor Phaenomenon, **neither Substance,** nor Apparition [Appearance *erased*], neither Body nor Soul—It is *Spirit*. The imagined Dilemma—whatever is thought of, must be thought of as Something or Nothing—rests on an Equivoque in the term "Something"—If by "Something" be meant something real in contradistinction from the merely imaginary, the I must doubtless *be* something Real, inasmuch as it is the very *Principle* of all Reality. But for this very cause that it is the *Principle* of Reality it cannot be real in the same sense with those Realities that are its products and derivatives. The reality, which alone the modern Metropothecaries and Physiologists admit, that which alone they *mean* by the word,[22] is merely a borrowed Entity, and only the *Reflection, the* Echo of that higher Reality which is its Principle. The Dilemma therefore, attentively looked at, reduces itself to this assertion: All is either a *Thing*, or it is a Nought; but this is evidently false inasmuch as there exists a higher conception that that of a THING, namely that of *Act*, POWER, FORCE, of which diversely inlineating and configuring the Things themselves are only the Modifications, or *Words*.[23]—All Space filling is in its very term an *Act*—and such and every *Thing* is only a given, a determinate *degree* of activity, by which a given Space is filled.

"It is for this reason that[24] we cannot say of the true I that it *exists:* for it is the *Ground* of Existence—it *gives existence* in all Things, but *is* not itself. The eternal "I AM," or the *timeless* Act of Self-affirmation, needs no Being to support it, has no Substance or Substratum, but self-upborne, self-sustained, reveals itself *objectively*, as the eternal *Becoming, subjectively*, as the INFINITE PRODUCING!"

Among the explanatory interpolations, the most noteworthy is the quotation "fit et facit, creat et creatur," which is from Scotus Erigena. Coleridge's acquaintance with this medieval Neoplatonic theologian[25] dates from 1803, when he read him with enthusiasm: "I have received great delight and instruction from Scotus Erigena. He is clearly the modern founder of the School of Pantheism—indeed he expressly defines the divine Nature, as *quae fit et facit, et creat et creatur (CL*, II, 954)." This quotation (without the name of the author) is twice repeated in *The Friend (F*, 90, 1st Landing, Ess. 3, and *F*, 313, Sec. 2, Ess. 7) and appears also elsewhere (*AP*, 58).[26]

The "illustration" of the diagram of concentric circles is also Coleridge's addition. "Metapothecaries" is a word coined by Southey and adopted by Coleridge in 1801 (*CL*, II, 168).

While some of Coleridge's interpolations give a more definite theistic coloring to the text, it is possible that in time he realized that the "I" in that text was not a personal God but an idealistic absolute, which Coleridge found he could not accept. This may be the reason why he never made any further use of this text.

iv

CHAPTER XIII of the *Biographia* takes up the philosophical argument where it had been left off at the end of Chapter XII. The new chapter begins: "Descartes, speaking as a naturalist, and in imitation of Archimedes, said, give me matter and motion and I will construct the universe. . . . In the same sense the transcendental philosopher says: grant me a nature having two contradictory forces, the one of which tends to expand infinitely, while the other strives to apprehend or *find* itself in this infinity, and I will cause the world of intelligences with the whole system of their representations to rise before you" (I, 195–96).[27]

This again is Schelling, translated, with explanatory interpolations, from the *System* (III, 427). The paragraph sums up the fundamental principle of Schelling's System: the interaction of two opposing forces which, repeated at different levels, produces all that is, both in the realm of Nature and in the realm of Mind. It is Schelling's characteristic procedure and Coleridge here adopts it unreservedly. The *System* follows this interaction in its successive phases, step by step, in a series of elaborate arguments which make up the body of the book.

Even the details of these arguments did not pass unnoticed by Coleridge, for he adopts from them two philosophical puns on German terms, one on *Emfpindung* (sensation) and one on *Urteil* (judgment).

Schelling, discussing the genesis of sensation, says: "The I therefore will be also able to only find (*finden*), i.e. only feel (*empfinden*), that negative element in himself" (III, 406).

Coleridge used this pun in *Church and State*: "all sensibility is self-finding; whence the German word for sensation or feeling is *Empfindung*, that is, an inward feeling" (Shedd, VI, 139–40).

This is a pun and not a genuine etymology, since the prefix *Emp* in *Empfindung* does not mean "in" or "inwardly," but is an assimilation of *Ent-* which may indicate either beginning or drawing away.

The pun on *Urteil* is still more elaborate. Schelling apparently (as Hegel [28] after him) takes the word to mean *Ur-* (original) *-teil* (partition, division), so that "judgment" is an "original partition" of subject and predicate: "Such an operation is the one very expressively designated by the word *Urteil*, since by means of it we first separate what up to now was inseparably united, the concept and the intuition" (III, 507).

In his unpublished Treatise on Logic Coleridge says: "The 'definition of the term Judgment' is most happily expressed in the Teutonic language by *Urtheil* and the Judgment itself or the judicial faculty *Urtheilskraft*, that is, the power of resolving a thing into its primary and original or constituent parts" (II, 61).

The idea of two fundamental principles, one of which is limited and the other unlimited, which we have seen at the basis of the Schelling-Coleridge view of the universe, probably has its roots in Plato. It is to be found in the *Philebus*, where Plato sets up four principles: the Limit, the Unlimited, the Combination of the two and the Cause which brings them together (23C ff.). This Platonic reference might have suggested to Coleridge some way of connecting the two great systems of philosophy which he admired, the Platonic and the Transcendentalist: a connection which, being based on a philosophical text, might have had a more solid foundation than Coleridge's talk of the two schools, "Platonic and Aristotelian," in the vague and unhistorical meaning which he gave to them. But apparently Coleridge did not make a study of the *Philebus*, though Schelling refers to it (*SW*, I, 356).

The elaborate arguments of the *System* are drastically condensed by Coleridge into one. From the three first expositions of the interaction (III, 392–93, 398 and 436–38) Coleridge gathers the ideas which he sums up in a terse conflict and one resolution. In one passage, Schelling sums it up thus:

"Self-consciousness (the "I") is a struggle between absolutely opposed activities. One which originally goes to the infinite, we will call the real, objective, limitable; the other, which is the tendency to intuit herself in that infinity, is called the ideal, subjective, unlimitable" (III, 398).

Coleridge follows suit (*BL*, I, 197, l. 23–24; cf. also *SW*, III, 433–38).[29] His aim was to show the results of interaction "in the living principle and in the process of our own self-consciousness" (I, 198).

But alas, as Dante said:

> All'alta fantasia que mancò possa
> (*Par.*, 33, 142).

and Coleridge broke off the argument, never to resume it.

By stopping where he did, Coleridge did not even carry out the "deduction" of the Creative Imagination which he had promised the reader. Instead, he wrote a famous letter to himself, with the advice to drop the subject as too difficult for his public (I, 199).

This breakdown at the crucial point, occurring in a book composed in the year 1815, as G. Watson has ascertained and wittily noted, may be designated "the Waterloo of English criticism." [30] Why, it has repeatedly been asked, did Coleridge break off at this point? Not because he felt unable to philosophize, for he went on philosophizing for the rest of his life. Or was it because of his notorious incapacity to ever follow a straight path and bring things to their conclusion? Possibly; but it would then be a psychological failing, and not a rational motive. I am inclined to conjecture a more philosophical, or at least theological motive. Coleridge had reached the brink of the absolute subjectivism which was at the centre of Schelling's idealism. This idealism would have done without the personal God whom Coleridge could not give up. So he stopped here in the *Biographia,* adding only a terse statement on the Primary and Secondary Imagination (which we will consider in the next chapter, together with other aesthetic ideas) and he left the battle with idealistic subjectivism to be fought out elsewhere, in a long series of skirmishes and engagements, of which his later writings, published and unpublished, give an idea, especially his marginalia on Schelling published by Sara (*BL2,* 379–400).

v

LET US NOW summarize in tabular form the derivations from Schelling in these thirty-odd pages of the *Biographia* (I, 168–202) and then venture upon some conclusions. Most of the derivations were noted by Sara, followed and amplified by Shawcross and later scholars.

BL, I.	SW	*Method of incorporation*
168–69	I, 443	Translation; Schelling named.
171–73	I, 444–46	Translation; Schelling named and work cited.
174–78	III, 339–44	Translation with some omissions and explanatory interpolations.
179	I, 403–4	Ditto.
180	I, 358	Latin quotation repeated.
180–84	III, 361–65	Free condensation with corrective interpolations (Theses I–VII).
184n	III, 374–75	Reference to "Kant's followers."
184–85	I, 367	Translation (Theses VII and VIII).
185–87	III, 354–56	Free condensation with explanatory interpolations (Theses VIII–IX). Thesis X is translated with slight alterations.
195–96	III, 427	Translated with explanatory interpolations.
196–97	III, 398	Condensed from a number of passages, the one cited being the closest.
202	III, 626	Adaptation.

This does not look very much like "genial coincidence"—rather, a manipulation of written texts.

Now the fact that Coleridge incorporated Schelling's arguments and ideas in his own book practically without acknowledgment, does not support the charge of plagiarism. That tiresome question has been argued pro and con too often and too long. This is not a matter of plagiarism, but a case of assimilation, carried out in a peculiar manner due to Coleridge's special conditions. To put it in the simplest terms, Coleridge was a peculiar genius; but all geniuses are peculiar, in one way or another. This is the very argument made in favor of Coleridge by his own devoted daughter, and apologist, Sara Coleridge, in the preface to her edition of the *Biographia* (*BL2*, 27), and "peculiar" is the very word she uses. Granting that Coleridge worked in a peculiar way, he also worked under discouraging impediments: "He was bad in health, had constant recourse to opium, was worried by financial difficulties, and had long been separated from his wife." [31] He was too much of a "mixture of carelessness and confusedness," as Sara said (*BL2*, 29*n*), to follow the exact requirements of scholarship all the time, and give chapter and verse references at every point. (We modern plodders may conform to these requirements, but we cannot write a *Biographia Literaria*.) Sara also acknowledged that he was somewhat subject to delusions in matters of authorship, but claimed that it worked both ways (*BL2*, p. 28, *n*. 22). He borrowed, but he usually borrowed creatively, incorporating other men's views with his own views as bricks in a wall, and reaching ultimate conclusions which were essentially his own. As a student of philosophy he often worked in an untidy manner, reading *in* an author (to use Stirling's phrase) as the mood inspired him, rather than going systematically through a treatise. As a thinker, he made his way sinuously between ideas sometimes dimly recollected from books, and ideas which he had glimpsed in a flash of insight, only to abandon them to follow some will-of-the-wisp in an irrelevant digression.

Since all this is well-known today, it should be unnecessary

to go into the statements that Coleridge repeatedly made, especially after he had attracted attention as a lecturer on
criticism, to the effect that he had anticipated Schlegel or Kant
or Schelling, reaching their conclusions before he read them
(e.g., *NB*, II, 2375; *BL*, I, 95 and 102–5, Ch. IX; *CL*, IV, 775
and 792–93). When there is agreement between his ideas and
those of his predecessors, he tended to claim priority: his
opinions were already formed before he read the Germans
(*CL*, IV, 792). But when he comes to reject those ideas, then
his claim is that he always had disagreed with them: "I was
myself taken in by them, retrograding from my own prior
and better lights" (*CL*, IV, 874), so he was always first. He
even affirmed that support for his claims would be found in
his "memoranda" and in his "letters and marginal notes." [32]
Alas! to-day we have, in print and splendidly edited, his notebooks from the age of twenty to the age of thirty-six, and his
letters from earlier still. Nowhere is there a trace of the stu-
pendous intellectual feat involved in the anticipation, all by
himself, of the whole development of German philosophy
from Kant to Fichte and to Schelling, even less of his having
anticipated "all the main and fundamental ideas" of these
thinkers.

I have found barely one entry in the *Notebooks* that appears to have even a remote similarity to a thesis of Schelling's
which Coleridge was to know afterwards. In December 1803,
before the earliest reference to Schelling, but after the study
of Kant's theory of space and time, Coleridge was speculating
on space, time, and motion. After a curious experiment which
he describes, Coleridge came to the conclusion that "our consciousness of motion" arises "from the interruption of motion,"
i.e., "the acting of the Soul resisted. Free unresisted action (the
going forth of the Soul) Life without Consciousness, properly
infinite, i.e., unlimited—for whatever resists, limits, and vice
versa. This is (psychologically speaking) SPACE. The sense of
resistance or limitation TIME—and MOTION is a synthesis
of the Two" (*NB*, I, 1771; cf. II, 2402).

This bears a distant resemblance to Schelling's theory of

sensation as a self-limitation of the Absolute Spirit, seen earlier, the act of limiting being subsequently forgotten and sensation falsely attributed to an external cause (*SW*, III, 411). Schelling deduces also space and time from this process of self-limitation (*SW*, III, 462). Perhaps this resemblance, vague as it is, may have given Coleridge the idea, on reading Schelling's theory, that he himself had somewhere said something like it, "toiled out" by himself and written down in his "memoranda," and so given rise to the illusion that he had anticipated Schelling. However, according to Coleridge's hypothesis the "action of the Soul" is resisted presumably by something external—there is no hint of *self*-limitation, as in Schelling. Furthermore, Schelling's theory concerns sensation and not "consciousness of motion" and the process is purely metaphysical, whereas Coleridge is "speaking psychologically." There is no real anticipation of Schelling.

What is true, as we saw in our first chapter, is that Coleridge had philosophical interests before he read the Germans; otherwise they would have meant nothing to him. He read widely in the philosophers that were accessible to him and his early philosophical tendencies, as we know, oscillated between the rationality of empiricism (but not to the extent of atheism) and speculations in the opposite direction, including Neoplatonism and such fantastic systems as Boehme's (but apparently not to the extent of pantheism).

Coleridge's generic and unsubstantiated claims to priority in philosophy were devastatingly criticized by a succession of Victorian critics particularly versed in German thought: Ferrier, Stirling, and Ingleby (the Shakespearean scholar, who in philosophy was a follower of Stirling)—not to speak of Hamilton.[33] Their tone was harsh and magisterial; Ferrier snorted: "Genial coincidences, forsooth!" This severity was due in part to ignorance of some of the facts that have since come to light about Coleridge, and in part to the indignation aroused in a philosophical mind by Coleridge's confusions and evasions, which stood in the way of a clear and adequate presentation of the idealistic systems, especially Hegel's (most of the critics were more or less Hegelians: Stirling strongly so, Ingleby a disciple of Stirling, and Ferrier somewhat sympathetic to Hegel). However, these critics were usually right in their factual statements on Coleridge's derivations and in their rejections of Coleridge's claims to priority. So that Sara, while protesting against the charges of actual plagiarism, candidly acknowledged most of the derivations, and provided material for parallels in her abundant notes to her father's works. Today it is rare that one still hears the old claim to "priority."

A more reasonable claim is to argue that some other philosopher, whom Coleridge read before the Germans, "prepared" him for them; as long as preparation is not a synonym for anticipation. Boehme, for instance, may well have conditioned Coleridge for the wilder flights of *Naturphilosophie* (*BL*, I, 95, Ch. IX), but not for the rigors of the critical philosophy of Kant and the logical deductions of absolute idealism. Neoplatonism of some kind or other may well have prepared the ground for the acceptance of a spiritualistic philosophy, but as Coleridge himself pointed out, it fell far short of the critical point of view (see his quoted observations on the Cambridge Platonists). To say, as some do, that Berkeley had already provided him with Kant's conclusions, is to confound subjective idealism with transcendental idealism. When all conjectures and evasions are set aside, what remains is that Coleridge was the first and most brilliant disciple of German idealism in England.

The fact that Coleridge incorporated so much of Schelling in his own book, either by translation or adaptation, simply means that, at that time, he accepted Schelling's arguments and adopted his philosophy. The frequent explanatory interpolations, the expansions and exemplifications, all go to show Coleridge's participation in the theory and his desire to present it to the reader in the most persuasive way. His own examples, as we have seen, are brilliant contributions to the discussion, and so are the additional arguments which he inserts. At this time Coleridge was an absolute or transcendental idealist. Historically, this is more than remarkable. It is a unique phenomenon in early nineteenth-century England, which has not yet been completely recognized even by historians of philosophy. For instance, the existence of these translations from Schelling has apparently remained unknown to the most recent and fully informed historian of philosophy, Father Copleston, who has this to say on Coleridge in Volume VII of his work: "In Britain the influence of Schelling has been negligible. Coleridge, the poet, remarks in his *Biographia Literaria* that in Schelling's philosophy of Nature and system of transcendental idealism he found a 'genial coincidence' with much that he had worked out for himself, and he praises Schelling at the expense of Fichte, whom he caricatures." [34]

Even in his later and fuller statement on Coleridge in the successive volume, Copleston does not say that the philosophical propositions he quotes from Coleridge are not merely under "the influence of Schelling," which Copleston clearly recognizes, but direct translations. He does conclude that "an important element in the mission of idealism, as conceived by its more religious adherents, was precisely that of giving a metaphysical basis to a Christian tradition," [35] which should make Coleridge one of those religious idealists.

Perhaps a better statement of Coleridge's relation to Schelling would be: "Schelling in Britain made one important disciple, the poet, critic and philosopher Coleridge, who became for a time an enthusiastic follower of his, expounding his philosophy brilliantly and cogently, translating and paraphrasing him in excellent English prose, and then on one side attempting an apologia of Anglicanism grounded on transcendental idealism, and on the other carrying on speculation of his own on the lines of the *Naturphilosophie*." It is surely a great merit in Coleridge as a philosophical thinker that he was able to grasp and assimilate a system of thought so alien, even in its external form, to traditional British empiricism. But one must also add, as we have done repeatedly, that Coleridge never adopted the whole of Schelling's philosophy and that after a while he reverted to orthodox theism, rejecting Schelling's absolute idealism as pantheistic. One interesting fact not generally known is that Schelling himself was well aware that he had found a kindred spirit in England and made in 1847 a gracious acknowledgment to Coleridge (*SW*, XI, 277 and 294; first noted by Pfeiler).[36] Schelling was even aware that Coleridge had made quotations from his works without acknowledgment, but he generously defended Coleridge from the charge of plagiarism, on the grounds of congeniality (*SW*, XI, 196*n*). If Schelling was aware of this fact, why should it remain unacknowledged by modern English philosophers and scholars?

Here is another instance of this ignorance. In a recent anthology of idealistic philosophers compiled by the English philosopher A. C. Ewing[37] (to whose Kantian labors I am much indebted) there are selections from Berkeley and from Kant, from Schopenhauer and from later thinkers, but only a second-hand exposition of Hegel (as if the explanations in the great *Logic* were not sufficiently lucid) and nothing at all of, or on, Schelling (or Fichte, for that matter). What could be better than to give the English reader Schelling in the translations and paraphrases of Coleridge, a master of English prose? Coleridge would then begin to assume his rightful place in the history of philosophical ideas.

CHAPTER 9

Schelling II—Art and Nature

i

WE WILL NOW consider the ideas that Coleridge derived from Schelling in the realm of aesthetics. They are not as many as those on metaphysical topics, but they are important, for they enter into some of Coleridge's best known doctrines in criticism. Here the adaptation of the borrowed material is perhaps greater. But let the reader judge.

Let us begin with the famous summary definition of the Imagination which Coleridge gives at the end of Chapter XIII of the *Biographia,* in place of the more fully developed one which he had announced, and which he still promises he will give in forthcoming works which were never published (I, 202). This definition, such as it is, has been the subject of much discussion in modern criticism, but I believe it will become more intelligible when seen in the light of Coleridge's connection with Schelling.

Coleridge makes a distinction between the Primary and the Secondary Imagination which is parallel to that which Schelling formulated in the last section of his *System* between the "productive intuition" and the "poetic faculty" (III, 626). For Coleridge the Primary Imagination is "the prime agent in all human perception," thus exercising a function analogous to that of Schelling's "productive intuition" (III, 427 ff.), which like Kant's in the *Critique of Pure Reason* is concerned with the cognition of nature, only that in the absolute idealists, Fichte and Schelling, cognition becomes creation. From the productive intuition of the absolute I, Schelling derives, as we saw, the concrete forms of Nature, such as Matter. It might be called the cosmic Imagination.

On the other hand, the Secondary Imagination is the aesthetic or poetic faculty, which, says Coleridge, "dissolves, diffuses, dissipates, in order to recreate"—to *re*create and not to create, because absolute creation belongs only to the primary imagination. Through this process of recreation, "it struggles to idealize and unify." In other passages, where Coleridge was less concerned with general philosophical questions, this inferiority of the poetic imagination to the cosmic is not mentioned, and he stresses instead the dynamic aspects of the poetic imagination, such as its "essemplastic" power (*BL*, Ch. X, I, 107), its capacity to create a unity out of multiplicity, and even a synthesis of opposites (*BL*, Ch. XV, II, 12). Indeed in Ch. VII he ascribed poetry to "a superior degree of the faculty" of Imagination (*BL*, I, 86, l. 13). But here it is only "an echo of the former" (*BL*, I, 202, l. 10).

There is a passage in which Schelling distinguishes between the poetic faculty and the cosmic intuition thus: "The poetic faculty is what in the first potency is original intuition, and vice versa: only the productive intuition, which repeats itself in the highest power, is what we call the poetic faculty. What is active in both is one and the same, the only [faculty] by which we become capable of thinking and understanding even the contradictory—the Imagination" (III, 626) as noted by Wellek.

The term for Imagination is *Einbildungskraft*, while the term for intuition is *Anschauung*, so the two faculties are distinguished even in their name. Yet the distinction seems to consist for Schelling in the fact that Imagination is the broader term, which includes as its species both the poetic faculty and the cosmic intuition. Coleridge does not bring out the unity of the basic power and its inclusion of the other two as its species or varieties, but otherwise his distinction is parallel to Schelling's.

Einbildungskraft is a word that haunted Coleridge. In one of his notebooks he wrote: "How excellently the German *Einbildungskraft* expresses this prime and loftiest faculty, the power of co-adunation, the faculty that forms the many into one—*In-eins-bildung!* Eisenoplasy, or esenoplastic power, is contradistinguished from fantasy, or the mirrorment—repeating simply, or by transposition—and again, involuntary as in dreams, or by an act of will" (*AP*, 236).

This is a remarkable passage for it contains in germ many of Coleridge's basic aesthetic theories and terms, so its date is important. It was dated 1810 by its original editor, E. H. Coleridge; but Miss Coburn's critical edition of the Notebooks has not yet reached 1810. However, the passage may be later if *In-eins-bildung*, as seems likely, comes from Schelling.

This eulogy of the term *Einbildungskraft* has been shown (*W*, 281) to be based on the erroneous assumption that its prefix *Ein-* was derived from *Ein*, one, and that the whole word meant "joining into one" or *In-eins-Bildung;* but etymologically this is not correct, the *Ein-* being not derived from "one" but being instead derived from *In-*, which like the English "in" means "inside, within," the etymology of the whole word meaning "to shape inside, within one's mind."

On this assumption Coleridge also constructed his famous term "esemplastic," making it out of the Greek phrase εἰς ἓν πλάττειν, "to shape into one." As for *In-eins-Bildung*, it is a rare German term, also to be found in Schelling, and in the very same *Philosophy of Art* (V, 390), which contains his definition of *Einbildungskraft* (V, 395). However this work of Schelling's, although given as a course in 1802–3, was not published in book form till 1859, so Coleridge could not have seen it in that form.[1] But *In-eins-Bildung* has been found in other works of Schelling which Coleridge knew: the "pamphlet against Fichte," as it is called by Coleridge (*BL*, Ch. IX, I, 105) and in the *Discourse on Academic Method* of 1807 (*BL*, I, 249).

In Chapter XIII of the *Biographia*, struggling with Schelling's so-called pantheism, Coleridge felt it necessary to add still another kind of Imagination, i.e., God's. Even the primary Imagination, being human, is finite and secondary. It is not really primary, being "a repetition in the finite mind of the eternal act of creation in the infinite I AM" (I, 202)—assuming of

course that the "infinite I AM" is the Christian God and not
the idealistic Absolute. This leaves us finally with three Imag-
inations: 1) God's, as exercised presumably in the creation of
the world; 2) Man's, as exercised in the perception of the
created world; and 3) the Poet's, as exercised in the creation of
poetry.

What the latter is said to "dissolve" and "recreate" can only
be the images received in perception by Imagination No. 2.
Coleridge did not say so explicitly here, but it is an inference of
modern interpreters, in keeping with his general assumptions.[2]

There follows in the *Biographia* the no less famous distinction between the Imagination and the Fancy: this makes a
fourth faculty in this area—Coleridge was not exactly "dis-
carding the heavy German panoply," as Muirhead said (p. 205);
rather, he was making it more cumbersome. Coleridge does
not seem to have derived this distinction from Schelling, although it is in Schelling (V, 395), but not exactly in those
terms and not in any of Schelling's writings that we are certain
that Coleridge read. It is in the above mentioned *Philosophy of
Art*.

We may perhaps conclude that this famous page with its
definitions of the various forms of the imaginative faculty (or
faculties) contains some Schellingian elements, although its
final form is Coleridge's.

Schelling's theory of Art was first presented in his *System*
(1800). Here the function of Art is to resolve the conflict between the conscious and the unconscious (III, 627), and between freedom and necessity (III, 619), by reaching to the
basic Identity of all these oppositions (III, 612). The artistic
faculty, as we saw, is the Imagination, which penetrates to the
ultimate ground of all reality and grasps this Identity of consciousness and unconsciousness. This is proved by the fact that
in the making of a work of art the conscious merges with the
unconscious: part of the work is made with full consciousness
and deliberate art, but part of it the artist produces without
being able to account for it and is therefore unconscious (III,
619). A work which is the result of complete consciousness

and deliberate reflection is artificial and not really a work of art, although fully intentional and obeying all the rules on the surface (III, 620).

Being the result of an eternal conflict between infinite forces, the work of art also partakes of the infinite, and therefore admits an infinite variety of interpretations (III, 620). Thus Schelling definitely anticipates modern poetics in its assertion of the infinite possibility of interpretation, and provides a philosophical foundation for it, although whether the foundation is solid is another question. As may be seen above in the definition of pseudo-Art, Schelling anticipates another modern doctrine: the rejection of the intentional fallacy. This also is given a philosophical foundation by Schelling, and that foundation is also subject to criticism.

Coleridge accepted wholeheartedly but without acknowledgment Schelling's basic conception of art in his Lecture "On Poesy or Art" (1818): "In every work of art there is a reconcilement of the external with the internal; the conscious is so impressed with the unconscious as to appear in it. . . . He who combines the two is a man of genius: and for that reason he must partake of both. Hence there is in genius itself an unconscious activity; nay that is *the* genius in the man of genius" (*BL*, II, 258).

The statement about "unconscious activity" is quoted as a discovery of Coleridge's in the otherwise most perceptive book by Humphrey House, on the same page that House minimizes "anything he learnt from Kant and Schelling." [3] Thus does the ignorance of Coleridge's sources lead even the most intelligent literary critics into error.

It may be proper to give here another instance of the same error, since it concerns another derivation from Schelling. R. L. Brett, in an interesting study of "Coleridge's Theory of the Imagination," wrote: "Coleridge, himself, went so far as to say: 'An IDEA, in the *highest* sense of the word, cannot be conveyed but by a symbol' (*BL*, I, 100)." [4]

Coleridge, himself, derived that doctrine from Schelling. First of all, the quotation should be completed: "by a symbol;

and, except in geometry, all symbols of necessity involve an apparent contradiction."

The corresponding passage is from Schelling's *Abhandlungen, Essay IV*, and it occurs in the argument, which we have seen above, against the Kantian "things in themselves." It was already given in part by Sara Coleridge (*BL2*, 267): "this supersensuous ground of all that is sensuous, Kant *symbolized* by the expression *things in themselves*—which, like all other symbols, contains in itself a *contradiction*, because it seeks to represent the unconditioned through the conditioned, to make the infinite finite."

However, she did not quote the end of the passage, which contains the key term "Idea": "Such contradictory and absurd expressions are, however, the only ones, through which we can generally represent *Ideas*" (*SW*, I, 406).

The one thought in Coleridge's statement that is not in Schelling is the reference to geometry. Otherwise the passage is wholly from Schelling, as noted by Wellek (*W*, 282). Schelling in turn derives from Kant, *Critique of Judgment* # 59.

We can begin to see now the genesis of one of Coleridge's most famous theories about the Imagination: "This power . . . reveals itself in the balance or reconciliation of opposite or discordant qualities" (*BL*, Ch. XIV, II, 12). We have seen above that Schelling defined the Imagination as "the only faculty by which we are able to think and understand even the contradictory" (III, 626). In Schelling, this is grounded on the metaphysical conception of Art as the reconciliation of the basic opposites, consciousness and unconsciousness. Coleridge, in the quoted passage, extends the sphere of reconciliation to "discordant qualities" besides the strictly "opposite," and among the former he includes a number of qualities that a philosopher like Schelling would have considered purely empirical: "the sense of novelty and freshness, with old and familiar subjects; a more than usual state of emotion, with more than usual order; Judgment ever awake and steady self-possession, with enthusiasm and feeling profound or vehement" (*loc. cit.*), which have been the object of much study by modern critics.[5]

No doubt Coleridge might have claimed that here he was being descriptive and suggestive, rather than strictly philosophical; and possibly these pairs of empirically "discordant qualities" might be resolved in more rigorous philosophical concepts; e.g., "emotion" and "order" might be taken to correspond to content and form, or to lyrical feeling and pure intuition. The reconciliation of "the general, with the concrete; the idea, with the image" (*loc. cit.*), which are included in Coleridge's list of pairs, had already been effected by Schelling, as we have just seen, in the Symbol and in other statements on the unity of the universal and the particular.[6] But the Symbol is also essentially poetry, and poetry is essentially symbolic, according to other aspects or developments of Schelling's views: so all these ideas were influential not only on Coleridge but on much more modern poetics. "Symbol" and "Myth" are key terms of Schelling's aesthetic thinking—indeed, "myth" is a key term of his philosophy, from his youthful essay *On Myths* of 1793 to his posthumous *Philosophy of Mythology*.

ii

THE UNION OF the conscious and unconscious in art is also the theme of Schelling's most famous discussion of aesthetics, the 1807 address "On the relation of the fine arts to nature." [7] This academic discourse is a dark, oracular pronouncement, which begins with a critique of the traditional formula "art imitates nature" from a transcendentalist point of view, and ends with a sketch of what will become Hegel's aesthetic: the arts seen as different embodiments of Mind in Sense, and their consequent dialectical development through three stages. The address does not follow an explicit logical framework, but proceeds freely with a continuous flow of ideas, many of them striking and original. Among these we may note the critique of the doctrine of "idealization of nature" (332), of Winckelmann (326 ff. and 337 ff.), of Goethe's theory of the Characteristic (338–41), of Greek tragedy (344–45), the concept of "charm" (342)—perhaps the most "aesthetic" of all—and the concepts of art as Form (329–37) and of Form as organic (330–34).

This Address was used by Coleridge especially in his essay "On Poesy or Art," which was the thirteenth lecture in the course of 1818, as shown by Sara in her notes (Shedd, IV, 482–87). But while Schelling's oration is much broader in scope than Coleridge's fragment, Coleridge touches on a number of topics not discussed by Schelling, such as music and architecture, and introduces ideas of his own, such as the definition of Beauty as "the union of the shapely with the vital" (*BL*, II, 257) and the distinction between imitation and copy, one of his favorite theories (as we saw in Ch. VI, *n.* 14).

To the derivations and parallels faithfully collected by Sara and carried over by Shawcross (*BL*, II, 317–20) I will add another possible reference. Schelling says: "If, as the excellent man of discernment remarked, every natural growth has only one moment of true and consummate existence, we may say that it also has only one moment of complete existence" (333). Coleridge states: "Everything that lives has its moment of self-exposition, and so has each period of each thing, if we remove the disturbing forces of accident. To do this is the business of ideal art." (*BL*, II, 259). This idea of the one perfect moment which the artist must seize may be the idea of the "one moment" in art to which Lessing devotes the third chapter of his *Laokoon*—and Lessing could well be described as an "excellent man of discretion" in an address which has also much to say in praise of Winckelmann.

More important, in view of later developments, is the concept of organic form in art, emerging in Kant as we saw in Chapter 6, and developed by Schelling in the address upon foundations which are ultimately both Platonic and Aristotelian.

iii

In his idea of setting up, within the system of idealism, a philosophy of nature that would show all natural phenomena deriving from a single principle, Schelling was in keeping with contemporary trends within science itself. A number of scientific discoveries seemed at the time to suggest a unified view of all natural phenomena: the new facts of electricity and galvanism seem to indicate a common ground to organic and inorganic nature in a general principle of polarity or the union of opposites; so did connections between chemistry and electricity. There were discoveries or theories in the realm of physiology which seemed to point toward a general principle in the notion of irritability, developed by Haller, or that of excitability, stressed by Coleridge's favorite, Dr. John Brown.[8]

So when Schelling began publishing his speculations on nature, he found followers even among the scientists. There were repercussions throughout the country and abroad, and great was the excitement in the Romantic group at Jena. Friedrich Schlegel wrote to Schleiermacher: "What with religion and Holberg, Galvanism and poetry, we have a pretty lively time of it here." [9] Holberg was a visiting Danish playwright. The excitement was still high in 1807 when a young Italian appeared in Munich, claiming to be a dowser and performing a number of other phenomena before Schelling, his friend Baader and his wife Caroline (ex-wife of August Schlegel), who related all this in her sprightly letters (cf. SW, VII, 487–95). Here was proof apparent of the interpenetration of Mind and Nature! Alas, the youth turned out to be a fraud.[10] But this did not even slow down the triumphant progress of *Naturphilosophie*, which being pure speculation did not need experimental verification. Eventually it degenerated into occultism and magic.

In the *System* Schelling had summed up the results of his previous dissertations on Nature, setting them in an account of the development of consciousness in a series of stages or phases,[11] sometimes called "Epochs" or "Potencies" (*Potenzen*). The three main phases were 1) *gravity*, deduced from the previous establishment of the concept of matter, seen in the preceding chapter; 2) a set of phenomena discovered by the scientific advances already mentioned, i.e., magnetism, electricity, galvanism, and chemistry, all brought under the general category of *Light*, and 3) *organic life*.

Not many natural phenomena are accounted for in the *System*, but Schelling encouraged the deduction of particular natural facts from the general principles of his philosophy, and a considerable number of disciples and adepts followed him on this perilous path. The best known are the naturalist L. Oken; the physicist H. C. Oersted; the theosophist Franz Baader, already mentioned, and Heinrich Steffens, whom we have met in Chapter 7 as an auditor of Fichte and a describer of his way of lecturing; but there were many others, both in Germany and outside. They form quite a long list in the fuller histories of philosophy.[12] This whole movement is called *Naturphilosophie* in a broad sense of the term, and it was a part of Schelling's system that made a deep impression on Coleridge and stimulated him to similar speculations.

These begin in *The Friend* (Sec. II, Essays 5 to 7). He there criticizes Linnaeus for not having perceived "the central Idea of vegetation itself" (*F*, 310, Sec. II, Ess. 6). Both botany and zoology are smothered under a multiplicity of particular facts not unified by any general Idea connecting the vegetable and animal kingdoms (*F*, 312, Sec. II, Ess. 6). And so on. This philosophy was developed in the years 1816 and following, in letters to Gillman in 1816 and to Tulk (who later was to translate Oken) in 1817 and 1818, and in other writings. The whole system has been reconstructed and logically presented—in so far as it admits of logical presentation—from the printed texts alone, by C. W. Miller in a recent paper.[13] A specimen of it will be found in the letter to Tieck of July 3, 1817 (*CL*, IV, 750–51), quoted early in our first chapter.

Coleridge's system of Nature is basically a development of *Naturphilosophie*, not only from Schelling but also from other members of the group with whom Coleridge was acquainted. "Of the Natur-philosophen," he wrote in 1817, "I think very highly," with some reservations; and among the members of the school he mentions, besides Schelling, also Steffens and Baader.[14] He concludes with his habitual claim of having formed his opinions in this field "before I was acquainted with the schools of Fichte and Schelling" (*CL*, IV, 792); and he may be referring to opinions formed in his youthful reading of Böhme, in whom there are many wild fancies of the kind. But in the mature Coleridge Schellingian conceptions, such as the key concepts of Identity and Indifference, are prominent, and most of all the attempt to interpret nature in terms of mind, by means of the construction of intermediate stages as the products of opposing forces.[15] His main difference from Schelling at this point is his Theism, his assertion of the Trinity—even if the three persons are interpreted as Ipseity, Alterity and Community (Boulger, 133–36).

The main fallacy of *Naturphilosophie* from the point of view of modern critical idealism is that the concepts of the natural sciences cannot be reduced to mental concepts, or philosophical universals, nor can they be brought by any device of dialectic into a single system with them, since the concepts of science are empirical or pseudo-concepts, as Croce called them, and the concepts of the philosophy of Spirit are speculative and universal.

Among the published works of Coleridge there is one which is definitely a specimen of *Naturphilosophie*: *The Theory of Life*, published posthumously in 1848 by a physician, Dr. S. B. Watson. Its actual date of composition has not yet been settled; but its central idea, that life is to be defined as a process of individualization, is already set out in the letter to Gillman dated 10 November 1816 (*CL*, IV, 690) and pages of it are in Coleridge's philosophical Lectures for 1819 (*PhL*, 339–44).[16]

The sources of this work were thoroughly analyzed by the same Swiss scholar, H. Nidecker (Ch. VII, *n.* 10), who edited Coleridge's marginalia in the years 1927–33. The genesis and transmission of this work are not perfectly clear; Nidecker believed it authentic, but made up from talks, notebook entries and translations from the *Naturphilosophen*, mainly Steffens, who in turn derives from Schelling. Only a few pages are directly taken from Schelling, with the usual slight modifications, and no acknowledgments: they refer to assumed experimental confirmations of the idea that magnetism corresponds to the spatial dimension of length and electricity to surface (Shedd, I, 413–14; *SW*, IV, 15–19), and are from the *Allge-*

meine Deduktion des dynamischen Prozesses (1810), not usually listed among the works owned by Coleridge. Another borrowing is the classification of different kinds of motion (Shedd, I, 392*n*) that Beach found in Schelling's *Ideen zur einer Philosophie der Natur* (*SW*, II, 28–29), which was one of the books owned and annotated by Coleridge.[17]

In the *Theory of Life* Coleridge endeavors to explain the nature of Life by means of a purely philosophical concept, the principle of Individuation, or "unity in multeity," to which he adds the principle of Polarity and the concept of Organism as formulated by Kant: a whole in which the parts are reciprocally ends and means (Shedd, I, 388). Through these general ideas he deduces all the forms and varieties of living beings, from the molluscs to man, distributed in three phases: productivity in plants, irritability in insects and sensitivity in animals. These three classes of living beings correspond to three classes of physical phenomena: magnetic, electric, and chemical. A modern biologist, who gave kindly attention to this work of Coleridge's, found in it some anticipation of the theory of Emergent Evolution, but also noted the connection with *Naturphilosophie*, and concluded: "he failed to realise the metrical and quantitative nature of scientific method." [18]

There is much more *Naturphilosophie* in the unpublished MSS. The whole of the volume once known as Say 1, and now as Victoria MS. 1, is such; so are several notes collected in the British Museum, Egerton MS. 2801, and in the still unpublished Notebooks: e.g., "Genesis and ascending scale of the Physical Powers, abstractly contemplated," in *Notebook* No. 23, pages 57–60.

Here is a short specimen of this way of thinking, from the long letter of September 1817 to C. A. Tulk: "Water is the Indifference or Balance of the four elements, each consisting of all the four elementary Powers but under the Dynasty of some one of the 4. Thus Carbon in the purest form is the Product of the *Powers* of Carbon, Azote, Oxygen, and Hydrogen under the predominance of the Power of Carbon, i.e., of Attraction. But Water being the product or indifference of the four elements, is of course 4 x 4 = the Cube. And so it is found in Nature." (*CL*, IV, 773).

This kind of reasoning resembles Hegel's discredited Philosophy of Nature: water for Coleridge is the indifference of the four elements, for Hegel it is abstract neutrality (*Encyclopaedia*, par. 333). *Naturphilosophie* proceeds by mere analogy helped out by the imagination and the improper use of philosophical concepts.

Another concept of Coleridge which derives from Schelling is "potence": for instance, "I shall venture to use *Potence*, in order to express a specific degree of a power, in imitation of the Algebraists. I have even hazarded the new verb *potenziate*, with its derivatives, in order to express the combination or transfer of powers" (*BL*, Ch. XII, I, 189).

"Potence" seems to be a transcript of the German *Potenz*, a rather obscure term in Schelling (e.g., *SW*, III, 331 and 356), who also uses the derived verb *Potenzieren*.[19] The noun in Schelling seems to mean "stage of being," hierarchically structured: e.g., consciousness is the highest potency (III, 331). Also, the higher stages have a higher "exponent,"[20] so the analogy is arithmetical ("in imitation of the Algebraists"): 9 is 3 raised to the second power, the exponent being 2. "*Potenzieren*" is "to raise to a higher power."[21]

Apparently after writing the passage in the *Biographia*, Coleridge decided to use the English equivalent "power" instead of "potence": see the letter to Tulk in which he expounds his philosophy of Nature (*CL*, IV, 768–69) and the unpublished note on "Powers" in Egerton MS. 2801, fol. 123. But on the whole the term is as obscure in Coleridge as it is in Schelling.

iv

A CURIOUS FACT is that Schelling in later times developed new versions of his philosophy which give up absolute immanence and find a place for God.[22] But Coleridge, a kindred spirit in this, does not seem to have made much of it.

Out of Schelling's interest in mythology came also a curious piece of erudition, the pamphlet *Ueber die Gottheiten von Samothrake*, published in 1815 (*SW*, VIII, 345–423). How Coleridge obtained it I do not know; it is not usually included in the lists of books of Schelling's that he owned. But read it he certainly did, for he made use of its out-of-the-way learning in classical and oriental languages, for a lecture of his own on Asiatic religion, which was the eleventh of the course of 1818. The fact is noted by Shedd (IV, 309n), but not by Raysor (*Misc. Crit.*, p. 191), and it was fully analysed by W. K. Pfeiler.[23]

This rather fantastic essay, which was used also for the *Prometheus* essay, was quoted in *The Friend* as the motto for the Second Landing Place, Essay 4: a sentence or two on the desirability of paying more attention to the Hebrew tradition of wisdom, by which Schelling meant the Kabbalah (*SW*, 416–17), and Coleridge, who somewhat altered the German text, "Rabbinic writings" in general (p. 246). In *The Friend* the author's name is given, but not the work, so the quotation has remained unidentified (Shedd, II, 340).

Muirhead has found in the later MS. notes of Coleridge "an attempt to establish a voluntaristic form of Idealism, or as he preferred to call it 'spiritual realism' " (p. 110). This consists in affirming "the Absolute as Will" or "Absolute Will" (p. 117). This attempt constitutes according to Muirhead an original contribution of Coleridge to English philosophy (p. 262).

There are certainly definite traces of this attempt in Coleridge's Notebook No. 37, dated 1828. One entry begins: "1. The Will is the Ground of all Being, the communicated Ground of all communicated Being, and the Ground is indestructible, even when all the Forms, Generations, and Manifestations, in Personeity, Reason or Being, Life are precluded and destroyed" (fol. 34). This continues for eight pages and deserves attention from any student of Coleridge's later thought and writing.

Furthermore, in that collection of Coleridge notes and fragments which the British Museum catalogues as Egerton MS.

2801, there are other voluntaristic notes, especially attempts at a systematic series of a priori propositions, the date of which is not ascertained. One begins:

"1) Spirit—i.e., Will *essential*, sive in *universo*.

2) Now, Will or Spirit contemplated finitely, must fall under the predominance of Subject $\times$ Object—that is, must be conceived by the Understanding now as subjective, now as objective, in antithesis to the power, in order to its final contemplation as the Identity of both in the Reason" (F. 104).

In both these entries the terminology is Schellingian: "Identity" in the latter we have already met as a key term of Schelling's philosophy, and "Ground" in the former corresponds to the German *Grund*, common enough in philosophy but prominent in later writings of Schelling such as *Of Human Freedom* (1809; *SW*, VII, 357–58, 376–78, 381–82, 403–6, 407–8).

The latter entry then proceeds to an outline of aesthetic theory which at first seems Crocean (by anticipation) in its assertion that "Beauty" is equal to "Expression." But it turns out to be not Croce's expression; rather it is "the Expression of the Life of Nature universally . . . found in Color and Transparency. Light being the Analogon or Exponent of the Life of Nature" (fol. 104 v). The thought then peters out into *Naturphilosophie*.

In the same collection is another note on "the intelligential Will" discernible in the universe, but it refers mainly to the already cited system of Dr. John Brown.

Certainly all these notes, and others that no doubt could be quoted, point to a deep interest in the Will as a metaphysical principle. This conception of Will has its roots in Kant's discovery of a noumenon in the ethical will of man, a discovery not lost upon the post-Kantian idealists, including Schelling. Indeed, students of the later phases of Schelling's speculation have often spoken of his voluntarism, to the extent of seeing in him a forerunner of Schopenhauer.[24] However Coleridge seems to have been ignorant of the later works of Schelling published within Coleridge's own lifetime (Schelling survived him by twenty years), and at the most a parallel might be drawn between them, not a derivation.

To sum up. Coleridge made a thorough study of Schelling's earlier philosophical speculations and expounded them lucidly and brilliantly. He evidently was deeply attracted to them as going beyond Kant. But the discovery of the ultimately subjectivist or immanentistic meaning of this phase of Schelling turned Coleridge back towards orthodox (objective) theism. This alternation of attraction and repulsion seems to have occurred more than once over the years and at different points, so it is not possible to assign a definite date to its phases.

Coleridge was also attracted by Schelling's philosophy of Nature and followed that line of speculation on his own. In aesthetics Schelling's ideas were influential on Coleridge's doctrine of the creative Imagination. But a definitive study of Coleridge's attitudes towards Schelling can only be made after the complete publication of the unpublished manuscripts.

CHAPTER 10

Hegel

i

Finally, the story of the development of German thought from Kant onwards requires for its completion an account of Hegel, whose system is the culmination of this whole trend. Coleridge was aware of him, so we must evaluate the extent of his knowledge of the last of the great idealists. It will be said at once that this knowledge was not very extensive or profound, so that it will not be necessary to go into the details of the most complex and most elaborate system of philosophy constructed after the medieval *Summae*. But a general idea of it will be given, if for no other reason to show what Coleridge missed.[1]

Like his predecessors, Hegel began his career as a philosopher in the modest garb, if not a disciple, at least as the associate of an already known philosopher, Schelling. However, Hegel was Schelling's senior, and he had developed views of his own in unpublished writings before he appeared in public as Schelling's ally. Having achieved a position of eminence, Hegel turned against Schelling and sarcastically exposed the weaknesses of his junior's system. At the time, Schelling's system was at the stage when he conceived of the Absolute as "Indifference," or indistinction, and Hegel called it wittily "the night in which all the cows are black" in the Preface to his *Phenomenology of Mind* (1807),[2] together with other gibes, substantially justified, but not in the most friendly manner.

One of Hegel's most pertinent criticisms of Schelling's system was its lack of logical method; so Hegel proceeded to work out a logical procedure of his own, the Dialectic. This is the well-known triadic process of Thesis, Antithesis and Synthesis, which we have seen emerging in Kant and developed by his successors. Kant called the three steps "moments" and this term is also used by Hegel; but Hegel's names for the single moments are Affirmation, Negation, and finally Negation of Negation. Hegel also claimed to have derived the dialectic from Kant's system of Antinomies, but as we have seen it is more clearly presented in the doctrine of the Categories, where not only the opposites but also the synthesis of the opposites are formulated.

By means of this dialectic Hegel, starting from the most general concept of all, that of mere, abstract, indeterminate Being, and proceeding by means of its opposite, Non-Being, to the first synthesis, the dynamic concept of Becoming (our acquaintance *Werden*, the Romantic concept), succeeded in building up an all-embracing chain of categories, covering the whole of reality, both physical and spiritual. The chain has three main divisions: the categories of Logic, the categories of Nature and the categories of the Mind—thus absorbing Schelling's Philosophy of Nature into a wider and better articulated system.

The Philosophy of Mind is probably Hegel's richest and most influential creation. Schelling in his *System* had already thrown out suggestive ideas for a Philosophy of History, a Philosophy of Right (or Law), and a Philosophy of Art; Hegel developed all of these into comprehensive treatises. His Philosophy of History, severely criticized as it has been, yet produced derivations which are still very much with us, since it is the core of the philosophy of Marxism. Furthermore Hegel developed new branches of philosophy, or philosophical sciences, as he called them, such as the Philosophy of Religion and the History of Philosophy, and in his aesthetics he presented also a History of Art and a History of Literature. On the whole, Hegel might be said to have realized Coleridge's ideal of "Unity with Progression" (*F*, 315, Sec. II, Ess. 7; *Method*, 2) to an extent beyond Coleridge's fondest dreams. All the great ideas which we have seen emerging from Kant and developing in the post-Kantians find their place in Hegel's system: the ideality of the world, the centrality of Mind, the dynamic nature of Reality, the Logic of the Sciences and of the Humanities, and the immanence of Reason in world history.

Hegel's *Geist*, which may be translated Mind or Spirit,[3] is conceived as the Absolute, and the Absolute is called the Idea, because it is the total system of all the categories dialectically connected. Kant's dualism of thought and reality, of knowledge and "things-in-themselves," is replaced by a thought, or Idea, which is the essence of reality and which is therefore "constitutive," as Coleridge would have had it, to the extent that "the rational is the real and the real is the rational," [4] to quote another famous dictum of Hegel. It follows that the universal (= the rational) is fully actualized in the particular (= the real) and one with it, becoming what Hegel called "the concrete universal." Coleridge too had firmly asserted "that union and interpenetration of the universal and the particular, which must ever pervade all works of decided genius and true science" (*F*, 304, Sec. II, Ess. 4). According to Hegel, it pervades all reality.

Hegel read widely, not only in philosophy and science, but also in history and in literature, he was sensitive to art and to music; so his doctrine of aesthetic,[5] though open to criticism in its dialectical structure, is based on a wide knowledge of all art, and contains a number of critical interpretations of great works, such as Greek Tragedy and Shakespearean drama.[6] In the field of drama he was building upon the foundation of A. W. Schlegel's critical works; but he went beyond Schlegel. In the history of art he is credited with the appreciation, if not the discovery, of Dutch painting,[7] no mean accomplishment for a professional philosopher. But he was living in the great creative age of German literature and German Romanticism, and nourished by the wealth of aesthetic interpretation which those movements had generated; in this sense he was himself a Romantic. In other respects, particularly in his ethical views and his concept of the State and society, he was definitely anti-romantic. It is impossible to cover in a short space all the aspects of such a great, and greatly controversial, thinker. But we will add something on his theory of the development of thought.

Kant's first *Critique* had revealed the operation of the transcendental mind: its forms of intuition (as aspicience, as Coleridge named it), its pure concepts of the understanding which build up the world of experience, and the unity of the transcendental self which is the foundation of all its activities. Sense, understanding and reason had been for Kant the three cognitive faculties, or functions, of the mind. Hegel in effect asked: what is the faculty, or function, which formulates this definition of the transcendental faculties? Sense of course does not make definitions, the understanding only categorizes sense, and reason may set up Ideas beyond that, but they are only regulative. What is the mental power that knows all this, and knows it for certain, constitutively? There is evidently here in action an organ of transcendental thinking, and it is the task of philosophy to become aware of it and define it. According to Hegel, it is the Idea itself that articulates its own distinctions and synthesizes them in the concept of itself.[8] Thus Hegel, while building upon Kant, goes well beyond Kant.

As far as the history of philosophy is concerned, this involves a new view of philosophical development, the movement of thought from one system to another, in a way that is not mere negation or supersession, but includes preservation and integration. It may be said to include acceptance, but not mere acceptance; nor is its final result a compromise, half of one and half of the other, but a new idea in which both the preceding system and its antithesis have their place, and yet are included in a new idea which goes beyond them both. Needless to say this is the dialectical movement. Hegel therefore applied it to the history of philosophy, claiming that for the first time he had made it scientific.

However, Hegel's dialectic, as applied to this field and to other fields of knowledge, presented a large number of paralogisms and arbitrary statements, which were the object of strong later criticism. While the errors of Hegel must be recognized and avoided, his dialectical system still presents a formidable challenge to contemporary thought. Are opposites really united and resolved in a synthesis? Is the world actually a process of awareness of an absolute and impersonal principle, acquiring consciousness through the events of history and the successive formulations of philosophy? Are all truths part of a single system, which can be expounded in its entirety and, being the foundation of all change, is not itself subject to change? Are individuals merely moments in the actualization of an eternal Reason or Idea, which manifests itself for a while in each and then transcends itself in the next? Is reality only to be found in collective units, such as the family, society, and the state or (in the Marxist version) in the class?

Positive answers to all these questions, with some difference in detail, were given by the idealistic systems, Hegelian and post-Hegelian. These were followed by a sweeping reaction in favor of the positive sciences on one side, and of the historical method in the investigation of human affairs on the other. Both the natural and the historical sciences made great progress and scored great victories in the nineteenth century, thus posing a further problem to philosophical thought. In particular, the historical sciences seemed to call for a new Critique, such as Kant had not written, a Critique of Historical Knowledge. This was initiated by William Dilthey and carried forward by Benedetto Croce in Italy and R. G. Collingwood in England. From Vico, Croce derived the idea of the cognition of the individual (*Anschauung*) as manifested in art and in language. These concepts were built into a new system, which provided a fresh solution to the philosophical problem of history.

ii

RETURNING TO COLERIDGE, let us see his connection with Hegel. Coleridge owned a copy of the work known as Hegel's greater *Logic*, in contradistinction to the shorter and more obscure version which is part of his *Encyclopaedia of Philosophi-*

cal Sciences (1830). Although Hegel's style is usually one of the most difficult and abstruse of all the German philosophers, the greater *Logic* is the most leisurely exposition of his philosophy and contains many sizable stretches of lucid argument. It was published in two volumes in 1812–13 and 1816, and Coleridge's copy is now in the British Museum (C. 43. a. 13).

Coleridge made annotations in it, which have been published by Snyder (pp. 162–65). They are mostly of an adverse nature; e.g., "This is Spinosism in it's superficial form" (Snyder, 165), and they do not go beyond Volume I, page 91. At the beginning of the present century the remaining pages were still uncut, "after the first division of Part I (Quality)," [9] so it may be safely assumed that Coleridge did not go beyond that.

But from what he read he may possibly have obtained the suggestion or the stimulus for an extension of the dialectic from three moments to four, through the addition of a preliminary moment, the Prothesis, as we see in a marginalium to the *Logik* (Snyder, 162). This is called by him the "Tetrad," and there are references to it in his unpublished writings (Egerton MS. 2801, fol. 125, and a fragment in *BL2*, 398). Not satisfied with four moments, Coleridge later extended the dialectic to five, and called it the "Pentad": e.g., see "The Pentad of Operative Christianity" printed in some editions of the *Confessions of an Inquiring Spirit*.[10] This Pentad is effected by the insertion of a fifth moment in the middle of the group, named "Mesothesis, or the Indifference," making it 1) Prothesis, 2) Thesis, 3) Mesothesis, 4) Antithesis, and 5) Synthesis (cf. *W*, 280, *n. 93*).

This might well be called to out-Hegel Hegel. Muirhead regarded it as "an extension which may here perhaps be neglected as belonging to the excentricities rather than to the essentials of his thought" (p. 86, *n.* 1). Such a five-step argument was too cumbersome for its author himself to make much use of; but it is remarkable development of the traditional dialectical process.

There are a few other references to Hegel. In one of his later *Notebooks*, No. 47 (Add. MS. 47, 525, fol. 21 v.), we find the following critical notice of Hegel's first triad, Being, Not-Being, and Becoming: "The error of Schelling and of Spinoza . . . is that they consider Ens and non-Ens as having no possible intermediates or degrees for even Oken and *as far as he means anything Hegel* who each in their way makes so much and such frequent use of Nothing constituting all things out of 1 and 0," etc. I do not quote the whole passage; for our purpose the relevant words are those I have italicized.

There are passages in the printed works in which Coleridge approximates Hegel's ideas. His definition of the history of philosophy in the *Biographia* (*BL*, I, 169–70) has something in common with Hegel's, but that may be due to suggestions from Schelling. Also, the statement on his "System of Philosophy" in *Table Talk* for September 12, 1831 (*TT*, 139), ending "to make history scientifical, and science historical," has a Hegelian ring.

On the other side, some of Hegel's definitions come close to Coleridge's: e.g., "Reason, the faculty of the unconditioned" (*Encyclopaedia*, # 45). Reason is also the faculty of Ideas and the Idea is "vindicated for Reason" (*ibid.*; see Wallace's commentary[11] for a reference to Coleridge). We also find the so-called Hegelians of the Right, who stressed the religious aspect of Hegel's system, arguing sometimes very like Coleridge in the *Aids to Reflection*: take the Italian Hegelian Sebastiano Maturi on "the Logic of the Finite": "If the logic of the finite invades the field of religion and of philosophy, it will only demolish and destroy everything.—Unity and Trinity at the same time and under the same aspect!—Impossible!—Divinity and humanity at the same time and under the same aspect!— This is folly!—And so on, at the gallop, at breakneck speed." [12]

Coleridge was not alone in post-Kantian metaphysics in his attempt to base a Christian apologia upon the distinction of Reason and Understanding.

However Coleridge's basic attitude toward Hegel probably was due to the fact that Coleridge remained to the end of his life under the belief that the last great German philosopher was Schelling. As he put it in the *Biographia*, "to Schelling we owe the completion and the most important victories of this revolution in philosophy" (*BL*, I, 104). Now Hegel's hegemony in Germany dates approximately from 1818, when he became professor at the University of Berlin, and an important person in the kingdom of Prussia. He was to die in 1831, three years before Coleridge. It looks as if Coleridge just heard of him as the author of a book on Logic, and so obtained a copy of the work so entitled. But he did not attempt to see whether Hegel had gone beyond Schelling (the Introduction to the *Phenomenology* would have been of help in this) and he never seems to have made a serious effort to grasp the fundamental principles of Hegel's thought, nor did he ever know what spectacular use Hegel had made of the distinction between the Understanding and the Reason.

If Coleridge could have seen Hegel's Aesthetics, which were not published till 1835, although previously delivered in lectures, he would also have seen that Hegel recognized the distinction between the Imagination and the Fancy.[13] The distinction then passed on to the greatest Italian literary critic of the nineteenth century, who made use of it in his *History of Italian Literature* (1871). From De Sanctis' criticism stems Croce's, who connected the essential theses of Romantic aesthetics with Vico's concept of the cognition of the particular. So the great tradition of speculative thought goes on from century to century, from Plato and Aristotle to Plotinus, from the Greeks to the Germans, from Kant and Schelling to Coleridge, from Hegel and his predecessors to Croce,[14] generating new forms of literary criticism and literary history all along the way.

CHAPTER 11

The MS. "Logic"

THE MS. "Treatise on Logic," to which reference has been made repeatedly in the course of our discussion, deserves more extended treatment. It is a MS. of about six hundred pages of text, clearly transcribed by amanuenses, and preserved in the British Museum in two bound volumes, Egerton 2825 and 2826. Its date of composition has been conjectured 1822–23 by Miss Snyder, who did a splendid pioneer job on it in her book of 1929.[1] After a number of vicissitudes, the MS. is now being edited for the Complete Coleridge by Prof. J. R. Jackson, so I will not repeat here the description of the external aspects of the MS., including its subdivisions, which I have given elsewhere,[2] but will discuss only its contents.

In spite of foreseeable shortcomings, this work has a number of qualifications which make it regrettable that it has not been published before. It is Coleridge's most sustained effort in pure philosophy, and it is more comprehensive in scope than any of his published writings on the subject. It has a definite place in the general plan of his unpublished *Opus Maximum*, to which it serves as a general introduction, or as Coleridge might have called it with a Kantian term, a Propedeutic.[3] Afterwards would come, presumably, the treatises, or part of the treatises, that were once called the Say MSS. and are now in the Victoria College Library of Toronto, mentioned in Chapter 6. To pursue this conjecture (for it is nothing more) to the end, the last part, or one of the last, might be the unpublished MS. "On the Divine Ideas" preserved in the Huntington Library, Then there are the notes collected in British Museum MSS., such as Egerton 2800, 2801, and Additional 34,225, and what

246

may be collected from the Notebooks. Altogether it will make a substantial set of volumes, particularly so when we consider for how long the *Opus Maximum* was considered a mere dream. True, even when all published, it is likely to be still fragmentary and unfinished. But some parts of it, like the "Logic," will stand on their own merits.

Being by Coleridge, the "Logic" is also rambling and digressive, devoid of a clear plan, and at times somewhat inconsistent. Yet it is more orderly and detailed than any of his published works that deal with philosophy or theology. It is not a miscellany like *The Friend*; it does not break down in the middle, like the *Biographia Literaria,* and then turn in another direction; it does not lose itself in a mass of quotations from another writer, like the *Aids to Reflection*; nor does it allow itself any excursions in autobiography, like most of these works; but it proceeds continuously with the main topic from beginning to end. The end itself is abrupt, and the work is usually considered unfinished; but we shall bring forward some reasons to show that it is not substantially so, or that not very much is missing. Among other things, it contains a number of illustrations and similes to the doctrines expounded, which, being by Coleridge, are often brilliantly conceived and written.

In the "Logic" we may find most of the traditional topics of ordinary logic: the definition of Concepts, or "conceptions" as Coleridge prefers to say (II, 42), of Judgments as the union of Subject to Predicate (II, 96), the Principles of Identity and of Contradiction (II, 79 ff.), and even the Syllogism, with its four traditional modes (II, 11 ff. and 106–16). But not in that order, as appears from the page references.[4]

The fact is that, while terms and definitions are initially traditional, Coleridge is continually passing from the traditional to the transcendental point of view. First of all, "conceptions" are resolved into synthetic acts of consciousness (II, 44–61). Then the Principle of Identity is resolved into a description of a mental process: "It is the mere narration of a fact, I reflect on Being" (II, 85), and the same happens to the Principle of Contradiction (II, 86). Syllogism in turn is resolved into three processes with new names, Clusion, Seclusion, and Conclusion (II, 18 ff. and 97), and the Kantian doctrine of the reduction of the four figures of the Syllogism to the first figure is adopted (II, 14 and 108); Kant being named and credited in the second passage.

Indeed the philosophy in the "Logic" is predominantly Kantian, with characteristic Coleridgean adaptations and hesitations, and some flashes of Schelling's absolute idealism. The Kantian derivation is amply acknowledged, even though Coleridge does not quote Kant at every point. But he repeatedly acclaims Kant as "the most profound of modern Logicians and the proper Inventor and Founder of the Transcendental Analysis" (II, 210) and "the greatest Logician since the time of Aristotle and the founder of the Critical Philosophy" (II, 27). For Coleridge, "Transcendental Logic" is a "more appropriate name" for the first *Critique* (II, 326 f.): the *Critique* "considered as *Logic* . . . is irrefragable" (II, 230). The most detailed acknowledgment has been quoted in Chapter 2: the Transcendental Aesthetic, the Transcendental Logic and Analysis are all acknowledged to be Kant's (II, 412), and we have also seen how Coleridge defended Kant from the charge of plagiarism (II, 209^v–211^v). Many other praises of Kant are scattered throughout the work (II, 308–10, 338, 401, 454, etc.).

Surely there are here enough acknowledgments to Kant to exclude even the faintest suspicion that "some phrases in the MS. sound almost like attempts to hide the true derivation of his ideas" (*W*, 117). When Coleridge speaks of "our Logic" or says "I have termed" something by a name derived from Kant (*loc. cit.*), he is using the professorial "we": for these pages appear to have been given originally as lectures to a small group of students (Snyder, 71–72). The lecturer's "we" means usually "what we, the class and myself, have seen, or will see, together," not "what I have invented or originated." There are perhaps better grounds for the complaint of no reference to Schelling for the ideas incorporated in the *Biographia* and here repeated without acknowledgment at I, 66 and II, 66 and 73, as noted by Miss Snyder.

This work is notable also for referring to other, lesser known works of Kant. Besides the *Dissertation* of 1770, from which the same quotation as in *BL*, I, 189–90 is made (II, 405–6), the "Treatise on the Dead and Living Forces" (II, 309), i.e., *Gedanken von der wahren Schatzung der lebendigen Kräfte* (1747) (II, 308, quoted also in *Aids*, 269), "the Dreams of a Ghost-seer . . . 1766, the most popular of Kant's works" (II, 329ᵛ); there are also derivations, noted by Miss Snyder, from the *Prolegomena* (1783) and from the *Logic* (1800). There is even a quotation from Kant on common sense which has not been traced (II, 306). There are references to other philosophers besides Kant, notably Moses Mendelssohn, to whom, as we saw in Chapter 1, Coleridge made a very early reference in 1796.[5]

The science of Logic, according to Kant and to Coleridge, is the province of the Understanding, as Coleridge repeatedly states: "the sphere of the Understanding . . . this alone is the rightful sphere of Logic" (II, 391, and see also I, 60, 83, 85 and II, 4 and 127). We have seen above the function of the Understanding (Chapter 5). It means that Logic is a purely formal science, dealing with the forms of cognition and not with its content.[6] Hence the book will discuss the forms of sensuous knowledge and those of intellectual knowledge, but will stop there, not touching the Ideas of Reason, which belong to a higher faculty than the Understanding (on Reason see I, 56–57, II, 40, 174–75 etc.).

Following even in this the example of Kant, who prefixed a sketch of the history of philosophy to his own treatise on *Logic*, Coleridge begins his treatise with an outline history of philosophy according to his own lights (I, 38–78). It starts with the earliest Greek attempts at ratiocination, indeed at speech, for Coleridge considered speech itself as a product of the abstracting power. From the beginning there is a distinction between ordinary speech or ῥήματα, and "select, considerate, well-weighed, deliberate words" or λόγοι (I, 44). Then, out of λόγοι, thought developed the genre of Fables "in speeches on delicate or hazardous subjects, addressed to kings or unruly popular assemblies": e.g., the fable of Menenius Agrippa (I, 45). Then

comes poetry in the guise of epos, followed immediately by
"chronicles" which develop into "histories" (I, 46–49): all are
λόγοι, in the sense above given. Next we have the emergence
of wisdom, in the person of the wise man or σόφος, who later
degenerates into the Sophist (I, 49–52).

Philosophy appears with Pythagoras, the first to call himself
a philosopher (I, 53). Anaxagoras introduces the concept of
Νοῦς (I, 56), which Coleridge defines as "pure reason," à la
Kant (I, 57), then proceeding to define the relations of Reason
to Understanding and to Sense with the help of a triangular diagram (I, 61), also in Egerton MS. 2801, fol. 77. This in turn leads
to a general classification of the sciences (I, 64) involving the
distinction of subjective and objective, for which Coleridge
draws on the arguments of Thesis I in the similar discussion in
the Biographia (BL, I, 174–75, Ch. XII), which we have seen
above in Chapter 8. Thesis I, it will be remembered, deals with
Nature, so "we will begin with Nature" (I, 70), i.e., the early
Greek "physicist" philosophers among the pre-Socratics. These
early efforts were merely "dreams and fancies, the hypotheses of
children" (I, 74).

Here Coleridge makes one of his few references to author-
ities: "see Stanley's History of Philosophy before Anaxagoras"
(I, 74). This is the "first part" of Thomas Stanley's History of
Philosophy (4th ed., 1743), "containing those on whom the
attribute of WISE [cf. σόφος above] was conferred," i.e., the
Seven Sages, etc. But Coleridge may have meant the Second
Part, which begins with Anaxagoras and contains the "Ionick
Philosophers," i.e., the Physicists, whose speculations on Nature
might receive in the nineteenth century the description given
above, of dreams and fancies.

Happily, Plato was at hand: "the greatest of philosophers, if
not the first who merited, as well as assumed, that name" (I,
74). But Plato turns out to be a mere pseudonym for Kant, not
for the first time in Coleridge, as we saw in The Friend. This
is how Coleridge presents Plato's thinking on Nature—or rather,
on "phenomenal Nature," as he calls it, introducing the Kantian
concept of phenomenon into Plato: "it [Nature] was true, ab-

solutely in and for the mind only; its proper being was in the mind, and contemplating it, the intelligence was contemplating its own acts and products" (I, 75). This is Kantianism and not Platonism.

Not only Plato, but the whole development of the sciences in ancient Greece follows a Kantian pattern: the sciences branch out "in accordance with the different faculties of the mind," which are classified in terms of Kant's Analytic: "First the sciences that refer to the acts of sense, either to the sense, which employs itself on ideal space, or the sense which has time as the material of its contemplation." There are "Arithmetic and Geometry." The next group of sciences has for its object the forms of thought, in their necessary dependence one on the other, i.e., "Logic" (I, 76).

This leads Coleridge to give his conception of Logic as a purely formal science (I, 77, 79–81), which as we have seen is in keeping with Kant. Then Coleridge gives a "table" or classification of all the sciences, rather like the one made for the *Encyclopedia Metropolitana* on the basis of his suggestions, i.e., it is strongly triadic.[7] It begins with the "metaphysical sciences":

"A—Noetics, the evidence of Reason
B—Logic, the evidence of the Understanding
C—Mathematics, to (?) the evidence of Sense" (I, 83).

Thus each of the faculties represented in the diagram above (I, 61) produces a corresponding science. There follows a class of physical or empirical sciences and a class of applied sciences (I, 84–85), into which we will not go since, as Coleridge says at the end of the section, our "immediate concern" is with the science indicated by B above, or Logic, which he now describes as "the perfect coincidence of a Conception or Proposition (that is words intended to express conception) with the laws of the Understanding" (I, 85). Incidentally, "conception" is usually Coleridge's equivalent for the Kantian "Begriff," as appears from II, 385–87.[8]

"Sense" also stands for the Kantian "sensibility" (II, 408), as confirmed by the following definition in a letter of 12 December 1817 to J. H. B. Williams: "in philosophical Language *Sense* means the *Faculty*, of which the different *Senses* are the *organs*" (*CL*, IV, 790). Here in the "Logic" we find the phrase "the forms of sense (*intuitus puri*)" (I, 84),[9] corresponding to the Kantian forms of sensibility or pure intuitions (*Anschauungen*) of space and time.

But the outline of the development of the logical thinking from the fable and the epic, fantastic as it is in some of its details, is almost Vichian in its suggestiveness and in its developmental pattern, Vico being also fantastic and arbitrary in some of his details. Coleridge however, in his own words, "began to read" Vico in 1825 (Notebook 20, p. 28, Add. MS. 47,517). If the "Logic" is earlier than that, there may be an echo of Warton or of Herder.

This confirms that Coleridge's aim in the "Logic" is to limit the discussion to the human Understanding, leaving the discussion of Reason and of the Ideas of Reason to another place. Notwithstanding all his false starts and his digressions, and the repetitions for which he himself apologizes more than once (II, 373–74, 422), this aim is kept in sight throughout the ensuing discussion. According to Coleridge the Understanding begins with the data of Sense, but achieves its proper organ in the concept, or as Coleridge preferred to say, the conception (II, 385–87), which is both the act and the product of the understanding. If Sense is below the Understanding, there is a faculty which is above (for this "above" and "below" see the definition at I, 61). Still more explicitly Kantian is the method proposed for the analysis of the Understanding, viz. the Transcendental, and Kant is named as the inventor of it, as we have seen above (Ch. 2).

In support of the statement that conception is both the act and the product of understanding, it may be said that Coleridge repeatedly makes the point that in mental acts "the producing act and the product are one and indivisible" (II, 354). This quotation actually refers to mathematics only, but in other passages Coleridge extends the same principle to other mental operations.

It applies to sensuous perception: in his full discussion of "Intuition" or "simple beholding," Coleridge refers to "both the act of beholding and the simple product thence resulting indistinguishably" (II, 214). He applies it also to "Intuitive Imagination" in a striking passage (II, 50) which is reproduced in Snyder (p. 111). This passage ends with a glance at Plotinus on Nature: "her contemplative act is creative and is one with the product of her contemplation." (Here Coleridge may not be quoting directly from Plotinus, but summarizing the passage quoted *in extenso* from *Enn.* III, 8, 4, in *BL*, I, 166*n*).

This unity of act and product is of course a principle of philosophical idealism: the product of thought being the objective physical world, thought is identical with its product and Mind is the same as Being.

From here to the end (II, 190–460), as noted by previous students of the "Logic," the work is mainly an exposition of Kant's Transcendental Analytic. Coleridge begins with discussing the workings of Sense, using most of the time Kantian terms: the forms of Intuition (II, 213–14), Sense characterized by "receptivity" (II, 219) and involving a "manifold" (II, 58 and 62); "representations" are "presentations" (II, 42), while "spontaneity" is characteristic of the Understanding and Reason (II, 427). The Understanding is defined as "the faculty of Rules" while the Reason is the "source of Principles" (II, 35). But Coleridge prefers "judicial" to "transcendental" (II, 210 and 212) and speaks of "Judicial Logic" (II, 212). We have quoted in Chapter 2 his discussion of "intuition" as a translation for *Anschauung*.

The Understanding is shown to operate by means of "functions": the term is fully discussed, II, 40^v–41^v and 419–30. These are of course the Categories of Kant, and as we have seen in Chapter 3 Coleridge here gives in full both the table of Judgments and the table of the Categories. Then follows the Kantian demonstration that the Table of Categories derives necessarily from that of the Judgments (II, 450). Wellek thought that Coleridge here showed greater sagacity than Kant and that he had rejected this derivation, thus anticipating later critics (*W*, 123). The passage that Wellek quotes does seem to say that:

however it is not on II, 399, but on II, 401, and belongs to a preliminary discussion, general in character, in which I do not believe that Coleridge was contradicting Kant. Indeed Coleridge, after making his faithful exposition of the two Tables, fully reiterated Kant's assertion of the logical derivation of the second from the first (II, 452).

Along the way Coleridge takes occasion to advance arguments against sensism and empiricism: there are critical references to Locke (II, 42 and 459) and a long discussion of Hume (II, 281–314) entirely in Kantian terms. Even the argument on II, 296, which Snyder apparently ascribes to Coleridge, is already in the *Critique*: "Then Coleridge endeavors to bring things to a head" by pointing out "a necessary preliminary to the solution" i.e., in Coleridge's words, "that of trying . . . whether the problem could not be presented under a higher and yet more comprehensive formula, whether there were not other connections $= x$ between A and B not included in A besides the causal connection?" (II, 296). The phraseology is Coleridge's, but the thought is the same as in Kant: of Hume he says, "He occupied himself exclusively with the . . . *principium causationis*. . . . If he had envisaged our problem the problem of the *a priori* in all its universality, he would never have been guilty of this statement" (B 19–20).

As mentioned in Chapter 2, Coleridge devotes considerable space to an exposition of Kant's distinction between analytic and synthetic judgments and the doctrine of synthetic judgments a priori (II, 265–396). That distinction had already been branded by Schelling as the object of a "scholastic dispute" (*SW*, I, 354). At one point Coleridge declared that "the antithesis between analytic and synthetic disappears" (II, 326; cf. *W*, 100–101). Other important deviations from Kant in this part of the *Logic* are Coleridge's concept of Reason, discussed in Chapter 5; his occasional flashes of idealistic speculation in the manner of Schelling, and finally his discussion of the synthetic activity of the mind, which does not appear quite to reach Kant's Unity of Apperception. Having already seen the first of these, we will now take up the last two.

In his exposition of Kant's Analytic, Coleridge stops short of the Transcendental Deduction. Nor is there a discussion of it in *The Friend*, the *Biographia*, or the other books published by Coleridge. It might seem that he never took any notice of it. However, in certain sections of the "Logic" Coleridge makes abundant reference to the Synthetic Unity of Perception, as the following quotations will show: "The representation which rises out of the logical function of unity and is called a common conception (*conceptus communis*) depends upon our power of combining a multiplicity of presentations in one and the same act of consciousness. Instead of common conception some writers have employed the phrase of complex ideas" (II, 42).

"Complex ideas" is a Lockean term (cf. II, 459), which Coleridge proceeds to criticize (II, 42–43). As for the Latin phrase *conceptus communis*, it is used by Kant in this context (B 134*n*).

In the following passage, the doctrine is explicitly attributed to "some Logicians" (Kant's *Critique* was always considered by Coleridge as a work on Logic): "This apprehension or primary combination of A (we will say) with b.d.c. in the act of *perceiving* the given object corresponding to the Impression A.b. d.c. has by some Logicians been called the Synthetic function of the Understanding, and . . . the reflex conciousness of this combination *as* a combination . . . the writers above mentioned have named the Analytic function of the Understanding" (II, 44).

After giving a number of interesting illustrations of his own (one is quoted in Snyder, pp. 111–12), Coleridge says even more definitely: "this primary mental act which we have called the synthetic unity, or the unity of apperception, is presupposed to, and in order to, all consciousness. It is its condition (*conditio sine qua non*) or that which constitutes the possibility of consciousness *a priori*, or, if we borrow a metaphor from space instead of time, *ab intra*. Both metaphors mean the same thing: an act or product of the mind itself considered as distinct from the impressions from external objects" (II, 56).

This comes very close to the Transcendental Unity of Apperception (cf. B 138). It is quoted twice by Wellek (*W*, 117 and 133). The terminology gets even closer in this passage: "Without the primary act or unity of apperception we could have nothing to be conscious of. Without the repetition or re-presentation of this act in the understanding which completes the consciousness, we should be conscious of nothing" (II, 59).

In this context, Kant speaks of the concept of the Unity con-ferred by the understanding upon the manifold in perception (B 130–31),[10] and Coleridge says of perceptions: "that which all have in common is the coexistence of the Many in the One . . . the One or Unity as the gift of the mind itself" (II, 60–61).

But Kant goes on to show that this concept of unity cannot be a category (or concept of the understanding) for "the cate-gory already presupposes combination," so "we must look still higher for this unity" (B 131). In the next paragraph (# 16) he finds the highest mental factor of unity in self-consciousness or the "I think," and calls it, as we saw in Chapter 4, "the Original Synthetic Unity of Apperception," as well as (in # 17) "the Supreme Principle of all Employment of the Understand-ing" (B 136). We do not find in Coleridge a clear, unmistakable statement of the "I think," or of the fact that "it must accom-pany all representations and be in all consciousness one and the same" (B 132).

This discussion has shown, however, that Coleridge was ac-quainted with this section of the *Critique*; it is also clear that he read it in the second edition, which was the one he owned. This is shown, positively, by the Latin phrase *conceptus communis* which occurs only in the second edition, and negatively by the lack of any reference to the threefold character of the synthesis of perception, which is very prominent in the first edition (A 98—A 104) and is absent in the second. But Coleridge did not fully grasp, or perhaps did not fully accept, the doctrine of the "abiding and unchanging I" of the first edition (A 123) or of the "I think," as it is in the second edition (B 132).

However, there are passages in the "Logic" in which Cole-ridge sums up the idealistic position of the post-Kantians in terse, striking arguments, like the following: "The mind affirms firstly its own reality. Secondly, that this reality is a unity. Thirdly, that it has the power of communicating this unity, and lastly, that all reality for the mind is derived from its own reality, and in proportion to the unity which is its form." (II, 63).

After having followed the idealistic argument so far, Coleridge turns back and returns to orthodox theism. The argument he presents here is not perfectly clear, but it might perhaps be summarized as follows. Self-consciousness, or the mind as absolute identity of being and knowing, is not ultimate. It "supposes reflection, and reflection an act antecedent thereto." Therefore "we have inquired for something more and higher than this self-consciousness" (II, 68). This presumably means that the antecedent act, or acts, imply the existence of the mind making those acts, so that the actual existence of mind, or its being, precedes its self-awareness. Now once it is admitted that Being absolutely precedes Thought, then Idealism, which affirms the identity of the two, is rejected. But an idealist like Schelling would probably have had an answer to this argument, i.e., that this "previousness," this "before" and "after," is psychological and not logical.

The vacillation which is observable in these pages is the same in substance as the one found in Chapter XII of the *Biographia Literaria*: a vacillation between the idealistic formula "*sum qua sum*, I am because I affirm myself to be" (II, 75; cf. *BL*, I, 183, Thesis VI) and the theistic formula: "*sum quia in Deo sum*" or "I am because I am in God" (*ibid.*). He repeats in the "Logic" the footnote already published in the *Biographia* (*BL*, I, 184*n*) upon the distinction between the "conditional finite I" and the "absolute I am, and likewise the inherence of the former in the latter in whom we live and move and have our being" (II, 75ᵛ), and so on, as in the *Biographia*. In other words, the Absolute is God and not the mind. Coleridge is safely back in the theistic fold.

More significant, perhaps, is the doctrine of "productive unity" which Coleridge develops in several passages (II, 381–82, 389–90 and 417–19), which was noted by Wellek (*W*, 120) and strongly stressed by Barfield.[11] Coleridge here draws a distinction between two kinds of unity, original and derivative.

The latter is produced by bringing together pre-existent parts, as in making "a watch for instance" (II, 417). Original unity instead pre-exists to the parts which compose it. Since it pre-exists to its parts, it may be assumed to have produced them, so it is both antecedent and productive.[12]

Now the Kantian origin of the doctrine should be noted. A pre-existent unity is precisely what Kant ascribes to Ideas. "An Idea," he says in his *Logic*,[13] "cannot be obtained by composition, for in it the whole is before the part." Hence this kind of unity must be described in Kantian terminology as a priori, and the mental act which cognizes it is an a priori synthesis. This synthesis is one of the most important concepts of post-Kantian thought, but Coleridge prefers to connect it with pre-Kantian speculation. As he puts it in a note, productive unity is "distinguished from a whole as elsewhere I have proposed to use the term Form as the technical antithesis of *shape*. As *Form* = *forma formans* [stands] to *shape* = *forma formata*, so the productive unity = *Totum suas ipsius partes constituens* [stands] to the whole (mass aggregate) = *Totum a partibus constitutum*. The former is the same with the Leibnizian monad and the Entelechy of Aristotle" (II, 381^v—382^v).[14]

The importance of this discussion for aesthetics lies in the fact that the distinction between productive unity and mass aggregate corresponds to that between organic form and mechanical form, which plays such an important part in literary criticism.[15]

Its relevance to metaphysics is made clear in the following passage: "if . . . I substitute the phrase of *productive unity* as that which gives existence, I venture upon a thought which, while it necessarily escapes the notice of sense, contradicts the first axioms of the Understanding, which as imperiously demands the Stuff for the Form as the Form for the Stuff and in whose creation a chaos necessarily precedes the world. From such contradictions there is but one way of escaping, viz. by assuming, by *willing* to assume, that the Truth passeth all Understanding, and that a contradiction exists in the heterogeneity of the faculty, not in the object, for which it was neither adapted nor intended" (II, 389–90).

This is another instance of Coleridge's adaptation to his own ends of Kant's doctrine of the Antinomies which we have seen already in Chapter 5. The antinomy or contradiction is resolved by "the heterogeneity of the faculty," i.e., the distinction of the Reason from the Understanding.

Among the topics also discussed in the "Logic" is language. Not only was Coleridge well aware of the close relationship between thought and speech, the idea and the word, but he was deeply interested in the subject in all its aspects, and continually reverts to it. He insists upon the necessity of technical terms in philosophy (I, 87 f., II, 378–81, etc.) and he defends their use against the often repeated request (possibly from his auditors) that he should use "common language." The latter is good for ordinary communication but not for Logic; however, the logician must always define his technical terms, and also warn the reader every time he deviates from common usage (II, 129). Words alone are never the causes of logical confusion, but "the pre-existence of such confusion" causes "their own existence as equivocations" (II, 159).

This deep interest in language is of course related to Coleridge's own magnificent capacity for verbal expression. Every reader of Coleridge's prose knows how meticulous he can be in the use of synonyms and antonyms, and how often he refers to the principles of "philosophical grammar." The "Logic" begins with a discussion of this very subject and includes a rather fanciful attempt to derive all the parts of speech from a few general categories (I, 25–31). Still more fanciful, but quite in keeping with the tendencies of German metaphysicians, are some of the suggested etymologies, such as that of *cogitans*, from *cogito* and *ens* (II, 68). Coleridge shows here also his love of the German language, already manifest in other works—nowhere perhaps so strongly as in the Shakespeare lectures of 1811–1812, where he says that the German language "is incomparable in its metaphysical and psychological force." [16]

Coleridge also shows his admiration for the German language in his attempts in the "Logic" to coin new English words modelled on German ones, for instance "inhold" from *"Inhalt"*

(II, 125) or "allcommon" for "*allgemein*" instead of "general": "if I might borrow a more expressive and more English form from our sister language, the German, the allcommon (*allgemein*)" (II, 382).[17]

However, Coleridge's concept of language in the *Logic* remains strictly intellectualistic: "words are themselves the earliest products of the abstracting power (I, 24) and "all language originates in reflection" (II, 388). This is probably due to the logical context of the book; but it is also possible that Coleridge was not aware of the other view, to be found among German philosophers and others, that considers language not the product of the logical faculty, but of the intuitional faculty—that particularizing faculty sometimes called *Anschauung*, a term which as we have seen was considered important by Coleridge. As Miss Coburn notes, "I have found no evidence that Coleridge read Herder on the origin of language, and K. W. von Humboldt's work appeared two years after Coleridge's death" (*PhL*, 416).

Finally, there is a note, written on the last leaf of Coleridge's copy of Jacobi, *Ueber die Lehre des Spinozas* (1789), in the British Museum Library (C. 126. d. 15, bound with Maass's *Versuch*), which reads like an epilogue to the "Logic," or a last sorrowful address to the class of students who had followed his lectures on logic:

"Readers of my Logic, or the Method of legitimate Thinking and Discussion, who yet expect to find short and easy Receipts on how to think without thinking at all—how to think without thought —how many! Alas! S. T. C.

"In order to understand by the Rule you must first Understand the Rule—and in order to ascertain this, it would be well to know what you mean by Understanding in general. And this is one main object of the present work.

"But who does not *know* this? Be it so. I say nothing to the contrary: and therefore I have not required you to *learn* what you ought to mean or should henceforth[18] mean, but know consciously what you actually, tho' without that reflective attention which constitutes distinct consciousness, always have meant by it."

The note continues ramblingly and ends with defining the aim of education, a topic discussed already in the "Logic," I, 32–38.

The references to "my Logic" and to "the present work" seem to refer to the MS. "Logic." "The present work" cannot be the book in which this is written, i.e., Jacobi's, which does not deal with "Understanding in general." And who can the "you" be if not the students? You whom "I have not required . . . to learn," etc.?

In conclusion, Coleridge in his "Logic" raised a building largely made up of Kantian bricks, but held together with Coleridgean mortar and designed after a Coleridgean pattern. Its goal was ultimate truth, which Kant in the *Critique of Pure Reason* held to be inaccessible, but which the post-Kantian idealists thought within reach. However, in spite of strong leanings toward absolute idealism, Coleridge in the end always returned within the fold of orthodox theism. But the attempt to reconcile idealism with theism, and to build a traditional metaphysic on a transcendentalist foundation, was made by Coleridge honestly and wholeheartedly.

The "Logic" has several secondary merits. First of all: "as an exposition of Kant, the "Logic" ranks high indeed and shows a far better insight into Kant than most of Coleridge's contemporaries could boast of and a much more precise knowledge of Kant's actual teachings than one would have expected from the loose phraseology of some of Coleridge's more popular writings" (*W*, 212–22).

The "Logic" also provides a foundation for his other philosophical works, both published and unpublished, and fills a gap in his general argument. It fulfills its titular purpose by being essentially a treatise on the functions and processes of the Understanding, to which Coleridge following Kant limits the sphere of Logic. When he had covered nearly all the functions that Kant assigned to the Understanding, the book comes to an end. True, there are further developments in the *Critique* which Coleridge omits, such as the doctrines of the *Schemata* and of the Principles of the Understanding. Coleridge was not ignorant of them, since he referred to them in *The Friend*. But in the "Logic" he stops short of them. There is also no formal conclusion or epilogue. Coleridge apparently had said all he had to say on the Understanding, and there the book ends.

Even if it were unfinished, it is regrettable that the work should have remained so long unpublished. The condition in which it was left also arouses regret that a mind like Coleridge's, whose capacity for philosophical speculation and grasp of transcendentalism does not appear to have been potentially inferior to, say, that of a Schelling, should have suffered from misfortunes and shortcomings to the extent of being unable to write a single complete philosophical treatise and then bring it to a finish, while Schelling was able to compose and to publish a number of striking philosophical works and so make a much deeper philosophical impact upon the world.

CHAPTER 12

Conclusion

WE HAVE DISCUSSED the claim put forward by modern writers that Coleridge had obtained from Cudworth the substance of Kant's philosophy (Chapter 1 and 5) and the claim, put forward by Coleridge himself, that he had anticipated all by himself the ideas of post-Kantian philosophy before reading the Germans (Chapter 8). But the tendency to deny absolutely or to minimize the German element in Coleridge's thought has been so persistent, that some attention will now be given to the arguments advanced in the past by some distinguished scholars in support of Coleridge's claims to originality in this field, and this will provide a recapitulation leading to the conclusion.

Muirhead in his valuable book of 1930—still the most comprehensive general account of Coleridge's philosophy—argues in favor of Coleridge's anticipation of the whole development of German philosophy after Wolff on the basis of Coleridge's claim in the letter of April 8, 1825 (p. 54), which, as we have already seen in Chapter 8, is a very improbable statement, and not borne out by any of the evidence. As for the earlier claim by Coleridge that *The Friend* "contains nothing . . . which is not traceable either to Greek philosophy" or to writers of the fifteenth–seventeenth centuries (pp. 54–55), this is refuted by the abundance of ideas in that book derived, as now everyone admits, from Kant (*W*, 102–3), such as the Kantian categories, the principles of the understanding, the categorical imperative, and all the others that we have seen already in previous Chapters; nor does "the absence of direct allusion to German influences" in this book give any support to the claim of originality, as Muirhead seems to think in his rather involved argument.

"But by far the most effective answer from this side to the accusation of the plagiarism of anything that was essential to his own system from Schelling is the running commentary" of hostile criticism to be found in the marginalia to Schelling (p. 55), already referred to in Chaper 8. It seems almost incredible that Muirhead could brush aside in this manner all the derivations of passage after passage from Schelling which had been already pointed out by Sara and by Shawcross in their notes to Chapters VIII, IX and XII of the *Biographia*, seen in detail in our Chapter 8. Perhaps these passages may not have been "essential to his system" in some undefined later version of it, but they are essential to those chapters of the *Biographia*, which would dwindle to a few scattered observations without them.

Previously Muirhead had stressed the influence of the Cambridge Platonists, while in a note he acknowledged Coleridge's dissatisfaction with them (p. 38 and *n.* 3). Here he happens to make a statement which is responsible for a number of confident assertions in later writers, but for which he adduces no evidence whatever. Muirhead affirms the existence of "the revival of Platonic studies in that University (Cambridge) through the translations of Thomas Taylor" (p. 38): this would have provided Coleridge with a philosophy independent of the Germans. But Taylor was not a Cambridge man; his education had been irregular and he was practically a self-taught writer who lived in London and there published his translations, which for a long time were ridiculed by scholars and by those who had pretensions to scholarship.[1] Finally, in 1802, a visit to Oxford is recorded, "where he was heartily welcomed" (*DNB*): to Oxford, and not to Cambridge. If he ever had any followers in that University, Muirhead did not name them. Really, this "Platonic revival" at Cambridge "in those very years" seems to have been invented by Muirhead out of the whole cloth.

Hanson is Coleridge's most detailed and most sympathetic biographer. Perhaps because of this sympathy, he goes out of his way to support (308–11) Coleridge's claim of 1825 that he had anticipated Kant and Schelling, with "at least five instances" that "can be adduced to show that his mind was already moving in many ways parallel to those of the German philosophers he was soon to discover." But what does "moving parallel" mean in this context? Does it mean coping with the basic problems of philosophy, the problems of Truth and Knowledge, of Freedom of the Will and Immortality of the Soul? This may well be true of Coleridge in 1797–98, but it does not mean that he anticipated the solutions that the German philosophers gave to these problems. Let us see in detail Hanson's "five instances."

1) The "Trichotomy" of the Germans was anticipated by Baxter (Hanson, 308–9). We have seen already in Chapter 3 how little substance there is in this argument.

2) Coleridge accounted for his speculations in 1797–98 in Chapter X of the *Biographia* (I, 135–37). But this is a dark and tortuous account, from which little that is definite can be extracted. Kantian terms are here used to denote ideas which he is supposed to have had before reading Kant, such as "sciential reason, whose objects are purely theoretical" (I, 135), which is simply Kant's theoretical reason distinct from the practical. Then we find a reference to the dilemma of the Antinomies: Reason challenged by atheism evinces "the equal demonstrability of the contrary from premises equally logical," while "the understanding" proceeds in a manner different from the Reason. Thus the Reason-Understanding dichotomy, which Coleridge was to emphasize in his later dealings with Kant, accounts here for the survival of Coleridge's early religious faith, but there is no evidence that his struggle with atheism was seen by him at that time in the light of his later conception of the Reason and Understanding.

3) In the same account Coleridge said: "there had dawned upon me, even before I met with the Critique of Pure Reason, a certain guiding light" (I, 134). This "guiding light" consists in looking upon the silver lining of agnosticism: if one cannot prove the existence of God, one cannot either disprove it. As we have seen in Chapter 1, this is not a very strong "guiding light" and no anticipation of transcendentalism.

4) Original anticipations of Schelling, or, alternatively (?), derivations from Boehme, are supposed to be the following:

a) the idea of being "a mere apparition, a naked spirit . . . I myself I" (1796). This may be perhaps Boehme (no reference is given), but it is not Schelling.

b) Coleridge's "ability to see things as a whole," as said in a letter of 1797. One might as well adduce Coleridge's ability to think at all as evidence that he had "anticipated" Schelling, because Schelling also was capable of thought.

c) Coleridge's "faith that 'all things counterfeit infinity'" (1797). This as we have seen in Chapter 1 is good evidence, not that he had anticipated Schelling, but that he had read Cudworth. In fairness to Hanson it must be pointed out that the derivation of the phrase from Cudworth had not yet been discovered at the time when Hanson wrote.

5) "And, finally, there is the general truth of the fact that the philosophy which he adumbrated (!) many years later, in 1818, could, as he claimed, be derived from "either the Greeks or the thinkers of the fifteenth–seventeenth centuries." This claim was adduced by Muirhead in connection with *The Friend* and already disposed of above.

These are actually more than "five instances," but none of them proves any anticipation from Kant and/or Schelling. At most, they prove that Coleridge was struggling with metaphysical problems before he read the Germans, and not that he had reached by himself the solutions that he was to find in them. There is nothing like Kant's critical method, his theories of pure intuition, of the categories and of the unity of apperception, and so forth, or of Schelling's system of transcendental idealism, based upon the interaction of two opposite forces which repeat the opposition of subject and object at different levels of being, but only some vague and general assertions of the existence of God that had been repeated for centuries by Christian apologists and pulpit preachers.

In a book which enshrines the myth of the anticipation of the critical philosophy in seventeenth-century thinkers—to which Coleridge himself took exception—another kind of argument in favor of Coleridge's originality is brought forward by the distinguished historian of literature and of criticism, L. I. Bredvold. He summed up Coleridge's relation to Kant in this sentence: "To put it briefly, Coleridge tried hard to make the Kantian epistemology point to a position beyond itself, a position essentially Platonic." [2]

To which the following remarks should be made: 1) the attempt to "go beyond" the restrictions that Kant placed upon speculation and to build up a positive metaphysics was made before Coleridge by Fichte, and Coleridge knew it; 2) the position that Coleridge ultimately arrived at does not seem to be so much "Platonic" (unless that much abused term is once more misused) as traditional Christian theism, a position which is not so much "beyond Kant" as *behind* Kant.

Furthermore, in all Coleridge's claims to have anticipated Kant and Schelling, there is implied a view of their historical position which was rightly singled out for criticism by J. H. Stirling when he said of Coleridge: "We suspect that he did not understand the exact nature of Schelling's obligation to Kant; and that, like most of his countrymen probably, he supposed Schelling to be a great *original* writer, who, of course read *in* Kant, as in others, but, on the whole, owed his triumph to his own 'magical brain.' The strict historical connection of the German philosophers was not then well understood in England, and such suppositions were, at least on the part of non-experts, very excusable." [3]

This lack of historical perspective is probably implicit also in Coleridge's attitude towards Fichte. It is true that Coleridge was well aware that Kant was the "master" of Fichte and of Schelling, but at times he considered the relation something purely personal: "Fichte and Schelling he said will be found at last wrong where they have left their master, towards whom they shewd ingratitude." [4] He spoke of them as "the Masters of the New and the newest Philosophy, the Kanteans and the Fichtians or Schellingites" (*NB*, I, Notes, p. 456) and in 1825 he differentiated them even more sharply: so-called "Kantean philosophy" really comprises three systems, those of Kant,

Fichte, and Schelling, "as diverse each from the other as those of Aristotle, Zeno and Plotinus." [5]

The closest he comes to seeing the "strict historical connection" between the three is, curiously enough, in his earliest statement on them, which is also the earliest mention of Schelling in Coleridge, i.e., January 1, 1806: "Spinozo-Kantian, Kanto-Fichtian, Fichto-Schellingian Revival of Plato-Plotino-Proclian Idealism" (*NB*, II, 2784).[6]

Coleridge at best could say: "With the exception of one or two fundamental ideas, which cannot be withheld from Fichte, to Schelling we owe the completion, and the most important victories, of this revolution in philosophy" (*BL*, I, 104). Apart from the already noted fact that this omits Hegel completely, the linear progression from the *Critique* to the *Doctrine of Science* and from the latter to Schelling's *System* is missed. As we have tried to show in our exposition, Fichte's absolute idealism derives its logic from the position of Kant's epistemology, and Schelling proceeded directly and logically (at least in his intentions) from Fichte in his earlier system, but Coleridge does not seem to be aware of this, or at least he does not give it its proper weight.

This may reduce Coleridge's claim as a systematic philosopher, but it does not seriously impair his merit as a learned and acute writer on philosophy, a man well versed in the works of Kant and other German thinkers, as well as of the later Platonists, endowed with a vast literary culture and an unusual keenness in psychological observations. As such, he has been the object of undeserved neglect, which has also caused the near oblivion of his unpublished prose works. When these are all available, they will provide instructive and stimulating reading to any student of philosophy. But as regards systematic coherence, the best judgment is perhaps that pronounced by Storr: "Coleridge must be judged, not by any hard and fast standard of rigid consistency, but by the general tendency of his thought, and in the light of its large principles." [7]

Too much insistence on Coleridge's desultoriness, his lack of formal consistency and his indebtedness to other writers may produce the impression that his work is of little permanent value. Yet even in its fragmentary form, Coleridge's work has still something to say to the modern world. His ideas gave to English criticism a depth which it had heretofore lacked, and has since sometimes felt the absence of. They enlarged the English intellectual horizon and opened new ways for the future, some of which still remain to be explored.

Notes

1. See the Life of Coleridge prefixed to his edition of the *Poetical and Dramatic Works of S. T. Coleridge* (London, 1877), I, cxl.

2. It is hard to find any attacks on religion in the "philosophical notes" appended to that poem. Rather, there is a series of aesthetic discussions; the difference between prose and verse, the sister arts: painting and music, similes, etc. E. Darwin, *The Botanic Garden*, a Poem in Two Parts, London, 1789 and 1791 (Brit. Mus., 448. fol. 16).

3. For lists of these unwritten works see *RX*, 1955, pp. 421 and 423, and the indexes to the Coburn edition of the *Notebooks* under "Coleridge, S. T., Projected Works."

4. "Christ's Hospital Five and Thirty Years Ago" (1820), *The Essays of Elia* in *Works*, ed. W. Macdonald (London, 1903), I, 42.

5. *Unpublished Letters*, ed. E. L. Griggs, II (1933), 274. This fact was noted by L. Werkmeister in her paper on "The Early Coleridge" quoted later (*n.* 8), p. 103, *n.* 22.

6. G. Whalley, "The Bristol Library Borrowings of Southey and Coleridge," *The Library*, Ser. 5, IV (1950), 114–32, and the same, "Coleridge and Southey in Bristol, 1795," *Review of English Studies*, N.S., I (1950), 232–40.

7. E. J. Morley (ed.), *H. C. Robinson on Books and their Writers* (London, 1938), I, 70. Wellek, *Kant*, quotes parts of this entry, p. 76, *nn.* 41 and 78, *n.* 59, but not the part relative to Proclus. For the subjectivist interpretation of Proclus, see *post* in this chapter, § iv.

8. Lucyle Werkmeister, "The Early Coleridge: His 'Rage for Metaphysics,'" *Harvard Theological Review*, LIV (1961), 99–123.

9. According to Miss Werkmeister, Plotinus taught that "misfortune . . . is not a divine punishment: the punishment lies in the suffering, and the suffering is reserved for the vicious. This, of course, is the Plotinian solution of the problem, borrowed from the Stoics, and on the whole it is to remain Coleridge's solution" (p.

270

110). But her references to Plotinus do not support this—indeed, one of these references (to *Enn.*, III, ii, 4) states that the punishment of the vicious is not the "suffering" that they may feel in this life, but to be "assigned to a lower sphere" in another life; and reincarnation does not seem to have ever been held by Coleridge. The other passages of the *Enneads* referred to do not deal with the punishment of the vicious. (On this subject, cf. W. R. Inge, *The Philosophy of Plotinus* (3rd ed.; London, 1948), II, 24.)

10. L. Werkmeister, "Coleridge's Mathematical Problem," *Modern Language Notes* LXXIV (1959), 691–93.

11. Circulating libraries had mainly "novels," as Coleridge tells us (*BL*, 1, 34, Ch. III). The "library in King Street" has been identified by J. B. Beer in *Notes and Queries*, CCI (1956), 264, but no catalogue of it is available.

12. J. L. Mosheim in R. Cudworth, *True Intellectual System of the Universe*, with Notes by Mosheim (London, 1845), III, 259, *n.* 5.

13. For the history of the concept of "inner Form" in later aesthetics, see references in my *Croce, Philosopher of Art and Library Critic* (Carbondale, 1961), p. 324, *n.* 34.

14. *Concerning the Beautiful Or, a paraphrase translation from the Greek of Plotinus, Ennead I, Book VI*, By Thomas Taylor, London, 1787, p. 13. On Taylor see F. B. Evans, III, "T. Taylor Platonist," *PMLA*, LV(1940), 1060–1079, and more fully G. M. Harper, *The Neoplatonism of W. Blake* (Chapel Hill, 1961), pp. 10–33.

15. Miss Werkmeister utterly rejects the hypothesis, first advanced by A. Brandl, that young Coleridge read Taylor's translation of the Book on Beauty: "the doctrine of the Beautiful is the one aspect of Plotinian thought which Coleridge disregarded" (p. 99, *n.* 1); for "Beauty . . . did not interest Coleridge at the time" (p. 109). However she does not say how Coleridge at that time could have found, or understood, a Greek text of the *Enneads* or a Latin translation.

16. For a fuller discussion of unity in multiplicity see Chapter 6, Section iii and note 20.

17. A fuller account of the "Platonic tradition" will be found in T. Taylor's "History of the Restoration of the Platonic Theology, by the later Platonists," in his *Commentaries of Proclus* (London, 1792), II, 211–320. Cf. G. M. Harper (above), pp. 14–15.

18. The only scholar so far to take notice of Trenchard is Werkmeister (pp. 105–6). She believes that Coleridge, during his hypothetical depression from a deep sense of guilt, found in *Cato's Letters* the doctrine that suffering was caused by Vice and so confirmed both the sense of guilt and the depression.

19. I quote from the 4th edition: *Observation on Man, his Frame, his Duty, and his Expectations*, by David Hartley (London, 1801), 3 vols., the third of which contains the commentary by the Rev. H. A. Pistorius. The paging of this edition is identical with that of the quarto ed. of 1791. For the commentary by Pistorius see H. N. Fairchild, "Hartley, Pistorius and Coleridge," *PMLA*, LXII (1947), 1010–1021. A good exposition of Hartley's system is in B. Willey, *The 18th Century Background* (London, 1940), pp. 136–54, and G. S. Brett, *History of Psychology*, ed. R. S. Peters (2nd ed.; London, 1962), pp. 436–43. The most recent discussions of his influence on Coleridge are by Haven, Appleyard, and Piper.

20. W. R. Sorley, *A History of English Philosophy* (Cambridge, 1920), p. 195.

21. For statements by Coleridge on Spinoza, see *BL*, I, 245; C. Carlyon, *Early Years and Late Recollections* (London, 1836), I, 193–94; *PhL*, especially 384–86, 463–64; Muirhead, 45–48; Appleyard, 51–52, 102, 153, 205; L. Metzger, "Coleridge's Vindication of Spinoza; an unpublished Note," *JHI*, XXI (1960), 279–93, the note being MS. Egerton 2801, fol. 1–10.

22. J. H. Stirling, "De Quincey and Coleridge upon Kant," in his *Jerrold, Tennyson and Macaulay, with other critical Essays* (Edinburgh, 1868), pp. 194 and 219. That Coleridge could read philosophy critically is shown by (among others) G. Whalley, in *Review of English Studies*, N.S. I (1950), pp. 328–29.

23. Article in *The Gentleman's Magazine* (1834) quoted in Shepherd's cited introduction to the *Works* of Coleridge, I, xx.

24. *The Secret of Hegel* (Edinburgh, 1865), I, 20.

25. J. A. Passmore, *Ralph Cudworth, an Interpretation* (Cambridge, England, 1951), especially Chapters V–VII.

26. Cf. Coleridge: we only "partake" of reason "κατὰ μέθεξιν," *Aids*, p. 186*n*; Shedd, I, 264*n*.

27. "Ectypal" and "archetypal" (i.e., "derivative" and "original") are two terms used in English Platonic (or Neoplatonic) philosophy of the seventeenth century, as shown by the Oxford Dictionary.

28. Passmore, *op. cit.*, pp. 114–15. The work, however, is included in the edition of 1846 cited in note 11.

29. *Op. cit.*, III, 426, and passim. Cf. E. Cassirer, *The Platonic Renaissance in England*, English translation (Austin, 1953), pp. 56 ff., and Lydia Gysi, *Platonism and Cartesianism in the Philosophy of Ralph Cudworth* (Berne, 1962).

30. Cf. G. Aspelin, "R. Cudworth's Interpretation of Greek Philosophy," in *Acta Universitatis Gotobergensis* (Göteborg, 1943), XLIX: 1–47.

31. However, "the word 'plastic' was common property" and though it suggests Cudworth's influence it does not prove it, as observed by Piper, p. 43, *n.* 2.—Piper is in error in speaking of "plastic natures" in the plural (45–46): for Cudworth there is only *one* "plastic Nature," as the quotation on page 46 shows. See W. Schrickx, "Coleridge and the Cambridge Platonists," *Review of English Literature*, VII (1966), 77–79.

32. For "unitive" see the Oxford Dictionary; for tracing "counterfeit infinity" to Cudworth, see Schrickx, *op. cit.*, 80–82.

33. James Martineau, *Types of Ethical Theory* (London, 1898), II, 442.

34. Quoted in the paper by Lovejoy (p. 265) cited in the next note.

35. A. O. Lovejoy, "Kant and the English Platonists," in *Essays Philosophical and Psychological in Honour of W. James* by his colleagues at Columbia University (London, 1908).

36. C. Howard, *Coleridge's Idealism: A Study of its Relationship to Kant and to the Cambridge Platonists* (Boston, 1924).

37. J. H. Muirhead, *The Platonic Tradition in Anglo-Saxon Philosophy* (London, 1931), p. 150; cf. p. 39.

38. T. H. Raysor (ed.), *English Romantic Poets* (New York, 1956), p. 112.

39. *English Studies 1949* (London, 1949), pp. 78–79.

40. S. T. Coleridge, *Notes, Theological, Political, and Miscellaneous* ed. by the Rev. Derwent Coleridge (London, 1853), p. 405. —There are satirical references to tar-water in *NB*, I, 893 (1801) and *BL*, 1, 201.—Further references to the *Siris* in Beers, especially 114–18 and 152–53. Cf. also Wilma Kennedy, *The English Heritage of Coleridge of Bristol, 1798. The Basis in English Thought for his Distinction between the Imagination and Fancy* (New Haven, 1947), pp. 19–42: it contains a facsimile of the MS. note on the

Siris discussed above. On the *Siris* see also N. P. Stallknecht, *Strange Seas of Thought* (Bloomington, 1958 ²), pp. 35–36. The above does not aim to be a complete study of the Coleridge-Berkeley relationship.

41. This MS. is described by Muirhead, 259. The argument from Berkeley is also quoted by F. Brinkley, *Huntington Library Quarterly*, VIII (1945), 291. Cf. Notebook 30, Add. MS. 47, 527, foll. 5–7.

42 For Coleridge's political opinions in relation to his times, see C. R. Woodring, *Politics in the Poetry of Coleridge* (Madison, 1961), Ch. II, "The Young Man in his Time." The latest study of Coleridge's political philosophy is David P. Calleo, *Coleridge and the Idea of the Modern State* (New Haven, 1966).

43. For Coleridge's early religious opinions, see Appleyard, 7–19, 17–21 and 38–42. On his later religious philosophy there is the monograph by James D. Boulger, *Coleridge as a Religious Thinker* (New Haven, 1961).

44. A transcript by E. H. Coleridge is preserved at Victoria College Library, Toronto, signature ET5. An edition of them is coming in the *Complete Coleridge*.

45. On T. Cooper see Piper, 26–27 and 64–65.

46. W. Schrickx, *op. cit.*, in n. 30 above, p. 83.—N. P. Stallknecht, *Strange Seas of Thought* (2nd ed., Bloomington, 1958), p. 73; A. E. Powell, *The Romantic Theory of Poetry, an examination in the light of Croce's Aesthetic* (London, 1926), p. 86n.

47. A. Gérard, "Counterfeiting Infinity: *The Eolian Harp* and the Growth of Coleridge's Mind," *Journal of English and Germanic Philology*, LX (1961), 411–22; W Schrickx, *op. cit.*, pp. 80–82.

48. B. Croce, *Conversazioni critiche* (Bari, 1924 ²), I, 340–41.

49. Cf. Piper, 42. Coleridge was "the earliest avowed disseminator of Vichian ideas" in England: M. H. Fisch, "Introduction," *The Autobiography of G. B. Vico* trans. by M. H. Fisch and T. G. Bergin (Ithaca, 1963), p. 83. See also pp. 69 and 84. Coleridge read Vico in 1825: see Notebook 20, Add. MS. 47,517, fol. 28.

50. M. F. Schulz, "Oneness and Multeity in Coleridge's Poems," *Tulane Studies in English*, IX (1959), 53–60.

51. Cf. I. A. Richards, Introduction to *The Portable Coleridge* (New York, 1950), p. 45.

52. See H. A. Wolfson, "Extradeical and Intradeical Interpretations of Platonic Ideas," in his *Religious Philosophy, A Group of*

Essays (New York, 1965), Atheneum Reprint, pp. 27–68.—A more extensive derivation of Coleridge from Philo is argued by D. K. Jones, "Coleridge's Scheme of Reason," in *Literary Monographs 1* (Madison, Wis., 1967), pp. 96–99.—For the differences between the various kinds of later Platonism see Leland Miles, *John Colet and the Platonic Tradition* (La Salle, Ill., 1961). Jacob Brucker, *Historia philosophica doctrinae de Ideis* (Augsburg, 1723): pp. 65–67 for the extradeical interpretation of ideas and pp. 72–73 for the unreliability of the later Platonists. Apparently young Milton's mind, working poetically, hit upon the same interpretation: *"seorsus extat,"* *De Idea Platonica*, l. 14. Coleridge usually speaks of the "later Platonists" and "lower Platonists" (*NB*, II, 2445*n*; *BL*, II, 230). For "neo-Platonic" see *PhL*, 427. The date of the abandonment of the Neoplatonic interpretation of Plato is discussed by J. K. Feibleman, *Religious Platonism* (London, 1959), pp. 218–19, who gives credit to Gibbon and to Schleiermacher. On ancient Platonism and and Neo-Platonism, see now A. H. Armstrong (ed.) *The Cambridge History of Later Greek and Early Medieval Philosophy* (Cambridge, 1967).

53. For Coleridge's acquaintance with German literature before he went to Germany, see F. W. Stokoe, *German Influence in the English Romantic Period* (Cambridge, 1926), pp. 120–22. Beddoes' article did not appear in the *Monthly Review*, but in the *Monthly Magazine* for May, 1796.

54. Part of these notes may be in the MS. now at the Huntington Library, "On the Divine Ideas," foll. 638–649. For Coleridge's German studies from now on, see Stokoe, *op. cit.*, pp. 116–43. For the 1957 dissertation by H. M. Goodman, see my paper, "Coleridge and Schlegel Reconsidered," *Comparative Literature*, XVI (1964), pp. 112–13.

55. Cf. R. F. Brinkley, "Coleridge on Locke," *Studies in Philology*, XLVI (1949), 521–43, and Appleyard, 77–86.

56. D. G. James, "The Thought of Coleridge," in *The Major English Romantic Poets, A Symposium in Reappraisal*, eds. C. D. Thorpe, C. Baker (Carbondale, 1964), "Arcturus Books," p. 107.

57. Both in the first version of *The Friend*, 1809–10, p. 80, and in the later, *F*, 340, Sec. II, Ess. 11.—For the difference between the two versions, see Dudley Bailey, "Coleridge's Revision of *The Friend*," *Modern Philology*, LIX (1961), 89–99.

58. Letter on Kant to J. Gordon, dated 14 January 1820 (*UL*,

II, 265), already quoted *à propos* of Coleridge's reading habits. The marginalium: "What since Kant is not in Kant as a germ at least?" printed in *IS*, No. 94, p. 122, where "germ" is rendered, implausibly, as "German." It was printed "germ" in its first publication by Helen Zimmern in *Blackwood's Magazine*, CXXXI (1882), p. 116. Cf. Ch. 4, *n.* 9. Acknowledgments to Kant abound in Coleridge's later writings; see also Ch. 11.

59. Published by A. Snyder in *RLC*, VII (1927), 529.

60. H. Nidecker, *op. cit.*, VII (1927), 738.

61. W. Schrickx, "Coleridge's Marginalia in Kant's *Metaphysische Anfangsgrunde der Naturwissenschaft*," *Studia Germanica*, 1959, pp. 195–96.—Other marginalia on Kant are in *IS*, 138–43.

62. A. D. Snyder, "Coleridge on Boehme," *PMLA*, XLV (1930), 616–17.

63. For Crabb Robinson's qualifications as a German scholar, see Stokoe, *op. cit.*, in n. 46, pp. 53–60.

64. A. D. Snyder, "Coleridge's Cosmogony: a Note on the Poetic World-View," *Studies in Philology*, XXI (1924), 616–25. The passage by Kant is from W. Hastie's translation of *Kant's Cosmogony* (London, 1900), p. 80. The numbers in brackets have been inserted to show the parallelism with Coleridge's statement. Coburn's note to this entry (# 2151) does not refer to the Kantian source or to Snyder's paper, although the latter was quoted in the note to # 93 in another connection. Cf. "Of Kant he spoke in high praise. In his 'Himmelsystem' he combined the genius of Newton and Burnet." Coleridge in 1810. H. C. Robinson, *Blake, Coleridge, Wordsworth, Lamb etc.*, ed. E. J. Morley (London, 1922), p. 31.

65. J. W. Beach, *The Concept of Nature in 19th Century English Poetry* (New York, 1956 (1936)), pp. 320–21.

66. Cf. Jacobi's exposition of Spinoza: "All becoming must be grounded on a being that has not become; every derived being on something which is not derived; every mutable thing on something which is immutable and eternal." F. Jacobi, *Letters on the Doctrine of Spinoza*, 1785, Ital. trans. (Bari, 1914), p. 105.

67. This is Kant's definition of "Dialectic," A 61, B 86. See Chapter 5.

68. For this phrase cf. the MS. "Logic," I, 84. For an account of the "pure forms of intuition" in Kant's transcendental Aesthetic, see the following chapter.

To all this Deschamps makes the amazing observation: "Une fois familiarisé avec l'esthétique transcendentale de Kant, il en vient tout naturellement (!) à considérer, et il ne se trompe pas (!), que Platon a anticipé Kant sur ce point" (p. 383).

69. See note 52 above.

70. The remaining notes of Coleridge on Proclus are less significant. In his marginalium to Chapter VII (I, 60) Coleridge objects to something which is not in the text he is annotating: "diminutions of Loss" in the Idea and in the Soul (pp. 457–58). The Ideas and the Soul being unalterable cannot be said to diminish. However the Soul may lose its contact with the Ideas and sink into a "dormant state" (I, 60); but there is nothing here about diminution or the rate of diminution; only "gradual advances" are mentioned (I, 60).

On Ch. X Coleridge supplements Proclus-Taylor by showing the depths to which a pure mathematician will sink if he forsakes philosophy (458). On Ch. XIII Coleridge defends Bacon against Taylor, claiming Bacon was a Platonist (458–59), as Coleridge does also in *The Friend*, Sec. II, Ess. 9; see *W*, 74–75 (on p. 75, "Archides" is perhaps "Archytas").

CHAPTER 2

1. As Royce noted in 1892, the literature on Kant is enormous, and its growth does not tend to diminish. For the works of Kant, I refer to the edition published by the Prussian Academy of Sciences, *Gesammelte Schriften* (22 vols.; Berlin, 1902–1942). The following introductory works are recommended for the English-speaking reader:

A. D. Lindsay, *Kant* (London, 1934), the most lucid general exposition of all of Kant's philosophy.

J. Hartnack, *Kant's Theory of Knowledge* (New York, 1967), the clearest account of the first *Critique*.

G. Rabel, *Kant* (Oxford, 1963), gives a compact account of every single work by Kant, major and minor, with extracts freshly translated.

A. C. Ewing, *A Short Commentary on Kant's Critique of Pure Reason* (London, 1938, reprinted 1950): to be read with the *Critique*.

For Wolff (R. P.), see list of Abbreviations.

F. Copleston's volume on Kant in his *History of Philosophy* (London, 1946 ff.), reprinted by Image Books, Vol. VI, Pt. II, is the most modern and lucid presentation, like all his *History*. The early works of Kant are dealt with in Vol. VI, Pt. I. All volumes have up-to-date bibliographies.

More advanced are: N. K. Smith, *A Commentary to Kant's Critique of Pure Reason* (2d ed.; London, 1930): not only an exegesis, but a critique, which may be found confusing by beginners. Smith's critique is in turn criticized by Ewing (above).

Paton (see Abbreviations) is the fullest analysis yet of the argument in the first half of the *Critique*; it excludes the Dialetic.

H.-J. de Vleeschauwer, *La déduction transcendentale dans l'oeuvre de Kant* (3 vols.; Anvers-Paris, 1934–37). A monumental piece of analysis, both historical and philosophical, in a lucid French style. The author made a compendium of it in a single volume, while enlarging its scope: *The Development of Kantian Thought* (London, 1962), also remarkable for lucidity.

Translations of Kant's works will be cited as we proceed. For a popular biography, see W. Klinke, *Kant for Everyman*, trans. M. Bullock (London, 1951).

2. For brief general accounts of rationalism see R. Eucken, *Main Currents of Modern Thought* (London, 1912), pp. 119–29, or E. Cassirer, "Rationalism," *Encyclopaedia Britannica*, 14th ed., (1929), XVIII, 991–93.

3. J. H. Muirhead, *The Platonic Tradition in Anglo-Saxon Philosophy, Studies in the History of Idealism in England and America* (London, 1931), pp. 40–41.

4. *Op. cit.* in Ch. 1, *n.* 12, III, 62; Ch. V, Sec. 1

5. *Ibid.*, III, 426; Ch. V, Sec. 4, and *ibid.*, III, 626; *Eternal and Immutable Morality*, Book IV, Ch. IV, Sec. 7.

6. *New Essays Concerning Human Understanding*, trans. A. G. Langley (New York, 1896), Bk. II, Ch. I, p. 111.

7. *BL*, I, 93; *PhL*, 383 (cf. note, p. 463); MS. "Logic," II, 370; *Aids*, p. 150*n*.

8. "My recollection of David Hume was the very thing which many years ago first interrupted my dogmatic slumber and gave an entirely different direction to my investigations in speculative philosophy." *Prolegomena*, Academy edition, IV, 260; trans. by L. W. Beck (Indianapolis, 1950), p. 8, slightly adapted.

9. See R. Mondolfo, *La comprensione del soggetto umano nel l' antichità classica* (Florence, 1958).

10. For the connection between Leibniz and Kant, see Wolff, 2–22.

11. Cf. *NB*, II, # 2555 (1805); *CL*, 474–75 (1815); J. W. Beach, *Concept of Nature in 19c. English Poetry* cited above, p. 333; and Piper, 40–41 and 222–25.

12. B. Willey, *The 18th Century Background* (1940) (Beacon Paperback, 1961), p. 172.

13. *Prolegomena*, translation cited in *n*. 8 above, p. 9. (adapted).

14. *Kant's Introduction to Logic*, ed. T. K. Abbott (London, 1963), p. 40. (adapted).

15. For the historical background of this term see Lindsay, 61, and Wolff, 95, *n*. 11.

16. W. Kaufmann, *Hegel: A Reinterpretation* (New York, Anchor Books, 1966), p. 149. For Coleridge's possession of Kant's *Vermischte Schriften*, 1799, see NB, II, 2315, *n*.

17. *NB*, I, 1710 and 1717; see discussion in Chapter 6. Cf. also *Notes, Theological*, etc. (cited Ch. 1, *n*. 38), p. 407.

18. See Kant, *Anthropologie in pragmatischer Hinsicht abgefasst*, 1800, a copy of which with Coleridge's marginalia is in the British Museum. But the marginalia (see them in H. Nidecker, *RLC*, VII (1927), 339–40) do not amount to much. There is no English translation of the *Anthropologie*; on it, cf. Brett, *op. cit.* (Ch. I, *n*. 19), p. 538.

19. For the faculty psychology in Coleridge, see *BL*, I, LXXXVI.

20. On "function" see the important note in MS. "Logic," II, ff. 40ᵛ–41ᵛ; also in Egerton MS., 2801, fol. 139. See also "Logic," II, 397 and 419, and W. Schrickx, "An unnoticed note of C's on Kant," *Neophilologus*, XLII (1958), 147, *n*. 3.

21. See the paper by F. Brinkley quoted in Ch. 1, *n*. 41, at p. 289.

22. "That without which experience is impossible, cannot be the result of experience, though it must never be applied beyond experience." Max Müller's translation of the *Critique* (2d ed.; London, 1920), Introduction, p. xlvi.

23. A. J. Ayre in *Language, Truth and Logic* (1946, Dover reprint, p. 34) states that Kant grounded the impossibility of metaphysics upon the constitution of the human understanding, which Ayre considers "a matter of fact." But for Kant the constitution

of the understanding is not a mere matter of fact. Rather it is a condition for the perception of all "matters of fact." Being a universal condition it is transcendental, and being transcendental it is *a priori.*

24. See also *Notes, Theological,* etc. (cited in Ch. 1, *n.* 40), p. 331.

25. The distinction between the three faculties is made repeatedly in *F*, 97, 1. Landing, Essay 5, and 110*n*, Sec. 1, Ess. 3.

26. G. De Ruggiero, *Storia della filosofia,* (3d ed.; Bari, 1947), Pt. IV, Vol. III, pp. 265–75.

27. *Op. cit.,* p. 270.

28. There is a complete conspectus of the *Critique of Pure Reason* in J. Chevalier, *Histoire de la pensée* (Paris, 1961), III, 606–7.

29. J. Laird, *Hume's Theory of Human Nature* (London, 1932), pp. 30 ff.; Lindsay, pp. 15 and 303; D. F. Bowers, *Atomism, Empiricism and Skepticism* (Princeton, 1941). The "atomism" of Hume has been denied by some other scholars, e.g. C. W. Hendel, *Studies in the Philosophy of Hume* (2d ed.; Indianapolis, 1963), pp. 380–402, but it is reaffirmed by J. Weinberg, *Abstraction, Relation and Induction* (Madison, 1965), pp. 33–34. Cf. Copleston, Vol. V, Pt. II, 1954, p. 72.

30. Cf. "we have always a continuous diversity of sensations even when these are qualitatively sharply differentiated." A. W. Ward, in *Encyclopaedia Britannica,* 11th ed., 22: 594 c. Cf. also the *Gestalt* theory.

31. The word "interspace" is found also in *BL*, I, 201, l. 15, Ch. XIII, in *NB*, II, 2398, January 1805 (already published in *IS*, 54), and in a marginalium to Petvin; see R. F. Brinkley in *Huntington Library Quarterly*, VIII (1945), 291. Also in *Z*, 187.

32. Henry Fuseli, of Swiss origin, was a popular artist of the Romantic era in England. There is more than one reference to his art in Coleridge, often as an art of "Horrors-Terrors," for which Hamlet would be "a fine subject," (*NB*, I, 742, June 1800). Cf. *CL*, I, 135.

33. R. N. Wornum (ed.), *Lectures on Painting*, by the Royal Academicians Barrie, Opie, and Fuseli (London, 1848), pp. 505–6.

34. See Rabel, *Kant* (cited in *n.* 1), p. xv, and C. J. Friederich, *The Philosophy of Kant* (Modern Library, 1949), pp. xxx–xxxi.

35. D. G. James, *Scepticism and Poetry* (London, 1937), p. 35.

36. See my *Croce* (cited in Ch. 1, *n.* 13), pp. 32–34.

37. P. Carus in *The Monist*, XXVI (1916), pp. 312–15.

38. For the immediate predecessor of Kant on this question, i.e., Leibniz, see Wolff, 3–8. For more background, see J. J. C. Smart (ed.), *Problems of Space and Time* (London, 1964).

39. W. James also speaks of the "chaos of crude individual experience" when it is conceived without the "apperceiving ideas" —i.e., the ideas of space and time and the categories, similar to Kant's. These ideas are for him "conquests made at historic dates by our ancestors." But it would be very hard for James to fix those "historic dates" since at the time they are supposed to appear there was no idea of time. Conditions of experience cannot be derived from experience. See "Humanism and Truth" (1914), in *Selected Papers on Philosophy* (London, 1917), Everyman's Library, p. 224.

40. "Judicial" means for Coleridge "transcendental." See the MS. "Logic," II, 210 and 212.

41. The text follows the exposition of J. H. Erdmann, *History of Philosophy*, Engl. transl. (London, 1892), II, 373. Cf. *Co*, 161–66.

42. MS. "Logic," II, 240–44, fully quoted in Snyder, 121–22. The simile is anticipated in II, 177–78 and also found in Z, 243.

43. Coleridge also knew Kant's Latin dissertation of 1770 (*De mundi sensibilis et intelligibilis forma et principis*) where the principles of the critical philosophy begin to emerge (Wolff, 11–22). Coleridge makes a long quotation from it in *BL*, I, 189–90, Ch. XII. Cf. *W*, 87, and page 74 above.

CHAPTER 3

1. In an undated marginalium on Kant, Coleridge affirms that the "coincidence" of phenomena "with the forms of the Understanding" is for Kant "the sufficient ground of our assurance of an external World" (*NB*, II, 2316n). But this concordance brings to Kant no assurance of an external world, i.e., of things in themselves. What this concordance produces is the "objective" character of our representations; but "objective" for Kant is not "external." Cf. Paton, I, 193, *n.* 1.

2. Fly-leaf of Coleridge's copy of the *Kritik*, ed. 2, 1797, Brit. Mus., Shelf Mark c. 126. i. 9.

3. See Vleeschauwer, cited in Ch. 2, *n.* 1.

4. Vleeschauwer, *op. cit.*

5. B. Croce, *Estetica*, Bari, 1902, Part I, Ch. XVIII. See also *n.* 8 below.

6. The fact that words are intuitive symbols of logical concepts was well-known to Kant; see the *Critique of Judgment,* # 59.

7. This is the main difference between poetry and reflective thought. In poetry the structure and the parts of the verbal forms are also the structure and the parts of the poem itself.

8. B. Croce, *Logica* (Bari, 1909), Part I, Sec. II, Ch. ii and iii.

9. Cf. R. Kroner, *Von Kant bis Hegel* (Tübingen, 1921), I, 35 ff.: "Platos Ideenlehre und Kants Transzendentale Logik."

10. There is an apparent error in the MS. here. Line 7 of fol. 434 says "after I have subtracted all that is mortal" and lines 9–10 say "I have excluded from it one portion, the non-mortal." The last word should be "mortal."

11. "Causality in its unschematized form is ground," Ewing (cited in Ch. 2, *n.* 1), p. 189, and cf. p. 146 and *Co*, 330*n.*

12. *The Friend*, 1st edition, 1809–10, No. 5, p. 80; page reprinted in Shedd, II, 539–40.

13. "Unpublished Letters written by Samuel Taylor Coleridge," *Westminster Review*, XXXVII N.S. (April 1870), p. 353.

14. Cf. R. Franchini, *Storia della Dialettica* (Napoli, 1961), pp. 206–7.

15. R. Baxter, *The Reasons of the Christian Religion* (London, 1667), p. 371.

16. Cf. "a notion under an indefinite and confused Form, such as Kant calls a schema, or vague outline," (?) marginalium on J. Taylor in Brinkley, 288. Pleasure and pain are said to be "schemata" in Notebook 17, Add. MS. 47,514, fol. 235. For "schematism," see *F*, 388, Sec. 2, Ess. 11. Schemata are also in Z, 162.

17. This principle is connected with the science of the day: see Ewing, *op. cit.*, p. 149. For its possible relevance to modern physics, see Luigi Scaravelli, *Saggio sulla categoria Kantiana della realtà* (Firenze, 1947), pp. 81–92.

18. Coleridge's reference to Kant's Principles of the Understanding was apparently not noted by the most attentive previous students of the Kant-Coleridge relationship. Wellek notes the concept of schemata in Kant, as quoted above in the text (*W*, 83), but no echo in Coleridge. Winkelmann should have mentioned the schemata on p. 170 (see *n.* 43) but did not do so.

19. D. G. James, *Scepticism and Poetry* (London, 1937), pp. 32–

39 and 42–43. Shawcross rightly observed that Coleridge's theory of the imagination owed more to Schelling than to Kant (*BL*, I, lx–lxviii), as we shall see in Ch. 9.—Coleridge was already familiar with Wolff's belief in the presence of the imagination in ordinary perception: *NB*, I, 902*n* and 905.

20. The sign "⊁" means "contradistinguished from." For mesotheta, see Ch. 10, Sec. 2.

CHAPTER 4

1. *Psychology*, ed. 1918, Dover reprint 1950, I, 160.
2. Hamilton's Reid, Edinborough, 1846, pp. 947–48.
3. Pulished by A. D. Snyder in *RLC*, VII (1927), 529.
4. T. Case in *Encyclopaedia Britannica*, 12th ed., 18: 245.
5. J. E. Erdmann, *History of Philosophy*, Eng. trans., II, 378–79. On the general subject see A. O. Lovejoy, "Coleridge and Kant's Two Worlds," *Essays in the History of Ideas* (Baltimore, 1948), pp. 254–76.
6. For a fuller discussion of this issue see M. Calkins, *The Persistent Problems of Philosophy* (New York, 1912), pp. 229–34.
7. "Man is thus to himself, on the one hand phenomenon, and on the other hand, in respect of certain faculties the action of which cannot be ascribed to the receptivity of the sensitivity, a purely (*bloss*) intelligible object" (A 546–7, B 574–5).
8. Cf. "Herder . . . called Kant an Averroist," P. Merlan, *Metapsychism, Mysticism, Metaconsciousness* (The Hague, 1963), p. 114.
9. Published by Snyder, *op. cit.* in note 3, pp. 529–30. The original note reads "a 1000 persons may all of each," but the critics who quote this passage correct it to "all and each." The last word in the passage, "the germ," means in Coleridgean language "the informing principle": R. H. Fogle, *The Idea of Coleridge's Criticism* (Berkeley, 1962), p. 12. For the general idea. cf. also *BL*, II, 112.

CHAPTER 5

1. H. W. Cassirer, *A Commentary to Kant's Critique of Judgment* (London, 1938), p. 45.
2. On the other side, see Shedd, IV, 408.—Coleridge also knew Kant's earlier discussion of the *Only possible argument for the demonstration of the existence of God* (1763), from which he

quoted an important paragraph maintaining the personality of God in *BL*, I, 134, Ch. X. Marginalia on this work were published by Wellek in *W*, 305–9, cf. 90–91.

3. I. Kant's *Logik* (Königsberg, 1800), p. 142. The B. M. copy (C.43. A.10) has marginalia by Coleridge. The translation quoted above is by J. Richardson, *Metaphysical Works of the celebrated I. Kant* (London, 1836), p. 128. The classification of "Logical Acts" in MS. "Logic," II, 18–22, is based upon Kant's doctrine of Logical Acts in his *Logic* (Ch. I, sec. 6, pp. 131–32 of the translation), as noted by Snyder, 82, and Chinol, *56n*, but it is not identical with Kant's. It is also in *Aids*, 149, Shedd, I, 247.

4. When did Coleridge first use the constitutive-regulative dichotomy? My first quotation is from Appendx E to the *Statesman's Manual*, 1816. Its next appearance seems to have been in *The Friend*, 1818, *F*, 318, Sec. 2, Ess. 7, in a somewhat obscure passage. Other references in Shedd, IV, 358–59 and V, 37; *TT*, July 2, 1830.

5. Cf. A. W. Benn, *The History of English Rationalism in the 19th Century* (London, 1906), I, 255–56. "In the *Republic* (511) the distinction is between *Nous* and *Dianoia*."

6. *Forma formans*: this interesting phrase is first found in Coleridge a year before the quotation in the text, as *forma efformans*, in *NB*, II, 2543 and 2550 (April 1805). The note explains it as "self-determinate form." But later it appears in juxtapostion to *forma formata*: " '*Forma formans per formam formatam translucens*' is the definition and perfection of *ideal art*" (1816, in *BL*, II, 187). This quotation (if it is a quotation) has not been traced; the only *forma formans* I can find in philosophical dictionaries goes back to Albertus Magnus: "vere formae sunt formantes alias, ut dicit Boethius" (I, qu. 6, in R. Eisler, *Wörterbuch der philosophischen Begriffe* (Berlin, 1930), s.v.). This would make it mean "a form that produces other forms," but that does not fit the definition in *BL*, which seems parallel to the previous statement "the ideal consists in the happy balance of the generic with the individual" (*BL*, II, 187, l. 8), so that in the definition *forma formans* is the universal which lives in, and produces, the individual, which is the *forma formata*. The two phrases are of course parallel to the better known *natura naturans* and *natura naturata*. See the first phrase also in the MS. "Logic," II, 382^V and 401–2: the latter passage is reproduced in Snyder, 126, but omitting the relevant sentence, which occurs after "Reflection": "as the existence of the *forma formans* must in every case be mani-

fested by and in the *forma formata*"; which goes to confirm the interpretation given above.

7. From the context the period referred to is not clear. Possibly "previous" refers back to the first version of *The Friend* (1808–9).

8. A. O. Lovejoy, *The Reason, The Understanding and Time* (Baltimore, 1961).

9. J. H. Muirhead, *The Platonic Tradition in Anglo-Saxon Philosophy* (London, 1931), p. 41. Cf. Lydia Gysi, *Platonism and Cartesianism in the Philosophy of R. Cudworth.* (Bern, 1962), p. 32.

10. *Types of Ethical Theory.* (Oxford, 1898), II, 442–43. The pedantical manner in which this book is arranged has probably blinded readers to the value of its historical content.

11. Some go even further: "One of Coleridge's contributions to the history of philosophy is his discovery that the thinkers of the seventeenth century had anticipated Kant" (Brinkley, 109).

12. One of Coleridge's favorite quotations: "E coelo descendit, gnōthi seautón," Juvenal, XI, 27. See *BL*, I, 173 and Shawcross's note, which quotes the poem he wrote on it in 1832. The quotation is repeated in *C&S*, 227 and MS. "Logic," II, 200.

13. See Chapter 1, note 25.

14. *Op. cit.*, III, 71. The same argument is repeated in *Eternal and Immutable Morality*, III, 628–29.

15. "Metaphysician or Mystic?" in E. Blunden and E. L. Griggs (eds.), *Coleridge* (London, 1934), pp. 179–97.

CHAPTER 6

1. See Vleeschauwer, English version cited in Ch. 2, *n.* 1, p. 116.

2. Ewing, in the book cited in Ch. 2, *n.* 1, p. 251.

3. Compare Kant on love with Coleridge on love, in a marginalium to the *Metaphysics of Morals* (1797) published by H. Nidecker, *RLC*, VII (1927), p. 338.

4. The note to # 1723 does not analyze the ideas in the two paragraphs of Kant and so misses the conflict between these ideas and the views expressed previously by Coleridge in # 1705, 1710, 1711 and 1717.

5. In September 1805 he spoke again of "the unconditional Obedience of the Free Will to the Law of pure Reason," *NB*, II, # 2664. See also A. O. Lovejoy in *Essays on the Hist. of Ideas*, 1948, pp. 254–76.

6. This seems to have been quoted already in *The Friend*: "the

pure will . . . the one absolute end, in the participation of which all other things are worthy to be called good" (*F*, 295, Sec. 2, Ess. 3) and in *NB*, I, 1705 (1), dated 1803.

7. The MS. has "whom," but "which" seems more correct.

8. Crabb Robinson, book cited in Ch. 1, *n.* 5, p. 31.

9. The English sources of Kant's aesthetics were studied by O. Schlapp, *Kants Lehre von Genie und die Entstehung der Kritik der Urteilskraft* (Göttingen, 1901), and many quotations from them were published in the notes to J. C. Meredith, *Kant's Critique of the Aesthetic Judgment* (Oxford, 1911). See also E. F. Carritt, *Theory of Beauty* (5th ed.; London, 1949), Ch. V, and his "The Sources and Effects in England of Kant's Theory of Beauty," *Monist*, xxxv (1923), 316–17; K. Gilbert and H. Kuhn, *History of Aesthetics* (Bloomington, 1953), pp. 321–23.—On Kant's aesthetic in general see R. Wellek, *History of Modern Criticism 1750–1950* (New Haven, 1955), I, 227–32.

10. W. Greiner, "Deutsche Einflusse über die Dichtungslehre von S. T. Coleridge," *Die Neueren Sprachen* (Neue Folge, February 1960), pp. 57–65.

11. Cf. J. A. Mazzeo, "A Seventeenth-Century Theory of Metaphysical Poetry," *Romanic Review*, XLII (1951), 245–55.

12. *The Sublime: a Study of Critical Theories in 18th-Century England* (New York, 1935; new ed., 1960). His account of Kant's theory of beauty is not entirely correct (p. 6): he does not mention purposiveness or pleasure, and makes Kant say that "the beautiful . . . implies an effort of the understanding," whereas for Kant it involves a harmony of the understanding with the imagination (# 27), and that "The sublime implies an effort of the reason" whereas for Kant it involves a conflict with reason (*ibid.*).

13. *Essays in the History of Ideas* (Baltimore, 1948), pp. 196–97. Other ideas derived by Schlegel from the *Critique* in this period are noted by V. Santoli in his translation of Schlegel's *Frammenti critici e scritti di estetica* (Firenze, 1937), p. xxxl, n. 5, and xl.

14. Cf. R. Wellek, "The Term and Concept of 'Classicism' in Literary History," in E. A. Wassermann (ed.), *Aspects of the 18th Century* (Baltimore, 1965), pp. 121–26.

15. R. Wellek, *History of Modern Literary Criticism, 1750–1950* (New Haven, 1965), IV, 415. For Coleridge as a critic, *op. cit.*, II (1955), 151–87. See also R. Wellek, "Coleridge's Philosophy and Criticism," in T. M. Raysor (ed.), *The English Romantic Poets, a*

Review of Research (revised ed.; New York, 1956), pp. 110–37.

16. R. H. Fogle, *The Idea of Coleridge's Criticism* (Berkeley, 1962), p. 175, *n.* 64.

17. J. Drinkwater, "The Notes by S. T. Coleridge in Milton's Poems by Tho. Warton," *London Mercury*, XIV (1926), 494.

18. Coleridge was sensitive to color in art, and to the harmony of colors even independently of the subject: "What Tone to colors, chiaro-Oscuro to Light and Shade; viz., such a management of them that they form a beautiful whole, independently of the particular images colored, lit up, or shaded." *NB*, II, # 2797 (1806).

19. T. M. Raysor, *Coleridge, Shakespearean Criticism* (new ed.; London, 1860), I, 177–78, *n.* Cf. *BL*, II, 318, *n.* 255, and *NB*, II, # 2211 and note.

20. See *NB*, I, # 556, 1561 etc.; and *BL*, II, 230, line 21, 232, lines 6–7 and line 21, etc. H. Richter in *Anglia*, XLIV (1920), 319, traced the formula "multeity in unity" to German aestheticians.

21. Other dialogues are of course relevant to this metaphysical problem, especially the *Parmenides*, which is too complicated to be taken up here. There are discussions of the problem in the vast literature on Plato. A recent discussion is by Rosa Padellaro, *Il problema cosmologico e l'antinomia uno-molteplice* (*dai presocratici ad Aristotele*), Milano, 1962.

22. See my paper "Coleridge and Schlegel Reconsidered," *Comparative Literature*, XVI (1964), pp. 99–118.

23. See T. M. Raysor, *op. cit.* above in *n.* 19, I, 197.

24. *The Mirror and the Lamp* (New York, 1953), pp. 174–75. —On the *Critique of Judgment*, see H. W. Cassirer's book cited in Ch. 5, *n.* 1, for a most lucid exposition and intelligent criticism. A remarkable study which will probably escape Anglo-Saxon readers, but deserves notice, is Luigi Scaravelli, *Osservazioni sulla Critica del Giudizio* (Pisa, 1955).

25. Coleridge also started from Kant's definition of the sublime and worked towards a definition of his own, which he found in incomparability: see J. Shawcross, "Coleridge Marginalia" (on Herder's *Kalligone*), *Notes and Queries*, 10 S., IV (1905), 341–42. If we can believe Carlyon, he had reached this definition already in his German visit: C. Carlyon, *Early years and late reflections* (London, 1836), I, 118–19. See also the interesting set of aesthetic definitions quoted in *BL*, II, 309.—For Coleridge on Taste see also *Shakespearean Criticism²* *cit.*, I, 158–63 and 220.

CHAPTER 7

1. J. G. Fichte, *Sämmtliche Werke,* ed. J. H. Fichte (Berlin, 1845), I, 5. This edition of Fichte's works will be cited henceforth as *GW.* Unfortunately there is no English translation of Fichte's major works in print.

2. The story has been told in detail by several authors: e.g., R. Kroner, *Von Kant bis Hegel* (Tübingen, 1921), I, 315 ff.; Vleeschauwer, *op. cit.* in Ch. 2, *n.* 1, Vol. III, "The Apostates," pp. 491–551; E. Cassirer, *Das Erkenntnisproblem in der Philosophie und Wissenschaft der neuen Zeit,* III (Berlin, 1923), Ch. 1; but not by Copleston.

3. Cf. R. Adamson, *Fichte* (Edinburgh, 1881), pp. 50–51.

4. W. Windelband, *Storia della filosofia moderna,* trad. ital. (Firenze, 1942), III, 48.

5. Or, better, a relation that posits its terms. See the later Italian idealist, D. Jaja, *Sentire e pensare* (Napoli, 1886), p. 190.

6. For a full discussion of the Fichte-Coleridge relationship, see W. Schrickx, "Unpublished Coleridge Marginalia on Fichte," *Studia Germanica Gandensia,* III (1961), 171–208, who shows how Coleridge's attitude was consistently hostile. However, Schrickx does not quote two of Coleridge's more favorable statements. The first is the undated marginalium "Fichte I understand very well, only I cannot believe his system. But Kant I do not understand," which Schrickx himself published in his "Unnoticed note of C. on Kant," *Neophilologus,* XLII (1958), 148. The other statement is "My Faith is with Fichte" and will be discussed below. Fichte is also honorably mentioned in *NB,* II, 2375 (1804) and *NB,* II, 2537 (1805).—Cf. Chinol, 35–39, for a different account.

7. Adamson, *op. cit.* in *n.* 3 above, pp. 160–61.

8. *The Popular Works of J. G. Fichte.* Translated from the German by William Smith. With a memoir of the Author, 4th Edition in 2 vols., London, 1889, I, 85, *n.*

9. *Op. cit.* (1st ed.; London, 1848), I, 101*n.*

10. H. Nidecker, "Praeliminären zu Neuansgabe der Abhandlung über die Lebenstheorie (*Theory of Life*) von S. T. Coleridge," in *Bericht der philosophisch-historischen Abteilung der philosophischen Fakultät über die von ihr genehmigten Dissertationen,* Heft 5, Dissertationen aus dem Jahre 1925, Universität Basel, Basel 1927, pp. 10 and 12, *n.* 13.—Other comments on Steffens by Coleridge are in

H. Zimmern, "Coleridge Marginalia," *Blackwood's Magazine*, 131 (1882), pp. 118–19.

11. Professor Wellek informs me that the Wall episode is mentioned even by Emerson, but attributed to Schelling. See R. Wellek, *Confrontations* (Princeton, 1965), p. 201.

12. This is *not* among the volumes with marginalia, studied by Professor Schrickx in the paper cited in note 6.

13. Shawcross quoted the "Wall" fragment (originally published in part in *Anima Poetae*, London, 1895, p. 15) to illustrate the Schellingian theses in *BL*, I, 269; but it is Fichtean. It was also quoted by A. D. Lovejoy, *op. cit.* in Ch. V, *n*. 8, p. 62, who misunderstands it as "a demand for immediacy of knowledge." G. Watson (*The Literary Critics* (Penguin, 1962), p. 119, *n*. 1) refers to it in the same Schellingian context. Deschamps (472, n. 83) quotes the Wall but no Fichte.—A shorter discussion of the "Wall" was published by me as "Coleridge, Fichte, and Original Apperception," in *Friendship's Garland*, edited by Vittorio Gabrieli (Rome, 1966), II, 72–74.

14. The word "Psiology" (in this section of the note) which puzzled Professor Coburn, may perhaps be a Coleridgian abbreviation for "Psychology," using the Greek letter "Psi" to stand for "Psych-."

15. *BL2*, I, 266*n*. Cf. *BL*, I, 246.

16. Cf. J. W. Beach, *op. cit.*, Ch. I. I, *n*. 64, pp. 54–62.

17. As in J. V. Baker, *The Sacred River, Coleridge's Theory of the Imagination* (Louisiana State U.P., 1957), especially p. 176. Baker should have noted that in Schelling's statement there quoted, *n*. 65, it is "intelligence," and not instinct or appetite, that is "unconsciously productive in the perception of the universe" (Introduction to *Naturphilosophie*, 1799). Cf. also the other passage quoted by Sara (*BL2*, 341, *n*.) from Schelling's *Abhandlungen:* "the *spiritual* in man, namely that which lies on the other side of consciousness" (*SW*, I, 442–43). Cf. Coleridge: "the aids of the Divine Spirit" reach "deeper than our consciousness can reach" (*Aids*, 43, Shedd, I, 153), but this is not the "depth" of depth psychology. There is a fundamental difference, not to say opposition, between the idealistic philosophy of Schelling and Coleridge, and the naturalistic or mechanistic philosophy of depth psychology. It has been suggested that the idealistic subconscious would be better termed "meta-consciousness." Merlan, *op. cit.*, p. 130.

18. *Popular Works*, I, 385.

19. *Notes and Lectures upon Shakespeare* etc., ed. Mrs. H. N. Coleridge (London, 1849), II, 287–305, Shedd, IV, 408–19.

20. Schrickx, *op. cit.*, p. 174*n*.

21. Helen Zimmern, "Coleridge Marginalia. Hitherto Unpublished," *Blackwood's Magazine*, 131 (1882), p. 122.

22. Schrickx, *op. cit.*, pp. 173 and 201–6.

23. In the latest study of Coleridge's political theory, D. P. Calleo, *Coleridge and the Idea of the Modern State* (New Haven, 1966), Fichte is not mentioned, although Hegel is discussed.

CHAPTER 8

1. Cf. Copleston, Vol. 7, Part I, pp. 120–32. For Coleridge's borrowings from Schelling's earlier works, see *W*, 97–99. Regrettably there is no *complete* English translation of Schelling's *System*.

2. *Newton's Philosophy of Nature*, ed. H. S. Thayer (New York, 1953), pp. 99–100.

3. "Equivocal generation" is a reference (and perhaps a punning reference) to the term *generatio equivoca* which is often found in Kant, with the meaning of "generation of living organisms from dead matter": see Rabel, *op. cit.*, Ch. II, *n.* 1, p. 223.—Cf. "the dreary (and thank heaven! almost impossible) belief that everything around us is but a phantom," *BL*, II, 259, ll. 7–8, in "On Poesy or Art," and the conclusion to *Aids*: "the twins" of "mechanico-corpuscular philosophy," i.e., empiricism: "Materialism on one hand, and Idealism, rightlier named subjective Idolism, on the other: the one obtruding on us a world of spectres and apparitions, the other a mazy dream!" (*Aids*, 268, Shedd, I, 359).

4. *Biographia Literaria*, Everyman's Library, new ed. by G. Watson, 1960, p. 149, *n.* 3. Another echo of *Essay* I is in *BL*, I, 86: as noted by Shawcross, it corresponds to *SW*, I, 357.

5. G. Whalley in *Transacts. Royal Soc. Canada*, Ser. III, Vol. LIV (1960), p. 21.

6. "an English character." The text has: "'*I* asserted that the world was mad,' exclaimed poor Lee, 'and the world said I was mad, and confound them, they outvoted me'" (*BL*, I, 179). Cf. this marginalium on Kant: "the man in the fever is only *outvoted* by his attendants. He does not see their Dream, and they do not see his,"

in W. Schrickx, "An unnoticed note of Coleridge's on Kant," *Neophilologus*, XLII (1958), 148.

7. N. Brooke, "Coleridge's 'True and Original Realism,'" *Durham University Journal*, LIII (1961), 59.

8. This passage from Plotinus is in modern editions from *Enn.*, III, 8, iv, and not from III, 8, iii, as in Shawcross' note to *BL*, I, 173, l. 24. This chapter is also quoted at *BL*, I, 166, l. 14, to which Shawcross' note says that "the same passage is also quoted by Schelling, *Werke*, I, ii, 78." But there is no quotation by Plotinus on that page.

9. Copleston, VII, i, 132.

10. B. Croce, *Saggio sullo Hegel* (4th ed.; Bari, 1948), p. 341.

11. Beach, *op. cit.*, Ch. I, *n.* 64, p. 330.

12. Cf. Beach, *op. cit.*, p. 598, *n.* 19. Kant is quoted from the edition cited Ch. II, *n.* 1.

13. W. Schrickx, "Coleridge's Marginalia in Kant's *Metaphysiche Anfangsgründe der Naturwissenschaft*," *Studia Germanica* (1959) p. 184.

14. Cf. Beach, *op. cit.*, p. 599, *n.* 21, who observes that the Latin phrases in the note are Coleridge's. Another discussion by Coleridge of this work of Kant's is to be found in MS. Add. 34, 255, fol. 144–45.

15. Émile Bréhier, *Schelling* (Paris, 1912), p. 34.

16. On the works of Schelling known to Coleridge see *BL*, I, 105; *W*, 96; Winkelmann, 124–25; *PhL*, 464–65.

17. Letter to Gillman, Nov. 10, 1816, *CL*, IV, 688 and 690; *Aids*, 119*n*; Shedd, I, 219*n*; *W*, 132.

18. *Letters*, ed. E. H. Coleridge (Boston, 1895), II, 735–36.— A curious allusion to Schelling is in *BL*, I, 95. Here Coleridge makes one of his rare acknowledgments of indebtedness, but he does not name Schelling, only "a contemporary writer on the Continent." Here, too, Coleridge says "I in part translate": he might have said it on several occasions. The work quoted in Schelling's "pamphlet against Fichte" (*BL*, I, 105); i.e., *Darlegung des währen Verhältnisses der Natur-Philosophie zu der verbesserten Fichte'schen Lehre* (1806), with the defense of Boehme.

19. A more definite approximation to absolute Idealism is to be found in the MS. "Logic," II, 92: "the νους is that, in which the Idea is at the same time the reality; the knowledge is the thing known; the *scire* one and the same with the *esse.*"

20. A more literal translation might be: "As little as the in-

dividual I is to be understood under the I as principle, so little, too, must the empirical I, found in empirical consciousness" (III, 374).

21. "Both are therefore differenced by their limits only" (III, 375).

22. "The reality that some consider true, that of things" (III, 375); the last three words are omitted by Coleridge.

23. "The being of things does not consist in pure quiet or inactivity" (III, 375): the whole sentence omitted by Coleridge.

24. "Since none of the predicates that befit things befit the I" (III, 375). The rest of this paragraph has been rearranged, but nothing else has been altered.

25. É. Gilson, *Christian Philosophy in the Middle Ages* (New York, 1955), pp. 113 ff.

26. Cf. *PhL*, 433–34. For the meaning of Scotus for Coleridge see A. W. Benn, *History of English Rationalism in the 19th Century* (London, 1906), I, 244. See also Shedd, IV, 355.

27. Quoted, without naming Coleridge, by the American transcendentalist Hedge: see Wellek's *Confrontations*, cited Ch. VII, *n.* 11, p. 159.

28. "Das Urtheil ist die Diremption des Begriffs durch sich selbst . . . Es ist insofern die ursprüngliche Theilung des ursprünglich Einen," *Logik*, 1812, II, 74. This is quoted from Coleridge's own copy of Hegel's *Logic* in the British Museum (C. 43. a. 13), but there are no marginalia on this page.

29. Like Schelling (*SW*, I, 430, n. 1), Coleridge had a high estimate of Kant's *Versuch, den Begriff der negativen Grössen in die Weltweisheit einzuführen* (1763): see *BL*, I, 197. Coleridge may have reached it before reading Schelling: there is a quotation from it in *NB*, II, 2502, although neither the work nor the author are mentioned and consequently the commentary misses it. This entry is dated March 1805, while the earliest known reference to Schelling by Coleridge is dated Jan. 1, 1806, *NB*, II, 2784.

30. *The Literary Critics* (Penguin, 1962), p. 118. For the date of the *Biographia* see Watson's edition, 1960, pp. xii–xv.

31. R. W. Armour, *Coleridge the Talker* (Ithaca, 1940). p. 28.

32. *Letters*, ed. cit. (1895), II, 735–36.

33. J. H. Ferrier, "The Plagiarisms of S. T. Coleridge," *Blackwood's Edinburgh Magazine*, XLVII (1840), 287–99. J. H. Stirling, "De Quincey and Coleridge upon Kant," *Jerrold, Tennyson and*

Macaulay, etc., Edinburgh, 1868. C. M. Ingleby, "On Some Points Connected with the Philosophy of Coleridge," *Transactions of the Royal Society of Literature*, Ser. II, Vol. IX (1870), pp. 396–420. *Works* of T. Reid, ed. by Sir W. Hamilton (6th ed.; Edinburgh, 1863), II, 890.

34. Copleston, *op. cit.*, Vol. VII, Part I, 181 [1962].

35. Copleston, *op. cit.*, Westminster (Md.), 1966, VIII, 151–55.

36. W. K. Pfeiler, "Coleridge and Schelling's Treatise of the Samothracian Deities," *Modern Language Notes*, 52 (1937), 163, *n.* 6. Schelling's defence of Coleridge was noted by D. Hirsch, Jr., *Wordsworth and Schelling*, New Haven, 1960, according to D. Calleo, *Coleridge and the Idea of the Modern State* (New Haven, 1966), p. 54*n*. The fact was known to Sara (Shedd, III, xxxiv).

37. A. C. Ewing (ed.), *The Idealist Tradition from Berkeley to Blanshard* (Glencoe, 1957). Also, the only idealist included in R. J. Hirst's anthology, *Perception and the External World* (New York, 1965), is Berkeley: no Kant, no Fichte, no Schelling!

CHAPTER 9

1. However, the course was divulged "in manuscript notes all over Germany": Croce, *Estetica* (9th ed.; 1950), p. 324. These may have been lecture notes made for the use of German university students. Coleridge himself bought in Germany the lecture notes of Kant's *Logic* from "the Nachdrücker or privileged Book Pirates . . . doubtless published by, or from the Notes of, one of his Lecture-pupils": H. Nidecker, *RLC*, VII (1927), 136. So texts of Schelling's *Philosophie der Kunst* circulated in Germany early in the century, and a copy might conceivably have reached Coleridge through some friend like Crabb Robinson. This is possible, but not established, so we can not rely on it for any inference. On Schelling's aesthetic see R. Wellek, *History of Modern Criticism* (New Haven, 1955), II, 74–82.

2. "It has indeed to break down the world of everyday perception," D. G. James, *Scepticism and Poetry* (London, 1937), p. 17. "Materials from experience, melted down into their elements —dissolved and diffused—become the object of the mind's conscious activity" in the secondary imagination," C. D. Thorpe, *The Aesthetic of Th. Hobbes* (Ann Arbor, 1940), 87*n*. In this note the author presents the theory of the two interacting forces without any hint

that it is Schelling's. The Secondary Imagination dissolves "the world of ordinary appearances" which is also the product of a creative faculty, but "in itself cold and inanimate," "the hard commonplace which so easily besets us," B. Willey, "S. T. Coleridge," *19th Century Studies* (London, 1949), pp. 14–16. I. A. Richards is less explicit: the Secondary Imagination re-forms "every aspect of the routine World," *Coleridge on the Imagination* (Bloomington, 1960 (1934)), p. 58.

3. H. House, *Coleridge* (London, 1953), p. 142.

4. *English Studies by Members of the English Association*, New Series, II (1949), 85. See now Patricia A. Ward, "Coleridge's Critical Theory of the Symbol," *Texas Studies in Literature and Language*, VII (1966), 15–32.

5. Alice D. Snyder, *The Critical Principle of the Reconciliation of Opposites as Employed by Coleridge* (Ann Arbor, 1918). See also H. House, *op. cit.*, p. 121; W. K. Wimsatt and C. Brooks, *Literary Criticism, A Short History* (New York, 1957), pp. 395–97; and especially R. H. Fogle, *The Idea of Coleridge's Criticism* (Berkeley, 1962), pp. 12–13 and 34–48. For the roots in Greek thought, see C. J. De Vogel, *Greek Philosophy* (Leiden, 1954), III, 342, § b.

6. "We do not ask for the individual, we ask to see more, namely its living idea. But if the artist recognizes the union and the essence of the idea creating within him and stresses these, he fashions the individual into a world of its own, a genus, an eternal prototype," Schelling, "Concerning the relation of the plastic arts to Nature," transl. M. Bullock in H. Read, *The True Voice of Feeling* (New York, 1953), p. 335. Cf. Croce, Estetica, ed. cit., pp. 324–28. And compare *BL*, II, 258. This intellectualist trend in aesthetics is of course much older than romantic philosophy, and Coleridge shows hints of it before he became acquainted with Schelling. The earliest, perhaps, is to be found in *NB*, I, 943: "Pomponatius de Immort. Animae:—says of abstract ideas—universale in particulari speculatur—which is the philosophy of poetry," dated April–November 1801. Cf. II, 2441; *C&S*, 250; *BL*, II, 77, 106, 159, 187–88; *Friend*, 304, Sec. 2, Ess. 5.

7. See the translation quoted in the previous note. For a just remark on the term "plastic" in this title, see Sara's note in Shedd, IV, 482.

8. Bréhier, *op. cit.*, p. 44.

9. H. Höffding, *History of Modern Philosophy* (London, 1900), II, 163.

10. E. De Negri, *Interpretazione di Hegel* (Firenze, 1943), pp. 265–66. For "interpenetration" (*F*, 304, Sec. 2, Ess. 4) cf. "Wechseldurchdringung" (*SW*, VII, 350).

11. Schelling, being poetically inclined, expressed his view of Nature even better, perhaps, in verse: see his "Epicurean Confession of Faith of Hans Bristleback," a substantial part of which was ably translated by J. Royce, *Spirit of Modern Philosophy* (Boston, 1892), pp. 186–92.

12. Copleston, *op. cit.*, VII, 1. 178–81. Cf. T. K. Österreich in überweg, *Grundriss der Geschichte der Philosophie* (12th ed.; Berlin (1928), 1951), IV, 56–67. A more favorable view of the contribution of the *Natur-philosophen* seems to be held to-day by historians of science: Oken's "mucus vesicle theory led to the cell-theory," S. F. Mason, *History of the Sciences* (new revised ed.; New York, 1962), p. 359. Also, Goethe's attempts at a philosophy of nature should not be forgotten.

13. Craig W. Miller, "Coleridge's Concept of Nature," *Journal of the History of Ideas*, XXV (1964), 77–96.

14. See Ingleby, cited Ch. VIII, *n.* 31, p. 413, for a borrowing from Baader, in *C&S*, 276.

15. E.g. "If we pass to the construction of matter, we find it as the product, or *tertium aliud*, of antagonist powers of repulsion and attraction," *Theory of Life*, in *Miscellanies*, ed. T. Ashe (London, 1885), p. 396. Coleridge came to criticize the phrase *Natur-philosophie* (see *BL2*, 270, *n.* 25) and apparently also the thing (*IS*, 118).

16. See J. Needham, "Coleridge as a philosophical biologist," *Science Progress*, XX (1926), 692–702.

17. Beach, *op. cit.*, in Ch. 1, *n.* 65.

18. Needham, *op. cit.*, 698.

19. Schelling, *On Human Freedom*, trans. J. Gutman (Chicago, 1936), p. 105.

20. Schelling, *The Ages of the World*, trans. with an Introduction and Notes by F. de Wolfe Bolman, Jr. (New York, 1942), pp. 38–39.

21. *On Human Freedom* cit., p. 105. See also H. M. Schueller, "Schelling's Theory of the Metaphysics of Music," *Journal of Aesthetics and Art Criticism*, XV (1957), 461–76, where the reader will meet several ideas and terms used by Coleridge.

22. Copleston, *op. cit.*, VII, 1, pp. 111–13 and 157 ff.

23. "Coleridge and Schelling's Treatise on the Samothracian Deities," *Modern Language Notes*, LII (1937), 162–65. Pfeiler's account does not ascertain how this rare and little known piece of Schelling's got into Coleridge's hands: it is not mentioned in the lists of books of Schelling owned by Coleridge that I have seen. But the derivation is beyond question. The fact was noted by Schelling himself, in the above quoted passage (*SW*, XI, 196*n*).

24. Bréhier, *op. cit.*, p. 298.

CHAPTER 10

1. All of Hegel's major works, with the sole exception of the greater *Logic*, have been translated into English, and more than one is available in cheap reprints. (Works on aesthetics will be quoted below.) For a philosopher who has been the object of so much adverse criticism, and even obloquy, he is amazingly popular to-day. Now there is also a first-rate introduction to him in the work by Walter Kaufmann, *Hegel, A Reinterpretation* (New York, 1966 [Anchor Books]), together with a supplementary volume, *Hegel, Text and Commentary*, also 1966. These will be cited henceforth as Kaufmann I and Kaufmann II. They are not only eminently lucid, which Hegel was not, but they provide that circumstantial detail, biographical, historical and literary, which make Hegel a person of flesh and blood. In his full bibliography the reader will find a useful list of critical works on Hegel.

2. Sec. I, par. 3. Kaufmann II, 26.

3. Whether to translate *"Geist"* as "mind" or as "spirit" is one of the debated questions of Hegelian terminology. For "mind" see W. Wallace, *Hegel's Philosophy of Mind* (Oxford, 1894), pp. xlix–lii. Against "mind" see C. J. Friederich, *The Philosophy of Hegel* (New York, 1953 [Modern Library]), p. xxv. For "spirit" see Kaufmann I, 145–46. For both "mind" and "spirit" see J. T. Merz, *History of European Thought in the 19th Century* (London, 1912), III, 466, *n.* 1. All these discussions throw light on Hegel's meaning.

4. Preface to the *Philosophy of Right* (1821), Hegel's last book.

5. R. Wellek, *History of Modern Criticism*, II, 318–42.

6. *Hegel on Tragedy*, ed. with an Introduction by Anne and Henry Paolucci (New York, 1962 [Anchor Books]). On his Shakespeare criticism see my paper, "Critica e filologis shake-

speariana nell'epoca romantica," *Rivista di letterature moderne*, 1956, pp. 5–16. For other merits of Hegel as a critic of literature and of art, see A. Guzzo, "La cultura artistica di Hegel," *Idealisti ed Empiristi* (Florence, 1935), pp. 233–77.

7. Lionello Venturi, *Storia della critica d'arte* (2.a ediz.; Firenze, 1948), p. 314; Guzzo, *op. cit.*, 250.

8. For an answer that smacks less of panlogism see B. Croce, *What is living and what is dead in the philosophy of Hegel* (London, 1915).

9. See Benn, *op. cit.* in Ch. 8, *n.* 6, I, 261.

10. *Aids*, 288. For references to the Pentad see *Aids*, 117–19, *n.*, Shedd, I, 218–19, *n.*, and *Omniana*, in *Notes, Theological, Political, and Miscellaneous* (London, 1853), 401–3.

11. W. Wallace, *The Logic of Hegel* (2nd ed.; Oxford, 1892), p. 401.

12. S. Maturi, *Introduzione alla filosofia* (Bari, 1913), pp. 146–47.

13. *The Philosophy of Fine Art*, trans. by F. P. B. Osmaston (London, 1920), I, 381.

14. For the relations between Croce and Coleridge see my paper, "Coleridge e Croce," *Rivista di Sudi Crociani*, I (1964), 444–53.

CHAPTER 11

1. A. D. Snyder, *Coleridge on Logic and Learning* (New Haven, 1929), pp. 71–72. Miss Snyder gives a detailed summary of the book (pp. 75–103) and a number of extracts from it (pp. 104–26). She has diligently traced most of the references to Kant and to other thinkers, but in her summary she occasionally misses a point owing to her unfamiliarity with the philosophy of transcendentalism.

After her book, came the following studies which touch upon the "Logic," and most of them also quote from the MS.: Muirhead's book of 1930, quoted at the beginning of this work; Wellek's book of 1931, also quoted above; E. Winkelmann, *Coleridge und die Kantische Philosophie* (Leipzig, 1933 [*Palaestra*, 184]); O. Barfield, *Romanticism comes of Age* (London, 1944); and Chinol, 1954, quoted above. They will all be cited by the name of the author, followed by the page of the book. Although quotations will be made only on special points, the present study of the MS. is indebted to all.

2. In *The Disciplines of Criticism*, ed. P. Demetz, T. Greene, and L. Nelson, Jr. (Yale U. Press, 1968), pp. 581–92.

3. Cf. *Logic*, I, 53, and *LR*, III, 157 and 416; Kant, A 841, B 869, and *Co*, 72, *n.* 5.

4. For Coleridge's merits as a logician see Muirhead, 61–65. Here he draws also from Kant's *Logic*: see above, Chapter 5, note 3.

5. Cf. A. D. Snyder, "Coleridge's Reading of Mendelssohn's 'Morgenstunden' and 'Jerusalem,'" *JEGP*, 28 (1929), 503–17.

6. This point is made particularly clear by Chinol, 54–55, 57–58, and 125, where he juxtaposes the text of Kant to that of Coleridge.

7. A. D. Snyder, *Coleridge's Treatise on Method, as published in the Encyclopaedia Metropolitana* (London, 1934), pp. xx–xxiii.

8. See also Egerton MS. 2801, fol. 79: "conceptions *(Begriffen)*."

9. The MS. has *"intuitus piori"* which does not make sense. But Egerton MS. 2801, foll. 85–86, which appears to be Coleridge's original note for this "lecture," gives the correct reading *"intuitus puri."* Other MSS. that give a few parallel texts to the "Logic" are the Table of Categories in Egerton MS. cit., fol. 74, parallel to "Logic," II, 445, and the discussion of Function, *ibid.*, fol. 139 recto and verso, parallel to II, 40^v–41^v. *Intuitus puri* appears also in *NB*, Notes, I, 456–57.

10. Cf. Paton, I, 396–97 and 405–8.

11. Owen Barfield, "The Philosophy of S. T. Coleridge," in his *Romanticism Comes of Age* (London, 1944), *op. cit.*

12. See also *Aids*, 41, Shedd, 1, 151. Baker, in the work cited in Ch. 7, *n.* 17, p. 13, erroneously attributed this Kantian concept to Hartley, of all people: "Moreover, a complex idea is more than the sum of its parts; it has a unique quality not present in the component parts taken separately." The note refers to *"Obs. on Man*, Prop. 12, Case 5, I, 74–75," but there is nothing of the kind in that text.

13. Kant, *Logik*, Ch. I, par. 3; see the 1800 edition used by Coleridge, p. 140; and cf. Richardson's translation, 1836, p. 128.

14. For *forma formans* see above, Ch. 5, *n.* 6. For the Idea, see also Ch. 5.

15. See my paper "Coleridge and Schlegel Reconsidered," *CL*, XVI (1964), 97–118.

16. *Shakespearean Criticism*, ed. T. M. Raysor (2nd ed.; London, 1960), II, 87.

17. Already in a marginalium on Kant, *RLC*, VII (1927), 136.

18. "Henceforth" conjectural emendation; the word is cut at the margin.

CHAPTER 12

1. See the article by F. B. Evans, in *PMLA*, LV (1940), 1068–69.

2. In Brinkley's *Coleridge on the 17th Century*, p. xxxiv.

3. J. H. Stirling, *op. cit.* in Ch. 8, *n.* 31, p. 198.

4. Crabb Robinson, *op. cit.* in Ch. I, *n.* 7, p. 31.

5. *Letters*, ed. E. H. Coleridge (Boston, 1895), II, 735.

6. This notable reference to Schelling is not indexed. The only index entry under Schelling is to # 2211*n*, which is purely negative.

7. Vernon F. Storr, *The Development of English Theology in the 19th Century, 1800–1860* (London, 1913), p. 320.

INDEX